Understanding Cultural Identity in Intervention and Assessment

MULTICULTURAL ASPECTS OF COUNSELING SERIES

SERIES EDITOR

Paul Pedersen, Ph.D., *University of Alabama at Birmingham*

Understanding Cultural Identity in Intervention and Assessment

Richard H. Dana

Multicultural Aspects of Counseling Series 9

SAGE Publications
International Educational and Professional Publisher
Thousand Oaks   London   New Delhi

For information:

SAGE Publications, Inc.
2455 Teller Road
Thousand Oaks, California 91320
E-mail: order@sagepub.com

SAGE Publications Ltd.
6 Bonhill Street
London EC2A 4PU
United Kingdom

SAGE Publications India Pvt. Ltd.
M-32 Market
Greater Kailash I
New Delhi 110 048 India

Printed in the United States of America

Library of Congress Cataloging-in-Publication Data

Dana, Richard H. (Richard Henry), 1927-
    Understanding cultural identity in intervention and assessment/by Richard H. Dana.
      p. cm.—(Multicultural aspects of counseling series; vol. 9)
    Includes bibliographical references and index.
    ISBN 0-7619-0363-1 (cloth).—ISBN 0-7619-0364-X (pbk.)
    1. Minorities—Mental health services—United States. 2. Psychiatry, Transcultural—United States. 3. Cross-cultural counseling—United States. I. Title. II. Series.
    RC451.5.A2D36 1998
    362.2'089'00973—dc21   97-45247

98 99 00 01 02 03 10 9 8 7 6 5 4 3 2 1

Acquiring Editor:	Jim Nageotte
Editorial Assistant:	Kathleen Derby
Production Assistant:	Denise Santoyo
Typesetter/Designer:	Marion Warren
Indexer:	Mary Mortensen
Print Buyer:	Anna Chin

Contents

Series Editor's Introduction

The recognition that cultural identity issues are complex and not simple in a population that is increasingly multicultural raises many urgent issues in the delivery of mental health services. Richard Dana's book addresses these issues in uniquely important ways.

First of all, Dana brings a powerful network of resources and lifetime experiences from multicultural sources that lends understanding to the complexity of culture beyond the simplistic solutions of rigid cultural categories. His historical survey helps the reader understand the progression of events that have increased the visibility of cultural issues in mental health.

Second, he recognizes the importance of the context of between-group differences and similarities for both the consumer and the provider. Both differences and similarities are nested in each cultural context and can be understood only with reference to that context.

Third, Dana brings a perspective of hopeful optimism to mental health service consumers and providers in multicultural contexts. Without diminishing the enormous problems presented by those who define mental health according to rigid criteria and categories, he guides the reader toward positive and practical strategies.

Fourth, he provides a balanced criticism of mental health service systems, acknowledging subjective as well as objective factors in mental health and showing how to work with a less-than-perfect, culturally biased mental health service system without giving up one's integrity in the process.

Fifth, he demonstrates specific ways to work within the *DSM IV* framework without imposing the DSM's implicit cultural bias on the mental health service consumer. Recognizing the importance of the *DSM IV* in mental health services, and recognizing the imperfections in any unimodal description of health, he guides the reader to skillfully compensate for cultural biases through culture-centered interpretation of behavior in its cultural context.

Sixth, he provides systematic guidelines for identity issues among African Americans, American Indians/Alaska Natives, Asian Americans and Hispanic Americans/Latina-Latinos, demonstrating similarities and differences across cultural categories.

Seventh, he focuses on issues of accurate assessment throughout the book both through a culture-sensitive model and through frequent examples that demonstrate accurate assessment strategies in each cultural context.

Eighth, he focuses on specific strategies for intervention in each multicultural context that is sensitive to unique features of each culturally different population. "A focus for these interventions is strengthening of identity as a source of inner harmony for individuals as well as self-sufficiency and greater internal cohesion for communities."

Dana makes cultural or racial identity the focus of attention for professional providers of mental health services, not as a marginalized or trivialized aspect but as a central issue. He helps the reader avoid pathologizing differences in their diagnoses by going back to basic underlying and culturally learned assumptions about mental health and mental illness.

Dana describes his book as a "primer" toward developing a legitimate assessment-intervention model with different approaches for each cultural/racial group. This ultimate goal will require the cooperation of professionals from many different cultural backgrounds who look for differences as well as similarities in research and practice on measurement issues.

The reader will find new perspectives on providing mental health services in multicultural settings in Dana's book. Reading this book will reward the reader with new insights and practical strategies for taking culture seriously.

Paul Pedersen
University of Alabama at Birmingham

Acknowledgments

My major source of professional support during the entire process of writing has been the Regional Research Institute (RRI), Portland State University. I want to especially acknowledge my gratitude to Dr. Bill Feyerherm and Dr. Nancy Koroloff for making this context available to me on a continuing basis. Ron Talarico, RRI Business Manager, helped me in numerous ways on a day-to-day basis.

A second source of professional support has been Southern Oregon University, where I taught a variety of multicultural mental health courses to students of diverse cultural backgrounds and life experiences. These courses altered my beliefs on how the content should be considered and this book is the product of several major changes in my understanding, which are elaborated in the preface. The university's library resources, particularly Interlibrary Loan and the willingness and understanding of Ann Beauchamp, Coordinator, enabled me to acquire many references. Kathleen Kinzie shared her understanding of how to translate American Indian history and beliefs into sound intervention practices.

Dr. Mike Conner has always been willing to forsake his own heavy workload to talk with me, read and comment on many papers, particularly my own, and to help me prevail with a laptop and an archaic word processing program in spite of my disinclination to become competent. His devotion in crisis and persuasive rationality diminished obstacles and kept me task oriented. As if these virtues were not sufficient, he has also been sharing the effort of formalizing the assessment-intervention model introduced in Chapters 3 and 9 into a flow chart to enhance comprehensibility and permit applications.

I have been privileged and rewarded by many Portland luncheons with Dr. Stan Sue that increased my familiarity and respect for his work in this area and enriched my knowledge of many cross-cultural issues.

Dr. Israel Cuéllar and Dr. Giuseppe Costantino, in their own very different ways, have taught me not only something of the meaning and extent of within-group differences but have provided many models of excellent products of research and clinical thinking that have informed this book. The enthusiasm and incisive commentary of Dr. Paul Pedersen, Sage Series Editor, on four chapters helped me greatly in completing this book.

I will always be grateful to Jim Nageotte, Sage Acquisition Editor, for the specific suggestions that not only have improved readability, but have also strengthened and given salience and cohesion to my intentions in writing this book.

My wife, Dr. Joan Dayger Behn, has been infinitely patient with my persistent attempts to enlist her in research projects and has been supportive, understanding, and encouraging during a long writing process.

Finally, I owe thanks to a legion of students, faculty members, and practitioners who have attended my workshops, classes, seminars, presentations, and symposia at universities and meetings in the United States, Portugal, and Spain. These nameless persons not only listened to me but provided acceptance, encouragement, and feedback.

Preface

As a first generation clinical psychologist, I have literally lived through most of the initial 50 years of my profession. This book has been written, rewritten, and unwritten many times as my understanding of culture and identity changes as a consequence of professional and personal experiences. Because my forebears came from England and Eastern Europe, my thinking and appreciation of circumstances are Eurocentric. I have, however, learned that although Eurocentricism is a legitimate worldview, its applications are limited for persons whose worldviews differ. Mental health services need to honor other worldviews and to modify their practices accordingly, but these services must also be reinvented by professionals within each racial/ethnic group to accommodate their different construals of reality.

Throughout my professional lifetime, I have been critical of professional psychology training, assessment procedures, service delivery, and managed care mental health practices, particularly with multicultural populations, and have attempted in each area to offer constructive alternatives. A second strand of my professional identity is a human science orientation, which has nourished a professional approach that is distinct from the learning theory, experimental psychology, and statistics proferred as my clinical training in the early 1950s.

This book is a reaction to my despair with the inadequacies of available mental health services for persons of color in this country. These inadequacies have changed only very slowly in response to an increasingly strident dissatisfaction by consumers. Interventions are described for groups that are either indigenous (American Indians/Alaska Natives); have histories of residence roughly equivalent to Europeans (African Americans, Hispanic Americans), although under very different circumstances; or are immigrants and refugees from many countries worldwide, but predominantly from Asia (Asian Americans) and Latin America. Many groups have been excluded due to space limitations. This book is written to foster cultural sensitivity and eventual cultural competence among Anglo American students and providers.

Chapter 1 describes the history of mental health services from a multicultural perspective. Chapter 2 examines the difficulty of providing credible mental services for multicultural populations from an Anglo American perspective. Chapter 3 explores the nature of quality care by describing ideal provider virtues and American Psychological Association (APA) ethical code omissions that render equitable services infrequent. A delineation of problems requiring care leads to assessments and interventions that acknowledge racial/ethnic identity and constitute one culture-specific intervention model. Chapter 4 describes identities of clients and their providers. Understanding these identities—cultural, racial, ethnic—is essential for providing beneficial services. Chapters 5, 6, 7, and 8 organize selected interventions within the model for four groups presented in Chapter 3. Chapters 7 and 8 begin with a description of services and health/illness beliefs in countries of origins followed by major problems requiring care. Nonetheless, these four chapters have major subsequent differences in organization due to several assumptions:

1. *Group differences.* For each group, the magnitude of its worldview differences from an Anglo American population are emphasized and differences are related to the cultural elements used to facilitate interventions.

2. *Cultural identity, racial identity, or both.* Evaluation and understanding of identity should precede any assessment, intervention, or referral.

3. *Psychiatric diagnosis.* Because the *Diagnostic and Statistical Manual of Mental Disorders* of the American Psychiatric Association was not designed for application to these populations, the use of an expanded problem context, acculturation evaluation, identity description, and cultural formulation provide the means for an improved goodness-of-fit with standard diagnosis and any subsequent intervention.

Chapter 9 offers a rationale for these assumptions and suggests why they are essential in any quest for professionally responsible and ethical mental health services for multicultural populations in the United States. These assumptions and the general assessment-intervention model outlined at the end of Chapter 3 are dovetailed with examples from Chapters 5, 6, 7, and 8. Cultural competence among Anglo American providers can be improved by application of this model whenever providing services to persons in the cultural/racial groups discussed in this book.

To Mitzi,
who gave me an essential human context for respecting cultural
differences and becoming a psychologist.

1

Mental Health Services
and Multicultural Populations

This chapter reconstructs the history of mental health policy, legislation, professions, and services from 1940 to the present from the perspective of multicultural populations (for greater detail, see Vega & Murphy, 1990). Prior to the 1960s, the needs of these populations were not more directly addressed because group differences were unrecognized in policy and minimized by most service providers. Cultural competence was not understood to be necessary for acceptable and beneficial services. As a consequence, available services were consistently underused.

The community mental health movement contained service opportunities as well as restrictions and impediments. Although the shift from hospital to community care provided innovative services and settings outside of the offices of providers, potentially salutary effects were largely mitigated by fluctuating policies. Since the 1980s, a business ethic for cost containment has been increasingly practiced by managed care organizations (MCOs). Public sector mental health services have been curtailed due to restrictions on funding. Private sector services have become medicalized, the numbers of available interventions have been dramatically reduced, and quality of care has been adversely affected. A merging of public and private sectors, as well as health and mental health policy, has particularly adverse consequences for these populations in the form of further restrictions on use and quality of available services. In spite of this contemporary climate, culture-specific agencies, programs, and services do exist. Research indicates that acknowledgment of race/ethnicity/language in service delivery improves quality of care. The numbers of persons from multicultural groups requiring a variety of mental health services will continue to increase and will be accompanied by political pressures from each group to define their own needs and assume major responsibility for interventions. This book is a forecast of an immediate future in which training for cultural competence can increase the use and beneficial effects of mental health services to multicultural populations.

Clinical Psychology Training

Mental health care during the early 1940s was largely custodial in hospitals, although shock treatments, psychosurgery, and some limited psychotherapy was available. The National Mental Health Act of 1946 provided funding for research, training, and community treatment programs sponsored by the National Institute of Mental Health (NIMH). The clinical psychology profession emerged in 1949 from a conference in Boulder, Colorado presenting the scientist-practitioner, or Boulder model, of training (Raimy, 1950). Funded internships were provided by Veterans Administration hospitals, outpatient clinics, and domiciliary facilities.

Many psychology students were soon dissatisfied with training emphasizing an experimental paradigm rather than addressing the human problems that fueled their interests in clinical psychology (Lipsey, 1974). This may have occurred because there were, in fact, two psychologies, scientific and humanistic (Kimble, 1984), but only the scientific perspective was legitimized by the Boulder model. Few psychology students encompassed both perspectives and found these training programs nourishing and relevant (Conway, 1982).

These perspectives have been described as Alpha and Beta, respectively (Dana, 1982, 1987). Many Anglo American psychologists embraced Alpha beliefs in an objective reality, a normative ideology, and social responsibility ethics, the hallmarks of scientific psychology. Early Beta students construed reality more subjectively and intuitively, however, using a humanistic ideology and personal conscience ethics.

Boulder model learning environments favored Alphas, although particular programs developed learning contexts to foster Alphas or Betas (e.g., Dana, 1978). One outcome of this training was an impersonal, technique-oriented, medicalized service delivery stance. This Anglo American training-specific etiquette fails to be sufficiently "credible" or "giving" for many clients from diverse cultural origins (Sue & Zane, 1987).

Many early Boulder model programs infrequently admitted and less frequently graduated students of color. Although the use of raw power in the service of racist motives has declined, covert restrictive and discriminative admission practices "cooled out" many students of color during an era of affirmative action.

George Albee (1970) criticized the Boulder model for espousing a psychiatric disease model that pathologized clients while racism, sexism, and economic exploitation were ignored. Albee (1982) later decried a preference among clinical psychologists for individual private sector psychotherapy practice instead of practice that addressed the entire spectrum of mental health needs using a prevention perspective. Scientist-practitioner training was also criticized for not distinguishing between research, or the practice of science, and clinical practice, or applications of science using situational, biographic, and historical data sources (Manicas & Secord, 1983). The Boulder model represented a value-neutral science, omitting awareness of an essential human element, the capacity to experience oneself as subject and object simultaneously. This human element can result in a proactive stance as watcher, commentator, and critic of oneself (Harré, 1984). Only a reciprocal interaction between researcher and research participant, or between provider and client, is able to directly confront this uniquely human characteristic (May, 1967).

Boulder model training in the 1940s and 1950s was available primarily for middle-class white males who became scientists first and psychotherapists belatedly. Most of these students personified a self-contained individualism with "firm boundaries, personal control, and an exclusionary concept of the person" (Sampson, 1988, p. 15). A more ensembled individualism, or collectivism, with fluid self/other boundaries and diluted control functions is limited to only a few Anglo American men (Lykes, 1985), although more prevalent among Anglo American women (Jensen, McGhie, & Jensen, 1991), probably as a result of different socialization experiences. An ensembled individualism is more characteristic of the 70% of the world's population that does not share a Eurocentric construction of reality.

During the 1940s and later, few blacks were seen in these training programs or as patients/clients. Ellison (1952) believed that blacks literally did not exist in the world of most Anglos and were in a hibernation described by the "pre-encounter" stage of Nigrescence theories in the 1970s (see Chapters 4 and 5, this volume). Poets like Countee Cullen and Langston Hughes sensed, experienced, and articulated a self-determined awakening. I experienced their struggle to be seen and heard as it was symbolized and enacted in Washington, D.C. cafeterias where black and white students sat down together in nonviolent protest. These restaurants reluctantly began to open their doors, if not their hearts, to black persons in the summer of 1947.

Gunnar Myrdal (1944), writing *An American Dilemma,* did not mention racism, which was understood at that time to mean "an ideology, an explicit system of beliefs postulating the superiority of whites based on the inherent biological inferiority of the colored race" (Robinson, 1995, p. 19). Research during this period by Anglo American psychologists was tainted by stereotypy and did not serve to even provide accurate descriptions of black culture or personality, with few exceptions (see Pettigrew, 1964).

Community Mental Health

Initiated by the report of President Truman's Committee on Civil Rights and the 1954 Supreme Court ruling against school desegregation, subsequent hallmark legislation included the Community Mental Health Center (CMHC) Act of 1963, the 1965 Voting Rights Act, affirmative action in 1971, and availability of public sector services for the poor. The passage of relevant legislation was a slow process because it involved power sharing and an anticipated shift in the balance of power. Within U.S. society, power issues were not openly discussed until K. B. Clark (1965) put into words the ideas and the passion that eventually stimulated the visual acuity of a nation. Later, these issues were presented to psychologists in his American Psychological Association (APA) presidential address (Clark, 1971). Issues of power in providing psychological services are not often examined by psychotherapists (e.g., Heller, 1985; Pinderhughes, 1989). It has been difficult to study persons who are in positions of power (e.g., Dana, 1964), although Rollo May (1972) had provided a vocabulary for uses of power.

During the 1960s, the CMHC Act (Public Law No. 88-164) established nearly 1,000 community mental health centers with catchment areas each containing 75,000 to 200,000 persons (Bloom, 1984). These centers provided essential services for inpatient and outpatient care, emergency services, partial hospitalization, and consultation/education with additional diagnostic, rehabilitation, precare, and aftercare services as well as training, research, and evaluation. Psychological, behavioral, and family therapies, innovative service delivery options, and psychotropic drugs were soon available. Medicare and Medicaid legislation in 1965 enlarged the population for these available services by initiating public health insurance for the elderly and poor (Frank, Sullivan, & DeLeon, 1994) with funds for serious and persistent mental illnesses (SPMI) and homicidal/suicidal persons (Santiago, 1992).

Shadish (1984) described societal and policy effects of releasing SPMI patients to the community beginning in the 1950s. Deinstitutionalization proved to be cost-effective and encouraged a variety of innovative treatment programs. For example, the Lodge Society (Fairweather, 1980) stimulated patients to re-enter society and maintained a low profile for these persons in the community under nonprofessional auspices. Behavioral treatment projects for schizophrenics and autistic children (Graziano, 1969; Paul & Lentz, 1977), and even the Community Mental Health Center (CMHC) program (Chiles, 1982), the Community Action Program (Heller & Monahan, 1977), and the Community Support Program (Turner & TenHoor, 1978) lost funding or adapted to the larger mental health system (Naierman, Haskins, & Robinson, 1978).

Mental health policy was not designed to represent the best interests of patients, but rather to fit the political, economic, and social constraints within existing social structures. Social system solutions must share common elements that include a professional aegis for innovative services, a belief in individualism resulting in assistance only at a subsistence level, and congruence with public attitudes and values reflecting stigma, intolerance, greed, and pragmatism (Shadish, 1984). As a consequence, nursing homes prospered and now care for 3 million persons, mostly women, aged 65 to over 85 (Selker, 1988). Mental hospitals have also regained some funds and reclaimed some patient populations. Multicultural populations have had insufficient power to focus attention on alterations in social structures to meet their needs or even to define and articulate these needs from their own perspectives.

Practitioner-Scholar, Community, and Counseling Psychology Training

In 1973, a Vail (Colorado) conference promised an alternative training model with a broader base of content, emphasis on design/evaluation of service delivery systems, accountability, and a focus on social problems including values and lifestyles of culturally diverse clients (Dana & May, 1986, 1987). George Albee's vision for a preventive community psychology could have been implemented by Vail Model training programs. The practitioner-scholar model in these Psy.D. programs encouraged specialization, an advocacy role in social system intervention, and concern with populations neglected by Boulder model elitism. Unfortunately, accreditation pressures by the APA led to increasing similarity between Boulder and Vail training models (e.g., Dana, 1992a) and proliferation of these practitioner programs with selective admission for those who could afford escalating tuition costs.

During this period, counseling psychology became another potential training avenue for doctoral professional practice in response to human values. The Greyston conference in 1964 delineated remedial/rehabilitative, preventive, and education/developmental roles (Jordaan, Myers, Layton, & Morgan, 1968). There were originally some unique areas, but by 1960 there was little to differentiate them from clinical psychology programs (Patterson & Lofquist, 1960), although admission criteria recognized student values/ humanity. These programs, however, fostered a conspicuous development of publication outlets for research on multicultural populations. When comparisons were made between articles appearing in the 1975-1986 *Journal of Counseling Psychology* and articles appearing during 1983-1988 in expanded publication outlets for culture-specific instruments (Sabnani & Ponterotto, 1992), there were increases of 10% and 31% for relevant articles during these two time periods.

Community psychology training and practice is still imbued by George Albee's values and their three journals became another publication outlet for culturally relevant research. Between 1965 and 1985, 13% of articles in these journals reflected cultural diversity goals (Loo, Fong, & Iwamas, 1988). Moreover, many of the journals responsible for dissemination of culture-specific research also began during the 1970s decade—these include the *Journal of Cross-Cultural Psychology; Journal of Multicultural Counseling and Development; Journal of Black Psychology; Culture, Medicine, and Psychiatry; American Indian/Alaska Native Mental Health Research;* and the *Hispanic Journal of Behavioral Sciences.*

Health Maintenance Organizations (HMOs)

In 1973, the HMO Act (PL 93-222) provided new federal funding for outpatient mental health care, crisis intervention, alcohol treatment, and referral services (DeLeon, VandenBos, & Bulatao, 1991). By 1978, there was a dearth of funding for appropriate treatment of cultural groups and federal support was increasingly used for training primary care physicians rather than psychiatrists. One result was that psychiatry, long a step-child among medical specialists, opted for realignment with medicine by altering its training toward a "clinical science" in order to share a common, medical frame-of-reference with other physicians (Greenhill, 1978). This realignment was largely achieved by remedicalization; a reaffirmation of biological factors in mental illness; an increasing reliance on psychopharmacological interventions; and dissemination of a diagnostic classification system, the *Diagnostic and Statistical Manual of Mental Disorders* (*DSM*) in 1980 (Dana & May, 1986). This manual provided the set of diagnostic labels now used by all mental health professionals in this country and has been adopted internationally.

The expectations of blacks for equitable mental health services were raised by the civil rights movement. This fact may account for their persistence in trying to continue posthospital contacts for outpatient aftercare in spite of receiving less adequate care than was available for Anglo Americans (Solomon, 1987; Warren, Jackson, Nugaris, & Farley, 1973). During this time period, they underused services and often relied on family members or ministers before presenting to emergency rooms in dire distress. Their perceptions of services in mental health centers were more positive during the late 1980s (Gary, 1987) when Anglo service providers were acceptable to most black clients. Many of these clients with an Afrocentric identity now believe that racism is a primary ingredient in psychopathology and prefer an African American provider who may share their beliefs and can provide acceptable treatment for racism and other issues as well (Helms, 1990a).

Prior to 1980, a majority of persons of color had received public sector mental health services due to lack of insurance coverage and substantially lower incomes than Anglo Americans. These public sector services had been designed by Anglo Americans primarily for Anglo American clients. The applicability of these services to persons of color was unquestioned by the mental health establishment, in spite of evidence that these services had been underused historically by all groups (Hoberman, 1992; Hui, Snowden, Jerrell, & Nguyen, 1991; Padgett, Patrick, Burns, & Schlesinger, 1994; Rosenheck & Fontana, 1994; Wallen, 1992; Woodard, Dwinell, & Aarons, 1992). Takeuchi and Uehara (1996) summarized reasons for underuse and high drop-out rates. These reasons included different health/illness beliefs, a non-English first language, discriminatory care that provided different diagnoses for the same problems leading to over- or underpathologization, as well as use of less costly services (e.g., group counseling/medication rather than individual counseling/psychotherapy).

Societal Transformation by Immigration, Outmarriage, and Segregation

During the 1980s, the size and composition of ethnic populations in the United States was transformed by immigration of 6 million legal immigrants and refugees from Asia and Latin America (Vega & Rumbaut, 1991). The 1990 census (U.S. Bureau of the Census, 1990b) reported that 65% of Asians in this country speak English as a second language. Non-Anglo groups now compose nearly 25% of the entire population (Aponte & Crouch, 1995) and will constitute approximately one third of the entire population within a few years (Jones, 1991).

Many of these new immigrants survived a "context of exit" that included massive trauma and torture as well as imprisonment. These persons then proceeded to a "context of reception" that invariably added a burden of resettlement and acculturation stress to the chronic, unresolved aftermath of these life-threatening earlier events (Portes & Rumbaut, 1990). Earlier immigrants to the United States also experienced exit and postentry trauma evidenced by mental hospital admission rates and high symptomatology prevalence rates in the Midtown Manhattan Project (Srole, Langer, & Mitchell, 1962). Social class and age were partially responsible for these differences, but the "social distance" between origin and destination accounted for culture shock and subsequent coping problems (Portes & Rumbaut, 1990).

Rumbaut (1985, 1989) compared exit contexts for stressful life events in the post-1975 Indochinese refugee immigration including death or imprisonment of family members, being alone and out of touch with family members, assault and fear of being killed during escape, bribes required to escape, and two or more years of refugee camp experience. These events were reported in descending order of frequency for Hmong, Cambodians, ethnic Chinese, and Vietnamese. The symptom rates decreased steadily over time, particularly among more educated males, as favorable present conditions gradually replaced traumatic past events during the first year, although "exile shock" in the second year reflected depression/demoralization that by the end of the third year had decreased dramatically.

By 1985, six preventable health problems among multicultural populations had been prioritized, including intentional/unintentional injuries and chemical dependency, which were major problems-in-living for these groups (U.S. Department of Health and Human Services, 1987). Two directions in dealing with these priorities were noted (Montes, Eng, & Braithwaite, 1995): (a) cultural norms and health/illness beliefs in culture-specific public health programs were being used as relevant factors for change, although the targets of change were behavioral; (b) problems were defined and solutions proposed on the basis of cultural uniqueness such that prevention programs initiated and sustained behavioral changes by adapting to a cultural context. Although there is scant evidence that this public health policy is being applied to mental health problems, the collapse of mental health policy into health policy suggests a probable future for use of prevention as intervention.

Some culturally competent and acceptable mental health services for multicultural populations have been available for many years in culture-general and culture-specific settings. Culture-general settings are usually unable to provide more than token services for relatively small culturally diverse populations, but have been able to tailor their services for large, diverse populations in Los Angeles and other major cities since the 1980s. Specialized, culture-specific service settings are not only used whenever available but are also considered acceptable and beneficial.

A *1992 Annual Report of the National Committee on Vital and Health Statistics* (Montes et al., 1995) indicated that multiple factors going beyond race and ethnicity influence health status and, by implication, mental health status as well. The gross reporting categories have become less useful over time for federal agencies in reflecting population diversity (Montes et al., 1995). In the 1970 census, a separate category was created for African Americans, formerly called "blacks," instead of lumping them in a "non-white" category. The next census will probably include biracial designations for the increasing number of persons who want their multicultural ancestries to be acknowledged. Asian Americans tend to outmarry with different rates and patterns for Chinese, Filipino, Japanese, Korean, and Vietnamese (Kitano, Fujino, & Takahashi, in press). Women outmarry with frequencies from 52% to 79%; men outmarry from 25% to 46%. Outmarriages have been most frequent among Japanese, ranging from 51% to 63%; Filipinos exceed 40%; Chinese exceed 30%; Koreans range from 8% to 34%; and Vietnamese are lower with 26% in 1989 and 6% in 1994. Third generation status is the best predictor for Chinese, Japanese, and Korean outmarriage (Kitano & Maki, 1996). Few blacks and whites, however, marry outside their racial groups, with 6% and 1.6% of men and 2% and 1.4% of women, respectively, although approximately 60% of American Indians marry outside their group (Mathews, 1996).

All cultural groups perceived the events of the 1960s and early 1970s as a promise of increased acceptance and equal treatment under the law. This promise has been fulfilled for many middle-class persons, particularly African Americans, but there remains a festering internalized mass of inchoate feelings of rage, powerlessness, and disappointment for millions of underclass ghetto residents. The American dream has eluded the appetites honed by television and the rhetoric of politicians in search of votes.

An increasing number of writers (e.g., Robinson, 1995; Steele, 1990; Wilson, 1980, 1987) believe that low self-esteem, survivor guilt, and "a self-defeating sense of victimization" (Robinson, 1995, p. 69) among blacks results in avoidance of personal responsibility, use of racism as an excuse, and "playing the race card." They cite a concentration of poor persons in an enormous urban ghetto underclass, an aftermath of urban deindustrialization, as responsible for psychopathology. Support has not been forthcoming for intensification of poverty as a result of outmigration of nonpoor blacks (Massey, Gross, & Shibuya, 1994), although black/white segregation has increased in housing and geographically in cities and neighborhoods (Massey & Hajnal, 1995).

Robinson (1995) also described loss of discipline and emotional support in black urban ghetto families, attributable to an increase in households with a female head from 25% to 50%. Concomitantly, the birth rate for unmarried mothers was nearly 64%; 45% of all children were below the poverty line between 1965 and 1990. During the last 50 years, black males suffered cumulative effects of discrimination in decreased lifetime earnings relative to white males, although younger black males are closer in income to their white cohorts (Thomas, Herring, & Horton, 1994). Similarly, the ghetto underclass is perceived as primarily responsible for the 25% of the African American male population in prison for 45% of violent crimes (Grekin, Jemelka, & Trupin, 1994).

The Mental Health Systems Act in 1980 would have supported community outreach services for urban and rural poor and underserved cultural groups, but in 1981, the Omnibus Budget Reconciliation Act (Public Law No. 97-35) introduced alcohol and drug abuse and mental health block grant programs and prevented any implementation of outreach and community preventive programs. As a consequence, responsibility for development of continuing mental health services has gradually shifted to the states. Each state has been allowed to decide on the level of mental health services and funds were redirected toward maintenance of the deinstitutionalized SPMI adults and children within the community in the CMHC system. There was no longer NIMH funding for research projects that identified racism, discrimination, or inequality. Block grant programs provided a death knell for community mental health centers and state mental hospitals. These facilities were replaced by short-term psychiatric inpatient care in general hospital settings using 70% of funds while prevention and outpatient services were minimized (Kiesler & Simpkins, 1992), another outcome of remedicalization in psychiatry.

Managed Care for
Multicultural Populations

During the 1980s, MCOs began to replace other health and mental health facilities, Medicare ceased serving the populations for whom it was designed, hospitals were established as profitable businesses, mental health policy linked earlier to social welfare policy became indistinguishable from health policy, and the public and private sectors began to merge (Dana, Conner, & Allen, 1996).

In early 1995, MCOs were responsible for standardized medicalized mental health services to an increasingly large segment of the population with the percentage impact differing greatly across states (Smith, 1995). These services are provided according to "medical necessity" contract language for mental health benefits that limits treatment to *DSM-IV* severe psychiatric disorders, "problems-in-living" capable of symptomatic improvement through "therapeutic management." Entire categories, including *DSM-IV* codes and Axis 2 disorders that do not contribute to medical issues, may not be covered because these disorders are not considered illnesses, are difficult to treat, or patients become chronically difficult to manage and are labeled "trouble makers" prior to termination of benefits. No precise definition of medical necessity is provided to patients prior to enrollment. One outcome of medical necessity has been pathologization by overuse of Axis 1 codes that contribute to legal and economic stigma of patients.

"Therapeutic management," or "business necessity," limits services to a few contact hours for a discrete episode with identifiable symptoms, using available treatments with a rapid response. Services are formulated to be symptom-reducing, solution-focused, predetermined treatment tracks ranked for cost and resource availability (Dana et al., 1996). Use of these tracks begins with psycho-education, progresses to group session(s), individual treatment, and finally community resources when benefit limits are exhausted or available tracks are ineffective (Glazer, 1992). In MCOs, quality of care has been replaced by cost containment, profit considerations, and displacement of treatment decisions from providers to insurers without excusing providers from accountability. Fewer than 20% of all persons in a national survey of mental disorders received treatment during a 12-month period while less than 40% had ever received treatment (Kessler et al., 1994).

Specialized services for non-Anglo American patients are not available in most MCOs, although these patients represented 25% of the total population by 1990 (Aponte & Crouch, 1995). Estimates indicate that non-Anglo Americans will constitute 34% of the population by the year 2000 and over 45% of all patients requiring mental health services will be from these groups (Kramer, 1995). Even when multicultural staff members are potentially available in health management organizations (HMOs), patients are assigned to them randomly. This occurs because of the assumption that all persons benefit from the same standard treatment tracks in spite of *DSM-IV* recognition of cultural formulations in diagnosis and ensuing interventions (American Psychiatric Association, 1994).

Research findings indicate that matching patients with providers for ethnicity or first language does not occur in HMOs, although such matching is efficacious (Flaskerud, 1990). Even if desired by MCOs, these specialized services could not be offered because acculturation status is never examined using interview or assessment data prior to onset of services and their personnel remain largely untrained to offer culturally sensitive services (Dana, 1993a). Traditional persons from many cultures, and those for whom English is a second language, are often unwilling or unable to accept these standard services.

The contemporary service delivery climate in MCOs goes beyond these issues to become even more aversive and dehumanizing. Whenever persons are funneled into homogenizing tracks, racial-ethnic origins and cultural identities are obliterated while potentially destructive and unacceptable mental health services are sanctioned and institutionalized (Dana et al., 1996).

Prologue

A psychology of human diversity assumes greater importance now than at any time in history. Huntington (1993) argued convincingly that the future of Western societies depends on an increasing knowledge of other civilization entities—Confucian, Japanese, Islamic, Hindu, Slavic/Orthodox, Latin American, and African. Cultural differences provide the major loci of conflict between these civilization entities. Cultural differences are less amenable to modification than political or economic issues, particularly because religion is an integral part of each civilization worldview. Groups representing all of these civilizations will compose more than one half of the population in the United States during the next century.

At present, multiculturalism in the United States is misunderstood partially as an outcome of a controversy at Stanford University that escalated to the public and political domains. Stanford University was forced to revise a "great books" requirement that had familiarized all undergraduate students with traditions, history, philosophy, and literature of Europe and Western civilization. This requirement was labeled Eurocentric; all students were subsequently introduced to a three-course sequence, "Cultures, Ideas, and Values," that emphasized a pluralistic perspective. The idea of multiculturalism came to be equated with a "politically correct minority perspective" that demanded "intellectual conformity in the name of a putative commitment to diversity" (D'Souza, 1991, pp. xii-xiv). It is no wonder that college campus life today has become segregated into black and white antagonistic camps that share increasingly negative stereotypes of one another (Phenice & Griffore, 1994). Institutional racism has a long history in mental health service delivery (De la Cancela & Sotomayer, 1993; Wade, 1993), but there is now a larger "backlash" that includes counsel to deemphasize multiculturality (Schlesinger, 1991) and recognize the United States as an Anglo American nation (Schwarz, 1995).

A multicultural perspective insists that "we must not only be equal under the law, we must also be able to understand ourselves as the authors of the laws that bind us" (Gutman, 1994, p. ix). This issue is central to mental health problems, research, diagnoses, and services. Ultimately, each multicultural group must provide the idiosyncratic perspective and cultural/racial idiom in which all providers become fluent. This is the meaning of culturally competent mental health services. Gould (1995) has correctly pointed out that cultural information provided to students preparing to be professional providers is not sufficient for cultural competence. Knowledge of different cultures must be augmented by an understanding of cultural identity, first in oneself and subsequently in other persons. The vital ingredient in this understanding is an internalized sense of personal identity. Such ethnorelativistic identity formation recognizes a "multitude of equivalent cultural realities within societies" (Gould, 1995, p. 202) and can mobilize affective ties as signals to other persons that these alternative realities are honored, cherished, and understood as equivalent realities. Implied here is an enlarged and more permeable Anglo American self that provides an internal locus for openness, curiosity, positive affect, and personal identity that can incorporate diverse others and has been called ethnorelativism by Bennett (1986).

The United States is currently beset by an array of interrelated political, social, and economic problems. These problems seem to defy responsible solutions from bureaucratized and self-serving social institutions and political leadership that is no longer in contact with the general population. Professional interventions alone are insufficient for the economic and social problems generated by poverty, unemployment-underemployment, poor housing, marginal education, illiteracy, poor health accompanied by insufficient/inadequate health insurance, and the immediate or long-term effects of racism. It is not surprising that these problems have eroded the quality of life for all persons.

As indicated earlier, there has been widespread disappointment among racial/ethnic groups that the New Society during the 1960s did not yield any relative improvement in economic conditions or a decrease in prejudice/discrimination that would improve the quality of life (Andrews & Withey, 1976; Campbell, 1981). The United States now has higher mortality rates for infants, children, and young to middle-aged adults as well as in the "years of potential life lost" (YPLL) index than 12 other developed countries (U.S. Congress, Office of Technology Assessment, 1993). Now that we have implemented managed health and mental health care, these indexes can be expected to worsen for everyone, but especially for persons from visible racial/ethnic groups (Dana et al., 1996).

This book is concerned with an amelioration of mental health services for visible racial/ethnic groups in the United States, including American Indians; and African, Asian, and Hispanic Americans with cultures and worldviews that diverge from the mainstream Anglo American. The interface between these groups and U.S. society generates problems, symptomatologies, and psychopathologies requiring ameliorative actions and interventions. For refugees, new living conditions and acculturative stress are often superimposed on histories of earlier trauma, imprisonment, and/or torture. These groups all cope with inequitable socioeconomic conditions, discrimination/racism, and struggles for political and economic power. In the long run, however, any exposition of credible and relevant services can only be implemented as a consequence of dramatic increases in control at the political level by each of these groups over the conditions of their own lives in the United States. In other words, the emergence of a genuinely multicultural society with an equitable distribution of power as a consequence of widespread ethnorelativism is a precondition for a professional climate of cultural competence.

2

Why Is It So Difficult to Provide Quality Care
for Multicultural Populations?

Historically, quality mental health care in the United States has largely depended on a common language and the shared beliefs that contribute to a process of mutual understandings between providers and clients. These shared beliefs derive from a Eurocentric construction of reality. This shared reality includes an acceptable professional service delivery style; the use of standard tests; explicit frames of reference for understanding personality, "normalcy" or dysfunctional/psychopathological behaviors and lifestyle; and a set of interventions and recognized provider skills for implementation. Quality mental health care in the United States has been primarily for Anglo Americans.

It is now politically correct to assert that cultural sensitivity is necessary because multicultural clients may be found in any service delivery setting, and consequently an openness to new cultural learning is required. Nonetheless, I do not believe that most Anglo professional service providers have accepted how different multicultural clients can be from themselves, or the extent of differences within each cultural group and, consequently, what is entailed within oneself in becoming culturally competent with even one group. To my knowledge, there are only a few self-report surveys that suggest cultural sensitivity among practitioners in states that have large multicultural populations (López & Hernandez, 1986, 1987; Ramirez, Wassef, Paniagua,

Linskey, & O'Boyle, 1994). The reported sensitivities did not include, for example, recognition of folk disorders and somatization. Similarly, possible social desirability responding cannot be overlooked in these studies.

Several years ago, in a social setting, an experienced Anglo clinical psychologist told me that it had required no special knowledge to provide services for members of several different American Indian tribes in a reservation outpatient clinic. Being pleasant, accepting, and understanding sufficed. She could not accept my astonished disagreement, perhaps feeling that I was questioning her professional skills instead of her cultural competence. There have been other conversations with many professional persons over time, especially in cross-cultural assessment workshops conducted during the 1980s that indicated a professional penchant for minimizing differences, assuming similarities, and pathologizing clients of diverse cultural origins. There was also pervasive belief that standard psychological assessment instruments, psychiatric diagnostic categories, and favored interventions were applicable to all clients. Many providers have accepted as universal a Euro-American worldview that is displayed in our professional technologies and professional acts with multicultural clients.

This chapter deals with issues that have made cultural competence infeasible in the past. A frame-of-reference will be provided for the entire book including attitudinal and technical limitations that foster ignorance of other persons who differ markedly from an Anglo American provider. These issues include (a) worldview and cultural/racial identities; (b) acculturation; (c) bias in the form of racism; (d) ethnocentrism-ethnorelativism; (e) research beliefs and practices; and (e) Anglo American standards for service delivery, assessment instruments, diagnosis, interventions, and training.

Worldview and Identity

Worldview is a cultural construction of reality that has developed as a basis for sanctioned actions to permit survival and adaptation under particular shared living conditions, geographic circumstances, and catastrophic events. A worldview contains the collective wisdom used to make sense of life experiences. An examination of worldview includes nonverbal behaviors, language, and assumptions concerning the composition of the world, human nature, the place of humans in the world, time, and causes of behavior (Kearney, 1975). Provider and client worldviews may coincide or clash to render services beyond understanding, and therefore unacceptable or underused (Ibrahim, 1985).

Group identity evolved from the history of the group and the nature of their cultural heritage. After 1933, a new term, *ethnicity,* began appearing in dictionaries and was defined as belonging to a particular group and having pride in one's group identity (Glazer & Moynihan, 1976). Ethnicity has become a group or nation referent that includes cultural background as one component (Betancourt & López, 1993). This cultural background includes a "subjective symbolic" or "emblematic" use of any cultural aspect for group differentiation (DeVos, 1975). Ethnicity is thus a primary focus for group identity and the shared characteristics of group identity are called culture.

Culture includes shared values, beliefs, language, behaviors, and customs. Values provide meaning and permit a construction of what is important and necessary for survival, given the nature of external reality. Values have been examined in many rubrics, but the Kluckhohn-Strodtbeck model of value orientations characterizes group similarities and differences, which provide some general expectations, although there are marked changes by generation and acculturation status (Kluckhohn & Strodtbeck, 1961). These values are human nature, person/nature relationships, time, social relations, and activity (for a review, see Carter, 1991).

Beliefs, particularly those beliefs concerning health and illness; loci of control and responsibility; and spirituality, which includes symbols to provide meaning, are found in all cultures. Language structures life experiences into thinking processes, provides labels for important feelings and salient environmental features, and permits communication with other persons who also speak the same language. Shared behaviors and customs foster mutual expectations and cohesiveness among culture members. These ingredients combine to shape perceptions of mental health services, providers, and service delivery styles and largely determine their acceptability and credibility to individual culture members.

Group identity and individual identity are components of cultural identity. Individual identity is described by the self and by personality. The self has a variety of components that differ by group and are affected by acculturation process and the acculturation outcomes described as cultural orientation status. An individual self has boundaries that vary in permeability, contents that may be admitted, a person concept (exclusionary or including few/many others), control, organization, and relative importance of particular contents (Dana, in press). Persons of various cultural identities typically will differ markedly on these self-contents and self-characteristics. Personality is formed by those characteristics considered to be important within the culture, particularly as a result of child-rearing practices and by living conditions that accrue from caste and class and include socioeconomic status and educational level as well as life experiences and trauma.

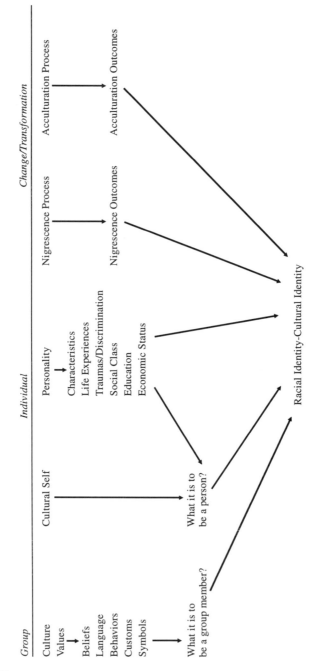

Figure 2.1. Group, Individual, and Change/Transformation Sources of Identity Formation

Figure 2.1 outlines the concatenation and relatedness of these ingredients as they form cultural identity or racial identity. This figure is provided to suggest the complexity of cultural/racial identity. In the first column, some worldview characteristics of the group describe culture and determine the perceptions of providers by clients and vice versa. The details regarding composition of the self, racial identity development (Nigrescence), and acculturation process and outcome appear in Chapter 4. This figure attempts to bridge the gap between group and individual identities and to expose the range and extent of within-group differences as expressed through the self and in the behaviors of individual group members.

The persistence of cultural/racial identities across many generations of residence in this country was not recognized by some earlier researchers who believed that ethnic identity was lost by the third generation. Recent work by Stanley Sue (1996) has indicated that for Asian bilingual and bicultural college students, culture significantly affects Minnesota Multiphasic Personality Inventory (MMPI) scale elevations regardless of generation in this country.

Because mental health services are primarily directed at understanding individuals not only as group members but as unique persons, a separation is made between "What is it to be a group member?" and "What is it to be a person who is also a group member?" By focusing on cultural/racial identity and self, this book attempts to bridge the gulf between research and practice.

Psychology has failed to define race scientifically or indicate its use as a concept (Yee, Fairchild, Weizmann, & Wyatt, 1993). As a consequence, "inaction has fostered a void that allows individuals and groups to assume and promulgate their own race meanings and agendas" (p. 1137). There is a growing conviction that the use of race as a political category has been responsible for the history of destructive group comparisons described subsequently in the Methodology section (Okazaki & Sue, 1995).

It follows that cultural identity and racial identity are difficult to distinguish and authors have strong preferences for using one term or the other. To avoid the use of the term race, Landrine and Klonoff (1996) use *ethnicity* or *cultural differences.* Carter (1995), however, prefers the use of *race* because all other experiences of black persons in the United States are superseded by the fact of race. Moreover, racial identity has been described as a process of Nigrescence whose outcome is the establishment of a comfortable racial identity or Afrocentrism/Africentrism (Montgomery, Fine, & James-Myers, 1990; Williams, 1981). These terms, *Afrocentrism* and *Africentrism,* go well beyond Landrine and Klonoff's description of cultural differences because pride is also included, a militant pride that insists on being acknowledged and demands justice, equity, and redress for a history of oppression from Anglo Americans.

I have tried to be careful in the use of ethnicity, culture, and race because they are complex terms, laden with surplus meaning, subject to politicization, and affected by racism (De la Cancela & Sotomayer, 1993). In addition, these terms are sources of bona fide controversy that need to be honored, particularly in the distinctions between racial identity and cultural identity.

Acculturation

Berry (1989) described acculturation as an adaptation or assimilation process by an ethnic/racial group to a host culture. This process is voluntary among immigrants, but happens involuntarily among refugees and indigenous peoples. Acculturation can also be an individual psychological phenomenon that occurs unevenly across many domains at the same time. For refugees, precontact, contact, conflict, crisis, and adaptation phases have been identified (Berry & Kim, 1988). These phases provide many opportunities for stressors, initially prior to immigration as well as during entry experiences, and often increasing during conflict and crisis. The accompanying distress may or may not be pathological in intensity.

The acculturation process, represented by these phases, is affected by ethnic group and majority group moderator variables (Aponte & Barnes, 1995). These moderators can be thought of as sources for potential corrections applied informally as part of an interview or more formally in questionnaire format. Typically, however, both interview and test sources of this information are helpful. The purpose of moderators is to have reliable estimates of contributions from various life experiences on the client. Moderator variables can change both the course of the acculturation process and the outcome.

Ethnic group moderator variables include not only the type of group, but cultural, social, and individual characteristics as well. Oppression, legal restraints, racism, prejudice, and discrimination adversely affecting the quality of everyday life are moderators from the majority group. These sets of forces influence both process and outcome as well as English language usage and fluency. Ultimately, psychological dysfunction and symptomatology by-products of acculturation may require mental health services.

Acculturation outcomes are varieties of adaptation that include traditionality, or maintenance of separation from a host culture; marginality, or adoption of some new cultural features and retention of others; biculturality, or integration; and assimilation to the host culture (Dana, 1993a). For American Indians, a transitional outcome has also been described in which individuals are bilingual but question their traditional values and religion (LaFromboise, Trimble, & Mohatt, 1990).

Historically, acculturation outcomes for American Indian tribes were evaluated and assessed by anthropologists, using a linear or continuum model. It soon became apparent, however, that separate dimensions of change for traditionality and acculturation were necessary. As measurement developed, the complexity of changes during the acculturation process required multidimensional acculturation scores or indices. As a consequence, not only was it possible to label the acculturation outcome, or cultural orientation status, but it became increasingly feasible to describe a cultural self on the basis of information from these measures (for detail, see Dana, 1993a, 1996b, 1997b).

Racism as Bias

As an outcome of racism, bias adversely affects our relationships with persons who differ from us. This effect can be conscious, inadvertent, or both. Consequently, it is necessary to label different forms of bias so that providers can examine these sources of bias within themselves as they interact with clients. Three sources of bias have been identified: cultural, individual, and institutional (Griffin, 1991). Cultural or group bias often appears in the form of stereotyping that defines the culture of one group as superior and by invidious comparison denigrates another cultural group. Individual or personal bias occurs in decisions that affect the life and well-being of persons in various cultural groups and in aversive encounters that individuals in these groups have with Anglo Americans. Institutional bias appears in the formal or informal policies of all societal systems at the national, state, and local or agency levels. These policies are often subtle and have indirect effects on cultural groups that serve to restrict, minimize, discourage, or deny mental health services.

Stereotypes, the most pervasive form of bias, will be described by studies of cultural racism in the general population and among professionals, particularly as applied to diagnosis and intervention. For example, Anglo Americans, surveyed as to whether various groups are "good" or "bad" for the United States, perceived persons of European descent—English, Irish, Jews, Germans, and Italians—as predominantly "good," whereas blacks, Japanese, and Chinese were perceived less cordially (Gall & Gall, 1993). Mexicans, Koreans, Vietnamese, Puerto Ricans, Haitians, and Cubans were even less generally favorably perceived, with one third to more than one half of respondents seeing these ethnic groups as "bad." Recency of arrival was the primary determinant of "good," while the degree of perceived difference influenced a judgment of "bad" (i.e., Cubans, Haitians, Vietnamese, and Puerto Ricans).

For blacks especially, stereotypes concerning inborn and physical differences have been used by whites to account for racial discrepancies in jobs, income, and housing. This history provided a basis for a 1993 telephone survey in Connecticut of a predominantly white, well-educated, middle-class population (Plous & Williams, 1995). Only 46% of these informants were willing to be interviewed, but approximately one half or more of these persons believed that white and blacks differed in at least one physical ability and that whites were superior in artistic ability and abstract thinking while blacks had superior athletic and rhythmic ability. Overall, although black respondents endorsed even more racial stereotypes, their relative numbers in this sample were very small.

Individual racism occurs in interactions between individuals and can be observed in behaviors as well as underlying attitudes and beliefs. Individual racism is also found in provider expectations for personality characteristics and behaviors. For example, Li-Repac (1980) found that Anglo American providers misperceived their Chinese American clients as anxious, confused, and reserved. Using the Survey of Afro-American Behavior, white professional providers in the 1980s endorsed negative stereotypes about blacks, particularly in the areas of family life, child rearing, and sexual values/behaviors perceived as inappropriate, while black providers held more positive attitudes in these same areas (Wyatt, Powell, & Bass, 1982).

Individual bias in epidemiological surveys, inpatient/outpatient admissions, and subsequent diagnoses, particularly of blacks, has been reported in a large number of studies over a long period of time. Two reviews are used to summarize this literature (Adibimpe, 1994; Lawson, Hepler, Holladay, & Cuffel, 1994). Recent data from the Epidemiologic Catchment Area survey suggested only modest racial differences in prevalence rates for mental disorders. There were, however, differences in help-seeking behaviors, the likelihood of involuntary commitment, representation in research samples, symptom presentation, and diagnoses. Blacks are still more likely to be involuntarily committed and hospitalized in public psychiatric hospitals where they receive more severe psychiatric diagnoses. Schizophrenia, especially, was misdiagnosed and consequently overdiagnosed. Using 1984 and 1990 Tennessee data, Lawson et al. (1994) found an overrepresentation of blacks in both inpatient and outpatient admissions as well as an assignment to several diagnostic groups, again including schizophrenia.

Because social stereotypes, when used as predictors of others' behavior, can induce the behavior predicted, the role of an intake provider will be complicated by any unexamined sources of group bias. Geller (1988) examined how construction of a patient image may impose restrictions during encoding of data, as well as distortions affecting information retrieval. Ninety psychiatrists and residents were placed in experimental groups using identical patient data except race and IQ. For two groups, the "black" or "white" patient had an IQ of 120, while in a third group the "white" patient had an IQ of 85. The "black" patient was rated as less able to benefit from psychotherapy regardless of an IQ equivalent to the "white" patient because he was significantly "less articulate, competent, introspective, self-critical, sophisticated about mental health centers, and psychologically minded" (p. 124). The "white" patient with an IQ of 85 was not deficient in the necessary skills to benefit from psychotherapy. It is no wonder that black patients have felt misunderstood by white therapists, as reported subsequently to their black therapists (Brantley, 1983).

Ethnocentrism and Ethnorelativism

Ethnocentrism, or the belief that one's worldview is reality, has pervaded human history. Bennett (1986) has described a model of ethnocentrism/ethnorelativism in which denial, an initial stage of ethnocentrism resulting from isolation and separation, is successively replaced by defense with postures of denigration, then by negative stereotyping and superiority, and, finally, by minimization of differences. Minimization trivializes differences and thus renders them unimportant using pseudoetics to rationalize and justify this position. The ethnorelativistic stages of *acceptance, adaptation,* and *integration* assume no absolute standard and that difference in itself constitutes the only absolute. Acceptance includes acknowledgment and respect for cultural differences, first as behavioral differences, then as value differences. Adaptation involves development of abilities to relate and communicate. Adaptation contains empathy, or "the ability to experience some aspect of reality differently than it is "given" by one's own culture" (p. 52). Pluralism, or the existence of many irreducible, equivalent ideas and values, means that differences can only be understood within the particular cultural context. Pluralism also implies biculturality, the simultaneous existence of two or more cultural realities. Integration posits a new type of human being whose worldview transcends an original indigenous culture. Contextual evaluation invokes the ability for analysis and evaluation from several chosen cultural vantages. Constructive marginality is used to describe the subjective experience of struggling with a total integration of ethnorelativism. Being outside of all cultural realities, such persons assume no "natural" cultural identity because of the conscious metalevel of any assumption. Marginality is constructive as a development from earlier states because it invokes a continuous creation of one's own reality.

Research Beliefs

The research beliefs held by most Anglo Americans are predominantly Eurocentric in origin and determine the conduct of their research, the likelihood of funding for support, and even the publishability of findings. An earlier research generation of visible racial/ethnic group social scientists who did not wish to conform to these Anglo American restrictions had the option of publishing in so-called fugitive journals, which were unavailable in most libraries, or of paying for publication in journals of secondary reputation or circulation. The use of these options has diminished over time, and an uneasy compromise has occurred between the demand to be heard and the use of conventional methodology and style of presentation to publish in mainstream or culture-specific journals. This does not mean that the social scientists have adopted alternate research paradigms (e.g., Hoshmand, 1989), but merely that it is now politically correct to publish research by non-Anglo American researchers when their work meets conventional standards on the basis of anonymity in peer review. Professional policy has been replaced by individual editorial prerogatives, with the result that some journals, especially in the area of counseling, not only are open to but welcome these authors of culturally relevant research.

Feminist scholarship has provided another impetus for change in publication policies that not only has broadened the range of acceptable methodologies but also has championed a less formal interactive process in which research participants are proactive and share in the development, conduct, and outcomes of research (e.g., see Billson, 1995). The importance of an advocacy motive for doing research has also been emphasized in this context (Wittig, 1985). This personalization of Anglo American scientific ideology, however, has not been subsequently legitimatized within psychology in spite of evidence indicating that who one is and where one works exerts a powerful influence on research outcomes.

Methodology. In addition to the development and awareness of new assumptions and methodologies, attention has focused on method deficiencies that can lead to reinterpretation of existing research literature. Okazaki and Sue

(1995) have described methodological problems in research design, sampling, selection of measures, establishing equivalence between groups, and data interpretation. If ethnic group members are included in a research design, they must be represented in sufficient numbers for meaningful comparisons that have been carefully planned in advance. Ethnic comparisons involve group matchings that are often extremely difficult to make on all relevant characteristics. There is no consensus concerning their identification, and there are extreme differences in the nature or distribution of these characteristics. When group-specific research is done, the psychometric properties of standard measures for the particular group should be established. Control of these variables post hoc by statistical analysis may also be complicated. Differences may exist in the variability of social-demographic characteristics that moderate the relationship between variables of interest. Nor is it generally feasible as a consequence of matching to extrapolate to other unmeasured variables.

Sampling techniques identify the ethnicity of participants. Self-identification by self-report, use of surnames by the researcher without participant confirmation, or identification of persons with mixed racial/ethnic identities are prone to gross errors. Even the assumption that ethnic identification per se leads to any common understanding of ethnicity among participants may be untrue (e.g., Sasao & Sue, 1993).

It has proven difficult to obtain samples of sufficient size for research purposes due to geographical differences in population distributions or reluctance to be "researched" because of suspicion, fear of exploitation, or unexpected and untoward negative consequences, although a number of suspect remediations for this dilemma have emerged. For example, recruitment practices may differ across participant groups, data from persons with common cultural origins may be lumped together, or unrepresentative college samples may be enlisted as research subjects as a general psychology course requirement. Community samples are preferred, although securing the cooperation of participants requires more finesse and knowledge of community social structures as well as avoidance of any unwitting overrepresentation by using subsamples. Similarly, the community geographic and political context may include particular ethnic group beliefs or intergroup relationships that can affect not only the sampling procedures but also the variables being examined by research.

Group statistical comparisons should be based on equal numbers of subjects, the representativeness of these subjects, random assignment or matching procedures, and control of all relevant variables (Okazaki & Sue, 1995). These conditions have been generally flouted or applied cavalierly, particularly by the use of very small and highly selected samples from cultural/racial groups (Graham, 1992). Moreover, matching fails because of differences between groups in social classes. Demographic composition by class and relative numbers of persons within each class may differ markedly. Failure to match on relevant variables such as acculturation outcome or racial identity stage instead of race can also dilute the matching process.

An example may be drawn from the MMPI literature in which matching on a greater number of variables did reduce the numbers of black/white MMPI difference items, but simultaneously rendered the black samples unrepresentative (Dahlstrom, Lachar, & Dahlstrom, 1986). An appropriate use of a cross-cultural framework assumes not only equating groups on all relevant variables, but using constructs and measures that have cross-cultural validity (Azibo, 1988).

In addition, cultural bias can compromise the assumptions for conventional statistics (Helms, 1992). Measurement bias is known to affect mean differences, latent factor structure, and population differences in test scores and external criterion-related measures. Cultural bias can, however, also occur using the Null Hypothesis as a no-difference proposition for cultural uniformity in assessment. Cross-cultural difference-variance could as readily be assumed as the basis for the Null Hypothesis (Malgady, 1996). A statistical basis for the unexamined assumption of minimal group differences has reinforced the apparent credibility of group difference research.

Finally, a persistent problem in the area of interpretation of comparative research data from a Western perspective has been the negative evaluation of differences. Evidence for this accrues from a pervasive inequity historically in the form of thousands of group difference studies that used a majority of available psychological tests. In these studies, not only is the premise of looking for group/racial differences suspect, but the biological/evolutionary explanations provided for obtained differences were generally untenable (Zuckerman, 1990).

A request from a test publisher to evaluate the Seven Squares Test provides a personal example. This intelligence measure was used in South Africa, and subsequent publication in the United States was desired. The task was to arrange seven squares. White subjects did arrange them, while the black subjects, coerced into testing by their supervisors, did as little as possible. This group difference in behavior was inappropriately interpreted at a construct level as "intelligence," without evidence that the test indeed measured "intelligence." An acrimonious journal debate resulted in the researchers losing their jobs, and the test was never published in the United States (Dana, 1965; Dana & Voigt, 1962). This example may sound simplistic, but it illustrates how methodology based on racial preconceptions can be faulty and can lead to erroneous research conclusions with potentially destructive social consequences.

Etic and Emic. There terms originally provided a linguistic distinction between phonemics, or sounds in one language, and phonetics, the generalizations from specific languages to a universal science of language (Pike, 1966). By analogy, emics and etics usually refer to culture specific or monocultural, and culture general or pancultural, respectively, although there have been radically different defining characteristics (Starr & Wilson, 1980). Emics are never cross-cultural, which may explain "a startling lack of encouragement or reinforcement to develop tests that are emic" (Trimble, Lonner, & Boucher, 1983). A pseudo simplicity has been apparent in measuring both emics and etics (Jahoda, 1977), which may be responsible for the failure to develop adequate emics or genuine etics.

Because these demonstrations of equivalence are difficult to accomplish, standard psychological tests have been used as pseudoetics. A *pseudoetic* is an Anglo American emic that is presumed to be an etic and, therefore, of universal usefulness. Davidson (1977) correctly anticipated the failure of translated pseudoetics to represent cultural differences as derived from mean score differences between two populations.

López (1996) prefers to use etic and emic as different lenses to provide helpful, alternative perspectives through which to examine cultural identity. In fact, he teaches his psychology graduate students to do this by a balanced consideration of "universal norms, specific group norms, and individual norms in differentiating between (a) normal and abnormal behavior, (b) considering etiologic factors, and (c) implementing appropriate interventions" (López et al., 1989, p. 370).

Personality. Most personality conceptualizations used for understanding clients have origins in Euro-American personality theories developed by male theorists. A notable exception to this is the structural approach to ego development by Jane Loevinger (1976) that relates specific interventions to particular stages and includes an assessment procedure. Psychoanalytic theories proffered a human developmental process never proven to be universal to become another example of a pseudoetic. Moreover, theories used in the United States typically focused on internal processes and subsequently minimized attention to external environmental or social demands as advocated by (Murray, 1938) and others (e.g., Leary, 1957; Stern, 1970; Swenson,

1973). This focus accorded with an Anglo American self as well as with psychoanalysis rather than with an enlarged self that goes beyond the discrete individual.

Similarly, although there are specific emic cultural/racial conceptualizations of personality, they have not generally been used to increase cultural understanding of intervention processes. A review of some of these non-Anglo American emics is available elsewhere (Dana, in press).

The identification of psychological universals or etics was described at a relatively early date in the history of cross-cultural psychology (e.g., Lonner, 1980). In addition, there have been demonstrations of genuine etic constructs by Eysenck (i.e., Introversion-Extraversion, Neuroticism, Psychoticism), Osgood (i.e., Evaluation, Potency, Activity), and Triandis (i.e., Individualism and Collectivism), and others. Although these are competent measures of etic constructs, they have not been used to augment appreciation of relevant personality characteristics in cross-cultural assessment practice (Dana, 1993a).

Non-Anglo American etic examples of personality theory include both the inner domain and the various intimate and extended worlds of other persons and society (Etzioni, 1968; Hsu, 1971). These theories have never been adopted or used by practitioners in the United States, while Euro-American theories have been used instead worldwide without evidence of cross-cultural construct validity to permit legitimate applications to non-Europeans. One outstanding cultural transmogrification of psychoanalysis by Doi (1971) has been used in Japan.

There is clearly too little etic or emic personality information at the present time to describe the cultural self with any degree of completeness or adequacy. Perhaps this has occurred because there are two separate traditions in psychology—the creation of personality theory and a research examination of constructs typically independent of particular theories. Conventional wisdom in clinical psychology, at least, has held that research knowledge should inform practice. The Boulder model of training was developed from this premise. There has been little incentive to examine deductions from personality theories, particularly because this research endeavor with psychoanalytic theory did not satisfy either practitioners who used psychoanalysis intuitively or research-trained clinicians who desired to practice on the basis of replicated research findings.

Research and Practice. It is my belief that a Eurocentric model for research and practice in the United States has fostered a dichotomy between research and practice because legitimate interventions have been identified almost exclusively on the basis of their empirical foundations. This research-practice dichotomy has been strengthened by a cognitive-behavioral construction of a technology-based therapeutic reality that pays only minimal attention to the human quality of the service delivery process. This statement is not intended to deny the efficacy of interventions for a variety of problems that can be replicated by different therapists with identical outcomes and applied to various cultural groups. This, however, provides only one legitimate direction for interventions that ultimately will be etic in nature. Moreover, as suggested by the service delivery constraint, an etic technology must be delivered in an emic format for maximum benefit to clients.

The endeavor to be scientists first and practitioners second in clinical psychology has failed to produce practitioners who can attend sufficiently to individual differences to comprehend cultural/racial identity as an acceptable focus for their interventions. Selection of students predicated on characteristics that make for potential excellence in research inevitably disregards a similar concern with selection for excellence in providing quality human care using other intervention technologies. Other areas, such as social work and counseling psychology, have been more focused on selection for human service practice in addition to excellence in scholarship and hence became less circumscribed by practice exclusively on an empirical-technological basis.

This book acknowledges both etic and emic traditions as well as emic/etic combinations as legitimate components of effective models for mental health services to non-Anglo American cultural populations. Bridging the research-practice abyss for effective multicultural services should rest on a clinical focus on client cultural identity rather than on Anglo American emic methods for diagnosis and intervention.

Anglo American Standards

Implicit Anglo American standards in four major mental health areas are a product of training, the kinds of services that have been available in this country, and the vested interests of test publishers and other professions, particularly psychiatry.

Service Delivery. Services have usually been available only in office settings. Service delivery for many clinical psychologists and cognitive-behavioral therapists has aped the medical model with distance, at least, if not an impersonal behavioral style. There has been scant attention to matching providers with clients for ethnicity or language, in spite of research that indicates that retention in treatment and favorable outcomes are associated with matching for several cultural groups. Except in the Rio Grande Valley area of Texas where providers are typically bilingual, most providers speak only English and are unaware that providing services in a client's second language, or using an interpreter, will drastically delimit the quality of services and distort the therapist-client interaction by stereotyping and misunderstanding of emotional content.

Assessment Instruments. As indicated previously, most standard psychological tests are pseudoetics. The assessment establishment prefers use of these tests without modifications to recognize cultural variance in obtained scores because the existing research is not deemed credible (e.g., Velásquez, Butcher, Garrido, & Cayiba, 1996). Nonetheless, even with adequate translations, the use of Anglo American standard tests in other countries or with non-Anglo Americans in the United States is feasible only under certain conditions (Dana, 1996a). First, an acculturation screening measure is required to indicate assimilated and bicultural persons for whom the tests may be appropriate, as well as traditional and marginal persons for whom the tests are often misleading or inapplicable (see Dana, 1993a, chap. 7). Second, standardization procedures typically select non-Anglo Americans either by representative sampling from the total population, which provides too few subjects, or by matching on selected "relevant" variables, as previously described, which minimizes group representativeness. As a consequence, cultural variance is reduced only for those persons rather than for the particular cultural group. Third, only the development of separate standard test norms for acculturation outcomes, or cultural orientation categories, would permit use of tests with traditional and marginal persons. This procedure avoids culture-specific or group-specific norms, which lump together persons with different acculturation statuses within the same cultural group.

Only the development and validation of new emic and etic tests, however, will answer the dilemma of fairness and potentially provide less stigmatizing assessment outcomes. We require a new generation of tests with adequate cross-cultural validation histories. Genuine etic tests can provide a construct vocabulary for personality similarities and differences across cultures. Some possible candidates include the Basic Personality Inventory (Jackson, 1989), the NEO Personality Inventory (Costa & McRae, 1992), the Interpersonal Adjective Scales (Wiggins, 1995), and the Personality Assessment Inventory (Morey, 1991). These tests and the models for personality study they represent are of relatively recent origin, and clinicians should examine available cross-cultural research applications (Narayanan, Menon, & Levine, 1995).

The use of new emic constructs has been limited due to failure to recognize ethnocentrism or examine Eurocentric assumptions. Instead, differences have been minimized to render others more like Anglo Americans. As clinicians become aware of information resources and there are many additional research-based constructs, this area can make a major contribution to cross-cultural interpretation. Nonetheless, new emic tests are also necessary as vehicles to examine the research-based constructs.

Psychiatric Diagnosis. All mental health service providers now use the *Diagnostic and Statistical Manual of Mental Disorders (DSM-IV)* (American Psychiatric Association, 1994). This manual was developed in a modern, secular, Western society on the basis of belief in dualistic epistemology, or mind-body dichotomy, that references a model of illness including pain reports, bodily experience, physiological dysfunctions, appropriate parameters of worry, social role functioning, and care seeking (Fabrega, 1991). A split consciousness has occurred among Europeans historically (Van den Berg, 1961), and, as Kleinman (1988) indicated, "this acquired consciousness interferes with total absorption in lived experiences" (p. 50). As a consequence, there is now an absence of highly focused attention (akin to trance states) and a dramatic, unreflective responsivity to crisis divesting the Western self of the literalness of bodily metaphors for intimate personal distress as well as access to gods, ghosts, and ancestral spirits. Instead, a psychological meta-language distances felt experience, has created boundaries for the self and, incidentally, has made for the appearance of Western culture-bound psychopathologies of borderline and narcissistic personality disorders. Hence, the *DSM* is devoid of meaning for many non-Western persons due to a culture-specific dualism and the presence of a "meta-self" or "critical observer" that has diluted our Anglo American life experiences and forms the silhouette humanity of modern persons (Kleinman, 1988). Nonetheless, the *DSM*—at least for Anglo Americans—fulfills and embodies the psychiatric vicissitudes of the contemporary human condition. One objective in this book is to render the *DSM* more reliable and useful for diagnoses of persons in multicultural populations living in the United States. Castillo (1996) traced the evolution of *DSM* paradigms from the biopsychosocial (*DSM-I*) to the beginnings of a shift in *DSM-II* toward a disease-centered psychiatry (*DSM-III*), and beginnings of another shift in *DSM-IV* because the research promise to undergird a disease model has not been forthcoming. Castillo believes that psychiatric anthropology and postmodernism can provide the impetus for *DSM-V.*

DSM-III and *DSM-III-R* were criticized for being poor science with disastrous social consequences for everyone affected by a diagnosis (Kirk &

Kutchens, 1992). A classification system should not only be usable with high agreement among diagnosticians but lead to intervention outcomes of demonstrated efficacy. Kirk and Kutchens find pervasive unreliability in the current diagnostic process, an unreliability that has been conveniently obscured using inappropriate statistics or simply denied. Misdiagnosis, pathologization, and over- or underdiagnosis are frequent outcomes. Only marginal agreement has been reported for *DSM* classification reliability between independent diagnosticians, accompanied by extreme variability in reliabilities across disorders (e.g., Kreitman, Sainsbury, Morrissey, Towers, & Scrivener, 1961). Nor does current *DSM* diagnosis necessarily lead to interventions of demonstrated efficacy, particularly for persons of color in this society. Only a new or radically revised *DSM* and a more sharply focused *DSM* would be able to provide a lexicon of culture-general and culture-specific psychopathology criteria and conditions. Many providers are acutely aware that *DSM* limitations render culture-fair diagnosis both elusive and difficult (e.g., Cervantes & Arroyo, 1994; Johnson, 1993). Even when clearcut *DSM* diagnostic criteria are applied to women and African Americans, blatant and pervasive psychiatric bias was apparent in an analogue study (Loring & Powell, 1984). Reliability issues are still germane and reliability trials have been proposed for *DSM-IV* (Kutchens & Kirk, 1995).

In *DSM-IV* there have been token attempts to create the illusion of cultural sensitivity in diagnosing culturally diverse persons (American Psychiatric Association, 1944). These attempts include a one-page introduction suggesting some inherent difficulties in diagnosing individuals from diverse cultural backgrounds, and the presence of some major culture-bound syndromes is recognized in a seven-page glossary. A total of approximately 15 text pages of specific culture, age, and gender features for many disorders are embedded in a context of 849 pages. It should be emphasized that gender and age content are also included in these brief statements, in addition to ethnic and cultural considerations. The *DSM-IV* suggests that a narrative summary be developed for multicultural clients. How to accomplish the task of cultural diagnosis is not specified in *DSM-IV.* In the interim, it will be necessary to develop the cultural formulations recommended in *DSM-IV* and to gain experience in using the *DSM-IV* glossary of culture-bound disorders. This is difficult because there is no consensus that it is mandatory to examine cultural identity as part-and-parcel of any diagnostic process. Castillo (1996) has provided guidelines for each disorder that are a necessary supplement to *DSM-IV.* The *DSM-IV* does provide the beginnings of a cultural sensitivity that has been applauded by the American Psychological Association (DeAngelis, 1994), although examined somewhat less enthusiastically elsewhere (Nathan, 1994).

Interventions. Most of the interventions to be described in Chapters 5, 6, 7, and 8 are remedial in nature, or tertiary, although the most effective interventions will continue to be societal in nature and preventive at the primary and secondary levels (Bloom, 1984). Tertiary prevention seeks to reduce the severity, discomfort, or disability of sufferers and ultimately to reduce prevalence rates. Secondary prevention affects these prevalence rates by reducing the duration of a disorder as a result of early casefinding and effective treatment. Primary prevention seeks to reduce incidence, or the rate at which new cases of a disorder develop. Any widespread usage of primary prevention for all populations will only be in response to health/mental policy as enacted into federal and state laws.

It is possible to reduce incidence rates for all kinds of disorders and problems-in-living by attention to risk and protective factors (Cole et al., 1993). Risk factors are germane to the probability of onset, increased severity, and prolonged duration of these disorders and problems. Risk factors were clustered by these authors into family circumstances, emotional difficulties, school problems, sociological context (i.e., neighborhood organization, racial injustice, unemployment, extreme poverty), constitutional handicaps, interpersonal problems, and skill development delays. Protective factors such as behavioral-cognitive skills, social supports, parental/adult warmth, discipline, monitoring, supervision, and adequacy of models for potential bonding can improve the resistance to risk factors. A casebook of selected prevention programs suggests a variety of approaches to reduce some of these risk factors for all groups (Price, Cowen, Lorion, & Ramos-McKay, 1988).

The available psychological interventions have been developed primarily for Anglo Americans, and their research histories suggest applications with this historic mainstream population. Recent evidence, however, strongly indicates that culturally competent service delivery by matching providers and clients for ethnicity, language, or both will improve service use, enhance client retention, and favor beneficial outcomes with available interventions (Sue, Chun, & Gee, 1995). Nonetheless, matching may simply provide culture-specific styles of service delivery to accompany intervention procedures that remain largely Anglo American in origin. Chapters 7 and 8 will begin with interventions in countries of origin and examine culture-general, combined, and culture-specific techniques as moderated by acculturation status and client preferences.

A still unaccomplished research task lies in specifying efficacious treatment options for persons in various cultural groups. To do this, research information is required on the contribution of specific cultural variables to the intervention process in addition to what is known about ethnic and language match effects. This research-based information, informed by cultural knowledge and experience, would be coupled with service delivery skills during assessment. As a result, assessment would have direction in the kinds of data to look for, what to examine, and what sources of extra-test data are required to use cultural information for diagnosis as a precursor to interventions.

Underuse of Services

Mental health services for racial/ethnic populations were underused historically because clients were denied access or presented with inferior, less costly, and culturally incongruous services often proffered using unacceptable service delivery behaviors and etiquette. In a recent review, Leong, Wagner, and Tata (1995) discussed several reasons for underuse including financial, institutional, and cultural barriers, as well as the availability of alternative resources. Because mental health services require either insurance coverage or ability to pay, reductions in public sector services most seriously affect those with the lowest incomes. Institutional barriers have included difficulties associated with going to central agency locations and arranging child care or transportation. Agencies typically have strict time schedules and formal procedures, and providers often focus on intrapsychic problems and are skeptical concerning the usefulness of indigenous therapies. There are also cultural barriers of language, values/beliefs, stigma among less acculturated persons, and scarcity of culturally relevant service settings (Rogler, Malgady, Costantino, & Blumenthal, 1987). Alternative resources including family, friends, folk healers, and clergy provide care within a community social context that has no cost or is relatively low in cost, immediately available, and culturally relevant.

3

Quality Care for Multicultural Populations

Quality care may be defined as a set of outcomes from ethnorelativistic thinking applied to the development of services and mechanisms for service delivery. Society has to esteem and value these services sufficiently to provide for adequate funding and minimize discrimination in access and use. This chapter will suggest ideals, describe realities, and assess current limitations. Such services begin with understanding the nature of the human contract between provider and client. The meaning of this contract can be reflected in the selection, training, and evaluation of providers as well as by the organizational standards, guidelines, and ethical codes developed by concerned professions. This contract is then implemented by state and national legislation, which includes licensure and enforceable rules governing subsequent practice.

The goal of this chapter is to develop a statement of cultural competence that describes quality care for multicultural populations. Quality care is approached via the character of the provider, including historical origins of strengths, relationships, and obligations. Over time, this idealized conceptualization has eroded. The 1992 American Psychological Association Ethical Code reflects this blurred provider image by omissions and limitations of services for multicultural clients. Suggestions are provided for continued development of codes, standards, and guidelines for ethical practice with multicultural populations. The range of problems requiring a high standard of care are described as an introduction to the application of culture-general as well as specialized assessment and intervention techniques for these populations. An assessment-intervention model contains some ingredients to render quality care more feasible for multicultural clients.

Becoming a Provider

The prototype for personal and professional characteristics of providers is the traditional healer. Historically, all behaviors of traditional healers were scrutinized by the entire community. There was informal monitoring by public opinion, and their multiple roles were discussed and evaluated in the manner applied to all other residents, although with special hopes and expectations (Boyer, Klopfer, Brawer, & Kawai, 1964). Their humanity (or lack of humanity) was palpable and known to everyone by reputation, or from first-hand experiences of persons in the community. Potential consumers had personal knowledge of the outcomes of services to many other persons over a period of time. This knowledge was always balanced by urgency of personal need for services, an ability to provide compensation for services, and availability of traditional healers, alternative services, or both. Under these circumstances, formal guidelines or sets of rules were unnecessary. Consumers and their families had sufficient information for decision making and were afforded some protection by the high level of community awareness. This awareness made censure for inappropriate behaviors possible in a variety of benign or violent ways depending on the cultural group. A modicum of social control over the behavior of providers could usually be exercised, often expressed only as part of the provider's reputation rather than reflected in any direct community actions. During periods of societal breakdown, provider probity and community regulatory mechanisms were sometimes adversely affected as a result of increased desperation for services, scarcity of providers, or both (e.g., Siskin, 1983). Even under adverse circumstances, however, consumers were in a somewhat stronger position than they are at present in the United States. We rely on a complex process of rules, with frequent flouting of these rules, and a time-consuming, difficult process to negotiate for personal or financial redress through ethics committees or by recourse to legal processes.

It is feasible to construct a model for ethical service delivery by human service providers. Any such model is an idealized conception similar to that contained in the Boulder model promise of a scientist-practitioner. This model provides a point of entry for discussing the APA Ethical Code (American Psychological Association [APA], 1992) as a vehicle for contributing to ethical services and quality of care for multicultural groups.

Provider Virtues, Relationships, and Obligations

Ethical services should emerge from provider probity based on an internalized set of community standards and a enlarged capacity for caring and acceptance of responsibilities. Table 3.1 contains an outline of idealized provider characteristics as related to obligations toward clients. This outline suggests an enlarged frame-of-reference with relevance to all client populations. Although the use of the term *virtue* may seem adventitious, virtue is used here in the Ericksonian sense to mean "strength" as in "strength of character."

Provider virtues include power, knowledge, and humanity. Power and perceived power have always been essential ingredients in providing services. Clients need to believe that efficacy for treatment is embodied in the provider, that their personal health/illness belief system dovetails with potential provider remediations, and that these remediations can be accomplished successfully by the provider. In other words, providers were endowed by the client with healing powers and an ability to exercise these powers for their benefit.

This does not beg the question of whether or not the provider, in fact, does possess immanent powers for healing. Healing is a "calling" in which bona fide providers believe they can be helpful to others whether by exercise of immanent powers, learned technologies, or persuasive social skills in the delivery of their services. Power is actualized by providers in different cultures on the basis of their own worldviews and belief systems. The power source for Western interventions lies in technologies that are believed to have both specific effects on presenting problems or behaviors as well as more generalized effects on personality structure, organization, and functioning.

Power in Anglo American culture has been identified and described by May (1972) as exploitive, manipulative, competitive, nutrient, and integrative. The application of nutrient and integrative power is particularly appropriate for providers, while exploitive, manipulative, and competitive power can be damaging and destructive in any healing process. Nutrient power is used for the care of others, while integrative power is shared because it can increase the personal power of others. Mental health providers in Western societies aspire to use nutrient power, but in earlier times and in many societies today, traditional healers still use integrative power. In these cultures, power is generated by an openness of the self to spiritual and natural forces that guide or directly assist the provider in healing ministrations and

Table 3.1   Service Delivery: Provider Virtues, Relationship Characteristics, and
Obligations

Virtue	Relationship	Obligation
Power	Trust	Be responsible in use of power for client (lifelong supervised self-scrutiny of own motives, needs, behaviors); not exploit, seduce, manipulate for own ends.
Knowledge	Closeness	Be fair, honest, prepared adequately with maintenance of skills over a professional lifetime.
Humanity	Dependency	Provide a standard of care: Advocating, affirming, advising, counseling, enabling, honoring, interpreting, mentoring, modeling, nurturing, sanctioning, sharing, supporting, and so forth.

rituals as well as by an informed use of natural substances. Such power may be used to invoke similar sources of self-emanating aid from spiritual or natural forces within clients that can contribute to a healing process.

Providers require knowledge to be effective and responsible. The cognitive professional knowledge of Western providers includes assessment and intervention technologies. These technologies are applied within a framework of diagnostic standards and practices as well as by an awareness of available community resources for intervention. A provider advocacy role may also be required to implement the use of these resources for clients.

Knowledge pertains to the context of a client's everyday life as well as the client's group history, including relationships with other groups. Knowledge of the beliefs, values, and perceptions that form the base for client behaviors is also necessary. In addition, facility in the client's first language is mandatory for effective communication and an accurate understanding of feelings and content of life experiences.

Providers exercise their own humanity in all transactions with clients. Humanity, in this sense, has at least four characteristics: (a) sensitive awareness, (b) understanding, (c) wisdom, (d) standard of care. Sensitivity refers to the ability to know what a client is communicating in words, behaviors, and feelings. Moreover, sensitivity implies that the provider recognizes that the meanings conveyed by his or her own communications are always culture specific. With sufficient knowledge and experience of a client's culture, a provider may be able to take the cultural standpoint of another person as a basis for interpreting communication and also as a means for altering and regulating the communicated meanings from the provider's own verbalizations and nonverbal behaviors. Understanding also implies the ability to put knowledge to practical use with a particular client and thus includes performance of an acceptable social etiquette in the delivery of services.

Wisdom affords perspective, particularly on the provider's own personal and group identity, on her or his life experience, and closure or coming-to-terms with a history of personal events, circumstances, experiences, and relationships. Wisdom is the outcome of a lifetime of learning from experience and is not necessarily related to age, gender, particular life experiences, or professional training. Although difficult to capture in words, clients do expect such wisdom from providers as a guarantee that provider humanity can envelop, sustain, enrich, and protect any intervention process.

Power and knowledge would be insufficient without a care-centered attitude that is part of provider humanity. This attitude creates an umbrella for the transactions, technologies, feelings, and difficulties in any intervention process. For the client, care centeredness implies a relationship that can represent any combination of many potential ingredients: advocating, affirming, advising, counseling, enabling, honoring, interpreting, mentoring, modeling, monitoring, nurturing, permitting or sanctioning, sharing, and supporting. These qualities of caring parallel the range of client needs. These are the "gifts" described by Sue and Zane (1987) that clients need to experience in a tangible, concrete, experiential manner during each encounter with a provider to sustain the belief that the provider indeed has the power, knowledge, and humanity to provide credible services.

Provider virtues are directly related to the quality of caring relationships with clients. Relationships should always be developed using a social etiquette that is recognized by clients as being culturally appropriate for the service delivery context. This relationship always entails trust and some degree of closeness evidenced by shared behaviors, which may or may not become prolonged, result in dependency, or both. Closeness invites transference in clients, a fantasy merging of provider power, caring, and protectiveness with images of significant, historic others, often mother or father. These transference feelings may or may not include distortion, but always provide glue to enrich, deepen, and strengthen the relationship between provider and client. Clients are bound to providers by hopes that the services are potentially efficacious, by convictions that the provider has the knowledge or wisdom to comprehend their life experiences and the requisite skills to meet their expectations and by feelings of immediate or potential sanctuary, safety, and security.

Providers have complex and often unverbalized obligations with regard to their clients. They are obligated not to misuse their power by demeaning, exploiting, manipulating, sexualizing, stereotyping, or pathologizing their clients. These abuses of power essentially benefit the provider and can destroy not only the relationship with the client but any remediation or restorative outcome of services.

Similarly, the uses of power can be compromised by greed, by provider motivation based primarily on rewards for services rather than an abiding concern with caring for other persons. One antidote for greed lies in taking a responsible place in the life of the community. This stance can include presence in and active participation at varying levels including providing pro bono services within the mental health service delivery system and voluntary participation in other systems (criminal justice, education, health, environmental planning, politics, religion, and so on). These activities encourage the development of a community perspective on what one does professionally within an enlarged social context. Only in this manner can there be a counterbalance for the professional immersion and encapsulation that often results in isolation from the panoply of community needs and resources. Such isolation can foster an elitism with expectations for special privilege as a result of education and professional occupation. The socialization experiences provided by medical, psychological, and legal training, for example, result in strong pressures for belief in personal rewards that include high income and special privilege.

Another obligation that accompanies power is to be continuously aware of countertransference and the necessity for lifelong self-scrutiny of the provider's own motives, needs, and behaviors. This is no idle obligation; in our society we lack public scrutiny and community monitoring of the provider's entire life experience that once resulted from an integumentation into the community and multiple roles with clients. Group practice, peer review, credentialing processes, continuing education, and personal counseling or psychotherapy are poor substitutes for the community aegis once provided by living in a figurative glass house in a small village.

Knowledge as an obligation means being prepared to provide services using comprehensive and up-to-date information and technical skills. Moreover, it is imperative to recognize that the life expectancy of this knowledge and accompanying intervention technologies may only be a few years at best. The obligation to be knowledgeable can be fulfilled by dint of continuous hard work to be aware of research and professional practices within one's specialty domains.

Obligations that accrue from the provider's personal humanity pertain to the responsibilities in providing services to other human beings. These obligations are complex and intertwined because quality of care is a behavioral outcome of sensitivity, understanding, and wisdom. There are no provisions in current professional training to ensure quality of care. In fact, the cost-effectiveness of intervention services often takes precedence over quality of care considerations, particularly in agencies and in private practice settings, which are increasingly monitored by insurance carriers to regulate and limit the kinds of compensated services. An unfortunate dichotomy between quality of care and cost-effectiveness limits the availability of quality care. Criteria that include specification of the number of therapy sessions for designated clinical diagnoses, approved interventions for these diagnostic categories, and clerical decisions by insurance carriers that override informed provider judgments all have contributed to an erosion of quality care.

The obligation to provide quality care is, nonetheless, contractual in the provider-client relationship. As a result, providers remain ethically bound to deal with these constraints on practice by personal, professional, and political activity. This is difficult because the time and energy-consuming task of perennial client advocacy in the face of restrictions from the provider's own profession, other professions, insurance carriers, and ultimately governmental regulation of services has been superimposed on provider obligations. Providing quality care now entails hypervigilance to protect the provider-client relationship from extraneous influences that impinge on the provider's sense of competency in delivering necessary services. Again, in this dilemma, only an understanding of the personal matrix of considerations in providing services to clients can enable perseverance and minimize despair. A mobilization of provider resources, both internalized and professional, is necessary for circumnavigating the obstacles of greed and external coerciveness as impediments to practice within the structure of a responsible humanity.

Ethical Standards

Ethical codes are guidelines or rules for professional behaviors designed to protect both consumers and providers. These codes provide a consensual statement regarding normative professional behaviors. In a society that deals with service obligations on a contractual basis, these rules are necessary as a standard for evaluating the behaviors of providers and as a potential means of assessing the quality of their services. The existence of ethical rules evidences professional intentions, capacity for monitoring provider behaviors, or both. Ethical codes, however, are enforceable only to the extent that there are interest and motivation for monitoring professional activities; developing the machinery for processing, evaluating, and adjudicating complaints; appropriate legislation; and adequate funding for this process as well as for dealing with subsequent litigation. These mechanisms are necessary as the structure of our society becomes increasingly complex and impersonal with a diminished sense of internalized values undergirding personal probity in interpersonal negotiations, and as society sanctions adversarial and competitive behaviors in business and professional relationships.

1992 American Psychological Ethical Code

Boulder model professional psychology began with a statement of character, personality, and training attributes believed to be essential for practitioners who care for others by providing psychological services (see Raimy, 1950, p. 213). Personal insight, sensitivity, acceptance of responsibility, a sense of ethical values, and an enhanced cultural background were included. This ideal, unfortunately, has only infrequently been implemented in selection criteria for graduate professional training in clinical psychology, although counseling psychology has a history of sensitivity to provider personal characteristics.

A 1973 Vail conference resolution recognized multicultural competence as a therapeutic skill and initiated an examination of ethical issues (Korman, 1974), but for years thereafter the APA Ethical Code reflected an exclusively Anglo American cultural standard for provider behaviors (APA, 1981). As a result, the code was ethnoculturally biased and inadequate as a responsible basis for practice with culturally diverse groups. During the 1980s, a concatenation of societal and professional events led to awareness among psychologists that a new code was long overdue. Sampson (1993) subsequently described a coming-of-age among collective movements in which *voice,* "the ability to express an opinion about an impending decision" (Cohen, 1989, p. 36), was increasingly exercised. These movements included the demand by visible racial/ethnic groups for a transformative voice in the determination of their own identities. The profession of psychology had used an add-on strategy that omitted a conspicuous avenue for understanding culture-specific views of the conditions affecting their individual lives.

These collective demands, concomitant societal changes, and informed description of competencies or standards for services to multicultural clients (e.g., Pedersen & Marsella, 1982; Sue, Arredondo, & McDavis, 1992) eventually resulted in the preparation of new guidelines (APA, 1989). These guidelines exerted some influence on the preparation of a new ethical code (APA, 1992).

For example, cultural sensitivity is not labeled in the 1992 code but described in very general terms in Principle D, as Respect for People's

Rights and Dignity while Principle A, Competence, recognized competence boundaries and limitations of expertise including education, training, or experience qualifications for providing services while omitting specific mention of cultural competence. Elaboration in Standards 1.04, 2.02, 2.04, and 2.05 specifies that competence boundaries should be established before services are offered. Continuing education and appropriate use of resources as well as unspecified "reasonable steps" are required for protection of patients.

Assessment materials should be used on the basis of research evidence with limits of certainty for individual diagnosis recognized by practitioners. Assessment with special populations should also "attempt to identify situations in which particular interventions or assessment techniques or norms may not be applicable or may require adjustment in administration because of factors such as individuals' gender, age, race, ethnicity, national origin, religion, sexual orientation, disability, language, or socioeconomic status" (APA, 1992, p. 1603). Caution, prudence, and clear noting of reservations concerning accuracy of interpretation are also required.

Principle B, Integrity, addresses only the psychologists' own belief systems, values, needs, and limitations by emphasizing self-awareness. Culture-specific assessment technology is not addressed, but psychologists are enjoined in Standard 1.09 to respect the rights of others to hold different values, attitudes, or opinions. Multiple or preexisting relationships are recognized by Standard 1.17 as difficult to avoid, but psychologists are cautioned against their possible harm and potential for client exploitation.

Language issues, including client first language, use of second language, interpreter, and translator are not discussed but subsumed in the word "language" included in Principle D, Respect for People's Rights and Dignity, as part of a long list of admonitions to try to eliminate bias. Standard 1.08 invokes the need for training, experience, supervision, consultation for competence or referral whenever 10 human differences, including race, ethnicity, national origin, religion, language, or socioeconomic status, affect work.

Ethical Code Commentary

A responsible basis for practice with multicultural groups is not feasible using the present ethical code. In this code, cultural sensitivity is equated with an awareness of cultural differences, respect for these differences, and an attempt to eliminate bias or discriminatory practices. This is an incomplete statement of cultural sensitivity and other contexts are required to augment this statement (e.g., Granger & Portner, 1985; Ridley, Mendoza,

Kanitz, Angermeier, & Zenk, 1994; Rogler, Malgady, Costantino, & Blumenthal, 1987).

Cultural competence is not distinguished in the code from professional competence per se. It was recognized, however, that not only will competencies vary by group but that recognition of their own competence boundaries by providers is mandatory. Without delineating specific competencies required for services to various groups, the code falls short of being able to protect the welfare of these clients. The statement that each psychologist is to exercise appropriate judgment and precautions suffices only to exonerate providers from liability.

Knowledge that is relevant to those services being provided for each group is also necessary, but acquisition of such knowledge requires awareness of professional competence boundaries. Providers are also expected to take unstated, albeit reasonable, steps toward competence in the absence of recognized training standards. Because assessment competence, for example, is based on research and other evidence that techniques may be used for their intended purposes with particular clients, an elaboration of conditions under which misuse of these techniques can occur should be stated. Such evidence is now available in published sources (e.g., Dana, 1993a).

The code makes awareness of limitations and any subsequent acquisition of knowledge a responsibility of the provider rather than a responsibility of the profession fulfilled by requirements for specific training, practice, and experience. Putting the onus for self-awareness of personal limits on practitioners instead of the psychology profession provides an unrealistic expectation for professional behaviors; providers regularly inflate or aggrandize their areas of competence with neither malice nor intent to do harm, but because of a desire to provide services for a larger range of potential clients.

Moreover, the limits of diagnostic certainty are not applied to special populations, but remain (by implication at least) embedded in the reliability limitations of the *DSM*. With special populations, however, adjustments in assessment or intervention techniques may be required. The nature and efficacy of such adjustments in assessment, for example, have not been determined.

The code does stipulate that interpretations must include relevant test and client characteristics that may affect judgment or accuracy without specific mention of cultural identity, cultural worldview, and culture-specific beliefs. The only cultural belief systems mentioned are those of the provider, which are typically derived from Anglo American culture. There is no stated recognition that other non-Anglo American belief systems—particularly health/illness, primacy of family expectations and obligations, and the impact of natural or spiritual forces on the self—affect client perceptions of providers and all of their preferred professional services.

Culture-specific technologies are neither recognized nor deemed necessary for competence. Because breaching boundaries of professional competence is explicitly forbidden, professional practice with individuals who have a traditional non-Anglo American cultural orientation is thereby limited and may be conspicuously inappropriate. Practice in new areas must be grounded on competence, but there is silence in the 1992 code concerning the nature of reasonable steps to foster such competence.

Culture-specific service delivery styles are not mentioned anywhere in the code. In fact, cultural competence requires culture-specific service delivery styles as part and parcel of cultural knowledge, including worldview, belief systems, and culture-specific technologies. Moreover, some understanding of specific client languages is required to use credible behaviors in the delivery of services. Because language shapes the thought processes and provides much of the distinctive and differentiating verbal content used to express culturally relevant behaviors directly, knowledge of another culture is incomplete without intensive language study.

Language is mentioned only twice in lists of potential differences among clients. Psychologists are enjoined to be aware of these differences and to seek remediation for their competence deficits in these areas. It is implied but not stated that psychologists need to learn the languages of their prospective clients. There is no indication in the code that competent services can be provided only in the client's first language or that there is abundant research that client welfare may be jeopardized by use of translators and interpreters, or by a lack of client fluency in English language service delivery.

Cultural knowledge must also include the histories of cultural contact as exposed in experiences of stereotypy, prejudice, discrimination, and racism, because these historical and contemporary social conditions directly affect the severity of problems or disorders arising on the basis of oppression. This knowledge should help providers to understand clients as cultural beings prior to offering them services (see Dana, 1994). This point was explicitly denied by Ethics Committee's Ad Hoc Policy and Education Committee inaction (S. E. Jones, personal communication, December 2, 1994). Similarly, no action was taken on the recommendation that the code be supplemented by guidelines that included (a) examples, vignettes, and/or case materials; (b) recognition of research status in that area, specifically of relevant assessment methods; and (c) need for a continuing self-examination by providers of their own racial identities (see Dana, 1994).

Clearly, there are differences among informed perceptions of what content should be included in an ethical code and what purposes a code should serve. An explicit albeit perfunctory presence of multicultural issues in the 1992 code has occurred in a context that empowers each practitioner to make decisions on all professional applications. Such empowerment continues the add-on strategy of accommodation deplored by advocates of a genuine voice for diverse groups.

In addition to these significant omissions, the new code standards were vitiated by the qualifying language of "lawyer-driven weasel words" (Bersoff, 1994, p. 384). Simultaneously, there has been a diminished commitment to the ideal of respect for the dignity and worth of individuals over time as expressed in the Preamble to successive versions of the code (Payton, 1994). Providers are now afforded primary protection to the detriment of consumers, particularly by the dichotomy between work-related and non-work-related activities in the new code. Two quotes illustrate the gravity of these code deficiencies:

> I fear that because of the litigious nature of society and the resulting fear of lawsuits, the current code has been diluted almost to the point of uselessness. . . . This does not bode well for diverse groups. (Payton, 1994, p. 319)

> The code's pervasive use of qualifiers and its deliberate ambiguity raise the question of whether it can be used to enforce anything but the most serious moral and ethical transgressions, behavior that is so egregiously wrong that no code would be necessary to condemn it. (Bersoff, 1994, p. 384)

Continued Development Agenda

This commentary indicates a necessity for continued development of the ethical code for protection of multicultural consumers, although there appear to be difficulties in implementation of code recommendations or adding new content. Recent book chapters have reiterated some of these issues and added other concerns (LaFromboise, Foster, & James, 1996; Pedersen, 1995). LaFromboise et al. (1996) commented that dual roles/relationships with multicultural clients can be desirable and prohibition evidences the individualistic orientation of majority-culture values. Because some providers exceed their competencies with multicultural clients (see Allison, Crawford, Echemendia, Robinson, & Kemp, 1994), these authors also recommend clear communication of intervention goals and procedures as well as alternative interventions before providing any services. Informed choice can only occur in a context of discussing potential treatment outcomes not only for the client but also as they affect family and community. An activist stance to human rights abuses of clients by the provider may be required to supplement client self-assertiveness for self-protection. Future directions encompass a review of the diversity in moral understanding across cultures, particularly notable in differences between individualistic and collectivistic cultures.

In Pedersen's (1995) words, "the weaknesses of . . . the APA . . . ethical guidelines are that they lack explicit philosophical principles, assume a dominant culture perspective, and generally minimize or trivialize the role of culture in ethical decision making" (p. 42). He recognizes general perspectives of relativism, absolutism, or dynamic universalism. Anthropologists as relativists may accept an emic level of discourse accentuating differences; absolutists are culturally encapsulated members of the mental health establishment (see Wrenn, 1962) who prefer constant comparative criteria that highlight pseudoetic differences, whereas universalists encompass both similarities and differences in a search for genuine etics.

Pedersen (1995) cites underlying assumptions by Ponterotto and Casas (1991) of altruism, responsibility, justice, and caring, which provide foci on real-life problems, relevance, fairness, trust, and a personal stake in helping, which may be compared with the independent derivation in Table 3.1. Pedersen (1995) calls attention to earlier guidelines (e.g., Tapp, Kelman, Triandis, Wrightsman, & Coehlo, 1974) to not only avoid harm but enrich and benefit by collaborative relationships in research settings that are also applicable to interventions.

There have been strong recommendations for the development of practice guidelines (Clinton, McCormick, & Besteman, 1994). Two recent sets of guidelines (APA, 1993; Guzman, 1993) provide a next step in development of a more relevant ethical code for multicultural populations. The APA guidelines acknowledge the importance and effects of ethnicity/culture on client behavior and psychological processes including influences from the collective culture, religion and spiritual beliefs, client language choice, experiences with racism, and socioeconomic and political conditions. Psychologists should address culture in their records, support client cultural identity, and take an advocacy role. Guzman's guidelines included a required examination of ethnicity and cultural influences on the intervention process for each client. This examination emphasized respect for "the roles of family members and community structures, hierarchies, values and beliefs within the client's culture" (p. 23) and for "clients' religious beliefs, spiritual beliefs and values, or both including attributions and taboos, because they affect their worldview, psychosocial functioning, and expression of distress"

(p. 24). Furthermore, services should only be offered in the client's preferred language and should specifically consider and document social, environmental, and political issues in assessment and choice of interventions.

Modern service providers do not have the visibility and community surveillance that once provided an external aegis for the practices of indigenous healers. As a result, there has been a gradual shift to formal credentials and reliance primarily on internalized standards for self-regulation of professional activities, particularly as codes of ethics become less enforceable by professional associations.

Two major avenues for increasing cultural competence at present are awareness of limitations of knowledge and skills and self-directed efforts to become more competent in areas of deficiency. The shift to individual provider responsibility puts a corresponding responsibility on consumers of professional services to learn for themselves at the onset of any professional relationship whether or not the provider is culturally competent. Many multicultural clients do this already before making a commitment to receive any services.

Problems Requiring Competent Care

Culture-General Disorders

These disorders, or *DSM* psychopathologies such as schizophrenia, depression, somatoform disorders, and anxiety reactions (including phobias), have significance primarily for acculturated persons. These descriptions overlap with other *DSM* disorders and with culture-bound syndromes, and their forms of expression in symptomatology and syndromes differ markedly across racial/ethnic groups because they can signify moral, religious, political, or social crises (Fabrega, 1991). As a consequence, these disorders require identification using cultural formulations.

Problems-in-Living

Problems-in-living are omnipresent and destructive in all cultural groups. They are group specific because of group differences in prevalence and effective interventions. There has been no consensus on a separate classification system for these problems, although a focus on psychological processes or symptoms that undergird *DSM* labels has been recommended (Persons, 1986). By investigating discrete symptoms, *DSM* reliabilities would be increased and continuities with natural phenomena emphasized.

All groups share difficulties in interpersonal relations often evidenced by physical abuse, sexual abuse, or both, of children, wives, women family members, companions, and elders. Poverty and lack of educational, social, and occupational skills are also problems affecting all racial-ethnic groups, although remediations for these conditions are beyond the scope of this book. Nonetheless, by depathologizing these problems, stigma is reduced and the population base for potentially effective interventions can be extended.

Relational problems have not been identified, described, tallied for frequencies, and considered for discrete individual, family, and community interventions. Recently, however, these problems have been examined as candidates for Axis I *DSM* inclusion (Committee of the Family, Group for Advancement of Psychiatry, 1995). In this model, severe dysfunctions, including family violence with physical abuse, sexual abuse, or both, of elders and children, are considered as relational disorders. Usually treated by couple and family therapy, these disorders involve control, communication, and conflicts that disrupt family functioning and are represented in generation-specific and intergenerational contexts. Teicher (1995) has proposed a Psychological Health Classification System to define the behavior conditions and dysfunctions germane to professional psychology practice. Such a system could, if developed, delineate some of the domains of professional psychological practice, although a social work diagnostic system, Person in Environment, to evaluate social functioning has already been developed (Williams, Karls, & Wandrei, 1991).

Alcohol/drug abuse and personality disorders appear in *DSM,* although these conditions may have special, culture-specific interventions because their meanings, circumstances, and frequencies differ as a function of culture. Managed care organizations often exclude personality disorders as untreatable, although they have been considered as deviations from Anglo American middle-class normalcy expectations requiring a *DSM* diagnosis (Alarcon & Foulks, 1993). Other problems-in-living are repeated traumatic losses, lapses in control including externalizations of anger erupting in violence or homicide, and internalizations contributing to accidents, injuries, and suicide.

One problem-in-living now receiving prominent *DSM* attention is post-traumatic stress disorder (PTSD). PTSD affects individual survivors of traumatic events including torture, prison, refugee camp experience, assault, and rape. PTSD also occurs as a consequence of generations of abuse and repeated individual tragedies, an accumulation of everyday experiences with abuse, violence, and death. Sustained living under conditions of recurrent trauma produces intrusive experiencing of the traumatic events, avoidance of trauma-associated aversive stimuli, and symptoms of sleep disturbance, irritability, and concentration difficulties together with anxiety, somatic, and dissociative symptomatology that differs by cultural origin and overlaps with major depressive disorder symptomatology. A summary of substantial portions of this PTSD literature is available (Marsella, Friedman, Gerrity, & Scurfield, 1996). The PTSD label may represent a variety of culture-bound syndromes or stress-related disorders rather than a single diagnostic category (Jenkins, 1996).

Oppression-Induced Conditions

During the 1960s, Franz Fanon (1967) described oppression in the Caribbean Antilles, which fueled personal anguish and exacerbated problems-in-living. Remediation was envisioned by rediscovery of African identity and by violence. Buhlan (1985) described Fanon's five kinds of alienation resulting from oppression. Alienation was from oneself, or one's "corporality and personal identity" (p. 188); from family and group; from the general other by "violence and paranoia characterizing the relation between whites and blacks" (p. 188); from one's culture, language, and history; and by the "denial, abdication, or both of self-determining socialized, and organized activity" (p. 188). Buhlan's account is required reading for Anglo American providers to comprehend blacks who have found strength and increased awareness in an Afrocentric identity. The blatant and cumulative effects of oppression, racism, and discrimination have neither been adequately recognized nor incorporated into *DSM-IV* (American Psychiatric Association, 1994).

There are descriptions of some conditions representing internalizations and externalizations of oppression. For example, idioms of distress for Puerto Ricans include anger dimensions of aggression, assertiveness, and vindictiveness as well as increased depression, anxiety, and somatization (Malgady, Rogler, & Cortes, 1996; Rogler, Cortes, & Malgady, 1994). For Asian Americans, oppression is often internalized and inhibits response processes by clients who accept a discrepancy between thought and action. As a consequence, the contents of personally oppressive events become difficult to express because of shame over exposure to aversive reactions from others (Toupin, 1980). Cultural norms militate against direct expression of feelings, counsel avoidance of confrontation, and support feelings of shame and inferiority. Somatization with culture-specific symptomatology becomes a recourse leading to medicalization of psychological problems. These expectations for behavior may have contributed to the erroneous perception of a "model minority" (Sue, Sue, Sue, & Takeuchi, 1995) as well as to the underuse by Asian Americans of mental health services.

One proposed classification for oppression-induced disorders among African Americans goes beyond simply suggesting consequences of victim status exposed in psychodynamics or psychopathology. Abkar (1991) proposed four categories of disorder for African Americans that may be applicable to other groups as well. An *alien self-disorder* occurs when mainstream societal standards are adopted and subsequent behaviors are not in one's own best interests. This disorder provides a formal label for Stage 1 of Nigrescence theories described in Chapter 4. *Anti-self disorder,* an identification with the oppressor, includes behaviors that would be described as optimal Anglo mental health. Hostility is directed at one's own group, however, because the "individual identifies with the projected hostility and negativism toward his group of origin" (p. 345). *Self-destructive disorders* encompass the range of survival behaviors typically used by marginal persons to endanger life and compromise community well-being. Examples include drugs, alcohol, prostitution, suicide, within-group homicide, crime, and gangs.

Stressors that result from oppression may lead to specific symptomatology and often contribute to chronic problems-in-living. There is always potential for confounding reactions to oppression with psychopathology, mislabeling persistent symptoms to provide a *DSM* diagnosis, or ignoring pathognomic effects of oppression. *Oppression-induced disorders* are unlikely to be represented soon among *DSM* categories. Nonetheless, cultural formulations to recognize them are required because the most effective interventions for these problems are culture specific.

Acculturative Stress

Acculturative stress is included because emotional distress and psychopathology are frequent concomitants of the acculturation process. Elements of the Lazarus-Folkman model sequence the occurrence of potential stressor, primary appraisal of personal relevance, secondary appraisal of possible remedial actions (e.g., coping, efficacy expectations, available resources), coping (problem or emotion focused), and adaptation outcomes (Lazarus & Folkman, 1984).

This model has been expanded for multicultural groups by incorporating culturally relevant events for each element using research on African Americans and Cambodian refugees (Slavin, Rainer, McCreary, & Gowda, 1991). Initially, the events that constitute potential stressors differ in their relation to minority status, discrimination, socioeconomic status, and specific customs. Primary appraisal of trouble includes cultural/family definitions of the particular event and how well the event fits with the cultural frame-of-reference for understanding these events. Secondary appraisal of potential actions includes cultural definitions of behavioral options, beliefs concerning operation of the mainstream system, group efficacy, and availability of family, community, and social networks. Subsequent coping efforts include culture-specific coping behaviors, or rituals, the group and mainstream sanctions for particular strategies, and the presence of bicultural skills for negotiation. Finally, the potential outcomes include culturally determined symptomatology and cultural norms for behavior. Expansion of the stress process model provides new awareness of the additional complexity of life for multicultural persons, an agenda for relevant research, and opportunities for effective interventions.

In addition to stressors from events and hassles in daily life, there may be stress from war and trauma for refugees and displaced persons (Hobfoll et al., 1991) as well as the stress accompanying exit- and entry-related trauma, and exile shock in the second year after arrival (Portes & Rumbaut, 1990). Stress has also been examined for precontact, contact, conflict, crisis, and adaptation phases of the acculturation process (Berry & Kim, 1988). New stressors appear during contact and increase during the conflict phase to become greatest during the conflict phase when family violence, substance abuse, or even homicide and suicide may occur.

Culture-Bound Syndromes

Twenty-five of these syndromes are described briefly in the *DSM-IV* Glossary I (American Psychiatric Association, 1994). Simons and Hughes (1985) have provided a greatly expanded classification of culture-general and culture-specific syndromes as well as folk explanations/diagnoses with more complete descriptions of symptomatology, locales, populations afflicted, and major references.

These syndromes have puzzled many Western psychiatrists and anthropologists who have labeled them as "exotic" and "unclassifiable" (Hughes & Wintrob, 1995). Their phenomenological reality and cultural validity stem from an absence of mind/body dualism in their cultures of origin and different conceptions of the self. These conditions occur most frequently among those persons who maintain a traditional cultural lifestyle and have actively resisted acculturation. American Indians, immigrants, refugees, and students or sojourners are prone to culture-bound syndromes because they are traditionally persons who do not speak English as a first language. There have been few descriptions and little research on the frequency of these syndromes for immigrant and sojourner groups. This book will include discussions of some culture-bound syndromes for each racial/ethnic group.

Multicultural Assessment Prerequisitites

Acculturation Evaluation for Cultural Orientation

Acculturation evaluation for cultural orientation status is part of client preparation for use of psychological tests and any subsequent intervention services (Dana, 1992b). A variety of measures or interview data can facilitate a decision as to whether a client is assimilated, bicultural, marginal, or traditional (see Dana, 1993a, chap. 7; 1996b). Assimilated and bicultural clients, with their informed consent, can be examined using standard tests. Cultural orientation status, however, is simply a label that informs clinician and client of the suitability or nonsuitability of standard tests and subsequent culture-general interventions. Whenever standard tests are not used, for example, with marginal or traditional clients, a description of racial or ethnic identity will be helpful for decisions to use "corrections" for standard tests.

Identity Descriptions

Identity description begins with cultural orientation statuses of marginal or traditional and may also include bicultural persons who choose assessment, intervention services, or both that go further than simply acknowledging identity by means of the service delivery etiquette. Some of the same measures that provide cultural orientation information can be used to provide racial or ethnic identity information, but their use now entails a descriptive elaboration of identity rather than simply a label to endorse or discourage the use of standard tests. Whenever identity is examined carefully, the intent is not only to avoid bias in standard assessment and clinical diagnosis but to suggest a combined or culture-specific intervention as well on the basis of this "portrait." There are two necessary ingredients for describing identity. The first is knowledge of a variety of techniques that go beyond acculturation measures to provide specific information concerning values, individualism/ collectivism, and worldview (Dana, 1993a). The second essential is to have a frame-of-reference that contains adequate resources of culture-specific knowledge for interpretation of these measures.

Identity descriptions are difficult for Anglo American clinicians to compose because they lack experience with a variety of culture-specific information sources, especially for personality theory and relevant empirical data. This context of knowledge is not available from Euro-American personality theories nor have the requisite volumes been developed to summarize emic contributions for each cultural group. There are at least six steps in an assessment process in which asking relevant questions can lead to use of a variety of emic and etic sources of information to provide cultural perspectives. These steps include the interview; cultural identity evaluation; standard psychological tests, culture specific measures, or both; the cultural formulation; and the report. A recent book chapter summarizes knowledge in this area (Dana, 1997b).

Modifications-Alterations of Standard Measures

Standard measures should always be administered to multicultural clients using a credible and acceptable service delivery style to gain rapport and encourage task orientation. Whenever modification/alterations are made, particularly for traditional and sometimes for marginal clients, these "corrections" may occur in test administration, scoring of particular items, interpretation, and feedback procedures. Unfortunately, clinicians often make these "corrections" in an unsystematic, unverbalized manner without appropriate empirical documentation. Guidelines for use of "corrections" are not currently available, although such compendia are now being considered and developed for various cultural groups (e.g., Allen & French, in press). For example, there are some culture-specific MMPI norms, the beginnings of a Rorschach comprehensive system research literature on cultural difference in norms for many scores and ratios, and some cultural orientation status norms for standard tests. There are few adequate emic (culture-specific) or etic (culture-general) measures in widespread use among clinical assessors.

Cultural Formulations

The development of cultural formulations to increase reliability of clinical diagnosis are now required for traditional clients and can be helpful for marginal clients. The outline for cultural formulations that precedes Appendix I in the *DSM-IV* (American Psychiatric Association, 1992), contains brief statements to note degrees of involvement with both the culture of origin and Anglo American culture or acculturation status, cultural explanations of illness, characteristics of the psychosocial environment, client-clinician relationship characteristics, and an overall assessment for diagnosis and care (American Psychiatric Association, 1994, pp. 843-844).

The preceding section on identity suggested that questions contained in an interview process as well as acculturation measures be used to gather relevant information in all the areas suggested for inclusion in cultural formulations. Information on the client's psychosocial environment should be used in a context of specific cultural knowledge to assess the nature, importance, and reactivity to stressors and reliance on family, religious, and community social supports. Cultural, social status, and language differences between clinician and client should be observed, although no mention is made of culturally credible styles of service delivery, except as an admonition to note communication difficulties.

There were pre-*DSM-IV* attempts to provide cultural formulations by Cuéllar and Gonzalez (1983) and Jacobsen (1988). Cuéllar and Gonzalez provided the earliest case example of how to make use of culturally relevant information. Jacobsen suggested assessment stages to gather information on ethnocultural heritage including the circumstances leading to relocation, perceptions of the family's subsequent niche in the host society, and, finally, consideration of the clinician's own cultural background. This formulation included culture but did not emphasize the inherent unreliability of the diagnostic process, although ethnocultural assessment should substantially increase reliability of both process and outcome.

There have been several recent contributions to augment the cultural formulation outline contained in *DSM-IV* (American Psychiatric Association, 1994). The aftermath of the pre-*DSM-IV* National Task Force on Culture and Psychiatric Diagnosis included historical context for cultural formulations by Mezzich (1995) describing proposed educational projects to facilitate their use as well as clinical and epidemiological research suggestions. Another clear, detailed, and helpful statement of culturally relevant information is also available (Lu, Lin, & Mezzich, 1995) as well as a new clinical cases section of the journal *Culture, Medicine, and Psychiatry* (Lewis-Fernandez, 1996a). These efforts were designed to assuage the disappointment experienced by task force members after their immense contribution in analyzing the cross-cultural literature had been neither understood nor incorporated into *DSM-IV* (i.e., NIMH-Sponsored Group on Culture and Diagnosis, 1993). Finally, Castillo (1996) critiqued successive *DSM* paradigms, presented applications of a cultural formulation outline for each *DSM-IV* disorder, and described a client-centered approach to diagnosis.

These approaches, although vital to competent use of cultural formulations, do not emphasize the *DSM* reliability deficits exposed by Kirk and Kutchens (1992). Cuéllar (1993) combined seven recognized steps in which unreliability may affect the outcome of a diagnostic process with a clinical judgment paradigm. He then illustrated each step using relevant sociocultural factors and clinician behaviors that potentially affected the diagnostic outcome of a case example. Dana (1993b) subsequently addressed diagnostic unreliability by juxtaposing culturally competent information with these seven steps. Table 3.2 uses material from both earlier papers and an unpublished paper (Cuéllar, Dana, & Gonzalez, 1995) to suggest how the reliability risk can be reduced using cultural competence skills at each step in the

Table 3.2 Cultural Formulation in the Diagnostic Process: Reliability Risk, Cultural Formulation, and Relevant Cultural Competency Skills

Reliability Risk	Cultural Formulation	Cultural Competency Skills
Interview	Cultural identity	Use client first language (if not fluent, consider interpreter, translator, or referral). Evaluate client behavioral style; use acceptable service delivery etiquette. Describe cultural orientation status (or use test data). Inquire re: health/illness beliefs, family history, present family structure/composition.
Define symptoms	Cultural explanation	Know culture-specific sources for diagnostic data. Be aware of culture-specific behavioral cues, particularly nonverbal cues, response sets, life contexts, idioms of distress, cultural norms.
Classify symptoms		Consider possible culture-specific syndromes (*DSM-IV* Glossary) for comparison with *DSM-IV* diagnostic categories.
Include other clinical information	Cultural factors re: psychosocial environment and level of functioning	Collateral history and life stress information from other sources (i.e., family members, community persons, mental health providers, medical records, and so on). Evaluate in terms of cultural background of source.
Include tests		Cultural orientation status evaluation will determine whether to use standard, culture-specific, combinations, or no tests. Be aware of any culture-specific norms for standard tests.
Reclassify symptoms	Cultural elements of relationship	Weigh all data, reevaluate new information, reexamine client-provider relationship/communication. Examine potential for provider bias, stereotyping, incomplete cultural knowledge/information/experience.
Consider presence/absence of etiological factors	Overall cultural assessment for diagnosis and care	Reconsider entire process by reexamination of culturally relevant data for etiology, course of illness, prognosis. Include protection of client/society and potential ethical issues.

clinical diagnostic process. In this table, the reliability risk column contains the seven steps and the cultural formulation column includes the areas specified in *DSM-IV* (American Psychiatric Association, 1994). The cultural competency skills column delineates behaviors and knowledge to inform each step. This process can increase *DSM* reliability and lead to a cultural formulation that reduces *DSM* cultural bias.

Intervention Model

Culture-General Interventions

In cross-cultural/cross-racial treatment interactions, the application of any culture-general intervention may require therapist role flexibility. To elaborate, Atkinson, Thompson, and Grant (1993) recommended a three-dimensional model in which acculturation level, locus of problem etiology, and intervention provide information on subsequent therapist roles. They listed roles of adviser, advocate, facilitator of indigenous support and healing systems, consultant, and change agent in addition to counselor and psychotherapist. An adviser can provide information on potential problems of discrimination or generational conflicts accompanying acculturation. Such information not only helps coping, but pinpoints difficulties as external in origin. Similarly, an advocate role for immigrants/refugees, following rapport and a comfortable relationship, results in an active stance with community, state, and national bureaucracies within the new society. As a facilitator, the clinician can mobilize the support systems available in the cultural community, including the family, religious groups, community spokespersons, or elders, and encourage interventions from indigenous healers when appropriate. As a consultant, a collegial relationship with highly acculturated clients can be used to minimize problems in housing, education, and occupation during family relocation, for example. As a change agent, the clinician can address deficiencies in a system that encourage discrimination by actively working to develop a multicultural view. This flexibility is necessary because therapist roles can conflict with cultural values and absence of flexibility can jeopardize an otherwise acceptable intervention.

Culture-general interventions are mainstream in origin and include psychodynamic, humanistic-existential, and behavioral-cognitive approaches. Each approach assumes specific role definitions for therapist and client that may be congruent in one culture but are incompatible with expectations for another cultural group (Suinn, 1985). In psychodynamic treatment, the therapist is the expert. These approaches require self-disclosure, expression of feelings, insight, and associations to symbols in dream interpretation as prerequisites for personality change. These ingredients are appropriate for many Euro-American clients, but are not universal in application. In humanistic-existential transactions, the client assumes the role of expert. Humanistic principles place the individual in the treatment foreground, but family and community perspectives may actually assume precedence for a particular client.

Hays (1995) deplored the "marginalization of cultural considerations" (p. 309) in applications of cognitive-behavior therapy and cites only three empirically based behavioral-cognitive outcome studies for anxiety reported by Casas (1988) for these groups. This dearth of studies suggests that Suinn (1985) is correct in stating that these interventions may conflict with cultural values, although they are directive and educational and can acknowledge some culturally relevant variables. Moreover, these approaches evoke meanings for behaviors, events, and words within a Euro-American scientific frame-of-reference. When Western science rules are followed for learning, behavioral changes often result, but the rules for behavior are culturally determined and culture specific. Behavioral approaches must acknowledge client cultural values and define problems in relation to cultural norms to be applied effectively (Tanaka-Matsumi & Higginbotham, 1989). Suinn (1985) cited "the use of a healing touch by a *curandera,* the prescription of an herb medicine, or the influence of ritual by a medicine man" (p. 675) as representing rules for behavior change derived from different conceptions of reality and derivative science.

Whenever culture-general, or standard Anglo American interventions are used, cultural considerations should never be ignored. To what extent a cultural context is necessary and how the clinician can provide an acceptable context for intervention are questions to be answered prior to treatment with all multicultural clients. Several steps described in the assessment section on identity are also relevant for decisions to use culture-general, combined approaches, or culture-specific interventions. Table 3.3 summarizes some of these questions, the kinds of information that can be helpful, and appropriate components for the three major classes of interventions. Chapters 5, 6, 7, and 8 will make use of this table to illustrate applications of the model.

Combined Approaches

These approaches adapt or modify a mainstream intervention by infusion of specific cultural values into service delivery, other intervention components, or both. To select an existing combined approach, or to develop a combined intervention, it is necessary to have cultural identity information

Table 3.3   Relevant Questions, Cultural Information,, and Suggested Components
for Culture-General, Combined, and Culture-Specific Interventions

Culture-specific interventions	
Questions	Client preference?
Information	English is client first language or bilinguality. Cultural orientation: Bicultural.
Components	English language. Client access facilitated by provider incorporation of cultural components to implement credible service delivery style.
Combined interventions	
Questions	Client preference? Client second language is English? Clinician is competent in preferred client language?
Information	Cultural/racial identity description. Cultural orientation status: Bicultural or marginal. Cultural formulation recommended. *DSM-IV* diagnosis using cultural formulation and glossary of culture-bound disorders.
Components	Modification of existing mainstream interventions to reflect cultural values using cultural identity information, and cultural orientation status derived from acculturation measures as well as language match, ethnicity match, or both.
Culture-specific interventions	
Questions	English not spoken or not fluent? Immigrant? Refugee?
Information	Cultural orientation status information. Traditional health/illness beliefs and cultural formulation required for referral to indigenous healers.
Components	Language match. Ethnicity match preferable but not mandatory under special circumstances. Cultural elements used to develop new interventions.

that goes considerably beyond a simple category label of cultural orientation status.

Culture-Specific Interventions

These interventions are used with non-English speakers or those persons with rudimentary English fluency who have a traditional worldview, health/illness beliefs, culture-specific symptomatology, or culture-bound disorders. The use of cultural formulations is required for diagnosis, referral to indigenous healers, and for selection of new interventions incorporating cultural elements in their development. These interventions should ordinarily occur using the client's first language.

Training and Evaluation

Multicultural competence training has improved dramatically in recent years, particularly in counseling psychology (e.g., Pope-Davis & Coleman, 1997). A philosophy for examining training motivations and subsequent focus on specific proficiencies has been recommended (Ridley, Mendoza, & Kanitz, 1994). Motivations for training should recognize combinations of external and internal sources. These sources include explorations of one's own culture and racial/ethnic identity and the development of a politically based ideology for equity, or awareness of sociopolitical history (see Chapter 1, this volume) and the continued presence of discrimination in providing managed mental health care services for multicultural populations (Dana, 1997a). It is now feasible to integrate awareness, knowledge, and skills in courses, curriculum, supervision, and evaluation. A multicultural immersion experience has been suggested that includes participation community groups/organizations for balance with course work and supervised experience (Pope-Davis, Breaux, & Liu, 1997). This experience includes keeping a journal and a presentation of activities.

Individual students or practitioners can be evaluated with four available instruments (Ponterotto & Alexander, 1996) and training programs can be examined with a multicultural checklist (Ponterotto, 1997). This checklist has 22 items for minority representation, curriculum issues, counseling practice and supervision, research considerations, student and faculty competency evaluations, and physical environment. A national survey of counseling training programs subsequently indicated that most programs addressed research and curriculum whereas less than one half included counseling practice/supervision, approximately one third provided student/faculty evaluation, and few programs included minority representation (Ponterotto, Alexander, & Grieger, 1995).

In a recent survey, doctoral-level, predominantly white, APA clinicians reported some training exposure to diverse faculty and staff, reasonably high exposure to diverse training cases, and current involvement with moderate numbers of multicultural clients (Allison et al., 1994). They reported feeling generally competent to serve European American clients, but less than one half perceived themselves as competent with African American clients, 26% with Hispanic clients, 21% with Asian clients, and 8% with Native American clients. Training experiences among clinical and counseling program graduates indicated self-perceived high competence levels with Euro-Americans, women, and economically disadvantaged clients; moderate levels with African Americans; but lower levels with Hispanic, Asian Americans, black

Hispanic, and American Indian clients (Allison, Echemendia, Crawford, & Robinson, 1996). Providers still fall short of the APA (1993) guidelines and these authors recommended current books, consultation, peer supervision, and the development of network directories of culturally competent psychologists.

Dimensions of Quality Care

Cultural Competence

Cultural competence is a prerequisite for a healthy society; it would embrace an ethnorelativistic citizenry who acknowledge, accept, honor, and understand differences as well as a responsive structure at federal, state, and local levels of government to provide health/mental health policy based on equity in services and service delivery mechanisms. Because neither of these conditions exists in toto at present, there has been an additive process that includes attention to provider, agency, and community levels. At the provider-level, recognition, understanding, and responsiveness to culturally prescribed communications, etiquette, and problem-solving approaches that occur on the basis of client cultural histories are now present in the educational, training, and experiential background of an increasing number of Anglo clinicians. Assessment and intervention services need to be integumented in a service delivery system consonant with agency policy that is endorsed, sponsored, and monitored by the cultural communities being served. As the interventions and service delivery systems described in this book will evidence, cultural competence among providers and agencies is now present but still embryonic. There are culturally competent culture-specific agencies and there are providers outside of these contexts who are also culturally competent. Recent research suggests that culture-specific agencies and matching providers and clients for ethnicity, language, or both, increase use and benefit intervention outcomes (Takeuchi & Uehara, 1996).

An Assessment/Intervention Model for Practice

Assessment and intervention for multicultural populations are inextricably linked because use of proffered interventions depends on the quality of the provider-client relationship, which is established during the initial contact. To be credible to the client, this relationship has to be accomplished using an acceptable behavioral/emotional etiquette; it must communicate cultural awareness and the absence of racism; and it must be consonant with expectations and health/illness beliefs. In addition, the outcome of even this initial contact has to be perceived as a "gift," not only promising genuine help over time but also providing an immediate, tangible benefit within a context of respect and understanding (Sue & Zane, 1987).

A six-step model begins with a relationship based on the extent of client-provider match on ethnicity, race, language, service delivery style, service setting decor, and client perception of provider personality and general professional competence. This match must be sufficiently acceptable to sustain the client during the initial session and result in willingness to return for additional meetings. An acculturation evaluation for category status provides a second step and for some clients will lead to a cultural identity description and subsequently a cultural formulation to assist in the third step, problem specification. Some or all of this information may be required for decisions leading to instrument selection in the fourth step, formal assessment, during which standard psychological tests, modified standard tests or pseudoetics, genuine etics, and culture-specific measures or emics may be used (Dana, 1993a). Feedback of the assessment results leads to informed participation by the client, family, and significant others. This feedback may constitute a legitimate intervention (e.g., therapeutic assessment), aid in a decision for applications of desirable and potentially effective interventions, or provide information for referral to another provider for subsequent interventions. The fifth step includes culture-general, combined, or culture-specific interventions. Finally, at the sixth step, the client and others evaluate the adequacy of the assessment/intervention process.

4

_____

_____

_____

Identities of Clients and Providers

This chapter is about the cultural/racial identities of clients and their service providers. For practical purposes, it is absolutely necessary to have information on client identity, including acculturation and a description of clients as cultural beings prior to the onset of any assessment or intervention services. Information on acculturation is provided by cultural orientation identification and is necessary because not all clients who appear to belong to a particular cultural group in terms of appearance, surname, or preferred language will share the worldview, values, beliefs, and perceptions of that group.

To avoid stereotyping based on appearances alone, cultural orientation information from an interview or test should be used. Cultural orientations reflect the relative contributions from an original culture and the acquired dominant society culture (Dana, 1992b). This information also suggests whether or not culture-specific services may be necessary, or even desirable, for a particular client. Furthermore, information on cultural identity permits increased understanding for purposes of establishing a valid diagnosis using a cultural formulation, and for planning potentially beneficial interventions.

This chapter will provide descriptions of cultural orientation categories for each of the four major groups—American Indians, African Americans, Asian Americans, and Hispanic Americans. Baseline estimates of the percentages of individuals in each category are included to provide some preliminary expectations for providers.

This chapter will supplement Chapter 2 with additional information on the worldviews of these groups, as well as specific discussions of some components that affect their use of mental health services. To appreciate the extent to which these worldviews may differ from an Anglo American worldview, components of an Anglo American worldview will be described for contrast with those of traditional persons from other cultural groups. Finally, the development of Anglo American identity in service providers affects all transactions with culturally diverse clients. Two major models of Anglo American identity development will be described.

A concluding theme in this chapter is how multicultural clients view their providers and the services they expect from them. The race of the provider and the provider's own identity development affect how clients perceive their providers. Because Anglo American providers will continue to be responsible for a significant proportion of services to multicultural clients for at least another decade, multicultural clients are more likely to receive services from these providers rather than from providers from their own cultural groups. The research literature on clients and providers includes client preferences for providers and client-provider matching. This discussion emphasizes the effects on perception of culturally competent services when client cultural orientations are matched with their potential providers.

Clients as Cultural Beings

The cultural beliefs of clients concerning psychological health and illness are part-and-parcel of a worldview that shapes their expectations for services, perceptions of providers, and willingness to receive available services. Because providers cannot assume that appearances provide unequivocal evidence for a particular cultural identity, it is necessary to make data-based judgments concerning cultural identification to know how and to what extent cultural issues should be acknowledged and addressed in services. Many multicultural clients share the values and worldview of the dominant Anglo American society and will benefit from the repertoire of interventions routinely used in this country. Even these bicultural persons, however, have to be accepted and understood on the basis of their original cultural origins and should be given a choice of culture-specific services whenever feasible.

Cultural Orientation

Cultural identification may be inferred from cultural orientation. The orientations to be described for all groups are traditional, bicultural, assimilated, and marginal. Traditional persons retain an original culture as a result of recent entry into this country, or as resident citizens because of preference, lack of contact and association, or both, with Anglo Americans.

Bicultural persons retain their original languages, but are motivated to learn the skills required for adaptation and comfortable functioning in the larger society. Some assimilated persons often want to forget, deny, or distance themselves from an original culture to become accepted by mainstream society.

Marginal persons are not comfortable with their traditional lifestyles, may not have opportunities to implement expectations for values and behaviors, or both, in the dominant society. Marginality always includes a mixture of Anglo American and traditional culture values and behaviors. Marginality poses a frequent problem for providers who attempt to be culturally sensitive because services that stem from the treatment ideology of either culture may be suspect and the development of trusting relationships with providers can be compromised. It is helpful to examine the specific mix of values and behaviors for each client to develop intervention plans that incorporate attention to personal identity conflicts and specific problems-in-living that are part of the dilemma of marginality.

Personality characteristics implied by the concept of marginality may be dysfunctional and lead to behaviors labeled by providers as personality disorders or transient situational disorders, although they may be behavioral reactions to societally imposed conditions restricting opportunities and preventing participation in either traditional or assimilated lifestyles. The concept of marginality has been addressed for many years by looking at the ambivalence created by divided loyalties and associated personality characteristics (Mann, 1958), which have been clustered to include ambivalence/ doubt, introversion/apathy, inner turmoil/depression, and paranoia/aggression (Kerckhoff & McCormick, 1955).

Cultural Orientation Information and Cultural Identity

Acceptable and potentially effective services acknowledge a client's cultural orientation and thereby recognize an intimate connection between client identity and responsible therapeutic acts. The ability to recognize a client's cultural orientation, however, will not automatically endow the provider with any special understanding or expertise, except perhaps for those clients who share the provider's own race/ethnicity and cultural orientation. To present culturally sensitive services, the behavioral style of the provider should conform to client expectations for relationships in these settings. In addition, any application of culture-specific interventions requires an in-depth knowledge of the client's culture as well as clinical skill in applying these interventions.

Descriptions of cultural identity have generally included three kinds of information (Olmedo, 1979): (a) language and customs, (b) culture-specific attitudes and values, and (c) socioeconomic/educational status. Specific psychometric measures can provide this information in the form of a "correction" using moderator variables for subsequent assessment using standard tests and technology stemming from a Eurocentric worldview.

A "correction" per se for a standard test, however, provides only a temporary substitute for the development of culture-specific assessment technologies for traditional persons. The use of "corrections" assumes that the Anglo American population standard is an acceptable criterion for beliefs and behaviors among populations of other cultural origins. As a result, client cultural differences from this population have been construed as a temporary by-product of contact with an unfamiliar culture and that these differences will diminish or disappear over time with assimilation and English-language fluency. This may not be a valid assumption because neither all cultural groups nor individual members within each group are necessarily motivated to assimilate and are facilitated during this process by their host society. Moreover, implicit in the acculturation experience is a disengagement from meaningful parts of the self represented by values and beliefs inherent in the original culture, which requires balance by acquisition of new understandings of the host culture.

In addition to serving as a "correction," a description of cultural orientation provides additional information about the client. Knowledge of cultural orientation can lead to inferences about the self, the importance of the family structure, and anticipated problems-in-living or culture-specific conditions. For example, an Anglo American patient may be understood as a discrete entity or closed system, encapsulated and responsible for thoughts and actions. Many multicultural clients, however, consider themselves to be a part of a larger system in which other persons, forces/powers, or all of these provide ultimate and required controls over thought and behavior. As a result, interventions should be predicated on an accurate assessment of who is the client. This self may be a self-contained individual with relatively impermeable boundaries or a person embedded in a larger matrix with more fluid and permeable boundaries. Psychiatric diagnoses using the *DSM* will be applicable only to persons who share an Anglo American composition of the self. Persons who have worldviews that sustain more extensive/inclusive or permeable self-boundaries will often be considered pathological because their cultural beliefs and behaviors have been confounded with Anglo American culture-specific or emic psychopathologies.

Traditional persons share a group identity based on their cultural heritage and their historic/contemporary experiences of contact with the dominant Anglo American society. An individual self that develops from this cultural identity is culture specific. These identities lead to constellations of shared values, health/illness beliefs, language, and perceptions. Culture-specific perceptions of services, service providers, and service delivery style affect client responsiveness and the potential effectiveness of subsequent interventions. Traditional, bicultural, and marginal cultural orientations will be described for four cultural groups.

African Americans

African Americans entered this country primarily as persons uprooted from their traditional cultures and forced to adapt to slavery. A legacy of this history for many persons was passive identification with the dominant cultural values. Advocacy movements provided some empowerment to create a climate of hope for alleviating second-class status. By 1970, African cultural identity reaffirmation took the form of cognitive developmental models of Nigrescence and an emergent racial identity of Afrocentrism for many persons.

Worldview. A residue of a group racial identity persists not only in the unconscious but also in everyday behaviors and even in a quality of expanded consciousness. This residual identity had to be articulated, described, understood, and made conscious for individuals by a rediscovery of their African origins and by a relearning what was once a coherent worldview basis for living. The impact of increased political empowerment and awareness of cultural roots strongly suggests that over time, this racial identity consciousness will include many more persons.

There is already evidence that a sense of racial identity increases over time in college settings (e.g., Cheatham, Tomlinson, & Ward, 1990). Socioeconomic status and racial identity, as measured by stages of Nigrescence, appear to be different constructs (Carter & Helms, 1988). In addition to a reconstruction of the historical Afrocentric concepts (e.g., Asante, 1987; Asante, 1990), there is also empirical evidence of West African origins for musical preferences, religion, and foods among African American children of working-class and business/professional-class families (Dodson, 1983).

Group identity in Africa was tribal in origin, and the individual self-concept was extended and permeable, including other persons (both ancestors and the unborn), spirits, plants, animals, and natural phenomena. Individual or personal identity is now expressed by a self, an extended family, and race. The interrelatedness of these self-components with nature, the spirit world, and the universe had been diluted for many persons in the United States. Group identity is now expressed by inseparability of materialistic and spiritualistic realities, interdependence, and collectivism. The language for interface with the Anglo American society has always been standard English, but there is widespread usage of Black English Vernacular for within-group communication.

Group identity in the 1970s included specific value orientations (Kluckhohn & Strodtbeck, 1961): human nature accepted as good and evil with subjugation to nature, a present-time focus, and a being orientation for human activity (Kendrick, MacMillan, & Pinderhughes, 1983). More recently, harmony in man/nature relationships, a future-time focus, and a doing activity orientation have been described (Carter & Helms, 1987).

The perceptions of mental health services by traditional clients are largely determined by their health/illness beliefs, which differ in etiology from those of Anglo Americans by the presence of spiritual factors (Millet, Sullivan, Schwebel, & Myers, 1996). Congruence between these beliefs and services is necessary if the services are to be experienced as legitimate and credible. There is an extensive range and variety of possible health-illness beliefs in traditional cultures as a component of worldviews. Cosmic, religious, moralistic, genetic, physiological, social, and psychological causes have all been recognized and each cause has many forms of expression (Lin & Lin, 1978) Table 4.1 presents the range of perceived causes of illness, varieties of providers, and credible remediations or interventions.

Racial Identity: Nigrescence. A Nigrescence model provides process conceptions for identity development in stages, while Afrocentrism has made descriptive content available for a culturally distinctive worldview. The original Nigrescence models developed by Thomas and Cross in the 1970s (Cross, 1978; Dana, 1993a, pp. 116-119) have been updated and expanded by Parham (1989; see Table 4.2). There is a progression from a Eurocentric worldview, with subservience to the Anglo American society and repression of rage (Stage 1); to beginning a motivated search for identity accompanied by pain, confusion, and self-denial (Stage 2); proceeding to a developing awareness of cultural identity initially expressed by intense rage/guilt/pride (Stage 3); leveling off with internalization/actions to provide personal linkages to African cultural values (Stage 4); and, finally, resolution by transcendence or internalization and commitment (Stage 5). This model documents the presence of a set of beliefs and cultural values that does not vary by

Table 4.1   Causal Illness Beliefs, Providers, and Interventions: Multifaceted
              Relationships Mediated by Culture

Belief	Provider	Intervention
Brain disorder	Community advocate	*Curanderismo*
Curse	Emergency room	Behavioral-cognitive
Demons/spirits	Family	Counseling
Diet	Family physician	Diet
Family life	Folk healer	Exercise
God	Friend	Exorcism
Heredity	Herbalist	Group process
Interpersonal	Indigenous helper	Herbs
Life changes	Mental health provider	Home care
Negative thought	Minister/priest	Hoodoo/voodoo
Physical illness	Self	Isolation
Punishment for sin	Self-help group	Medication
Spirits		Psychoanalysis
Supernatural		Psychotherapy
Taboo violation		Relaxation
Witchcraft		Religious/spiritual:
Worry/school		Confession, meditation,
		prayer, ritual
		Santeria
		Self care
		Shango
		Voodoo/hoodoo

SOURCE: Narikiyo and Kameoka (1992, Table 1, p. 365). There are specific additions especially to content
in the belief column, but the format and intent follows the original table.

gender or socioeconomic status (Allen, Dawson, & Brown, 1989; Jackson, McCullough, Gurin, & Broman, 1991).

These conceptualizations have been translated psychometrically into moderator variables to provide racial identity data for studies of process (Helms, 1990a; Milliones, 1980) and outcome (i.e., Africentrism, see Baldwin & Bell, 1984). Afrocentrism constitutes a traditional culture orientation described by the later stages of Nigrescence models. Burlew and Smith (1991) have described four approaches to racial identity represented by existing tests: (a) developmental (i.e., Nigrescence model); (b) Afrocentric (e.g., African Self-Consciousness Scale [Baldwin & Bell, 1984 and Belief Systems Analysis Scale] Montgomery, Fine, & James-Myers, 1990); (c) racial stereotyping

Table 4.2   Racial Identity Developmental Stages for African Americans

Stage	
1.	*Pre-encounter:* Lack of self-awareness as racial being. Denial/devaluation of black culture. Tacit acceptance of Eurocentric worldview and white normative standards result in pro-white/anti-black attitudes.
2.	*Encounter:* Experiences with personal and social vulnerability and trauma. Inconsistency of these events with image of self as human being. Realization that frame-of-reference is unsatisfactory. Decision to acquire black identity. Beginnings of painful search for black identity.
3.	*Immersion/emersion:* Preoccupation with idealized black culture. Withdrawal from whites and other groups. Denigration of whites. Rage/guilt/pride. Tension/emotionality/defensiveness.
4.	*Internalization:* Development of personal ties to black culture/experience. Increased self-confidence/inner security/resolution of conflicts. Proactive black identity with racial tolerance/flexibility/openness diminished anti-white feelings. May include focus on social action, political activity to channel negative feelings.

SOURCE: Helms and Carter (1991); Parham (1989).

(e.g., Cultural Mistrust Inventory [Terrell & Terrell, 1981]); and (d) group orientation (i.e., Black Group Identification Index [Davidson, 1975]). Since this 1991 review, Landrine and Klonoff (1996) have constructed the African American Acculturation Scale to describe cultural identity as distinct from racial identity or Afrocentrism.

Cultural Orientations. Valentine (1971) believes that all African Americans are essentially bicultural because they have been socialized by two distinct cultures. Although a bicultural orientation may have been preferred by many African Americans in the late 1960s, such identification was often problematic and limited by the presence of distinctive skin color. Nonetheless, identification with the dominant culture by striving for middle-class status and overachievement was once accompanied by an attempt to deny a distinctive African racial identity (see Stage 1, Table 3.1, this volume).

Cultural orientation data from tests for Nigrescence (Whatley & Dana, 1989) indicate that approximately 23% of a small urban, male, African American student population were in Nigrescence Stages IV and V, or Afrocentric, the equivalent of a traditional cultural orientation. Although generalizations from this limited college data to the entire African American population is not feasible, Hacker (1992) stated that 20% of this entire population preferred to be considered as African American, 78% black, and

2% Negro. Less than 25% of these persons preferred African names for their children. Hacker's figures were based on large and representative samples in studies conducted by political scientists.

Marginality implies an absence of any clear cultural tradition and describes black persons who are trapped by the "victim system" stemming from poverty and racism (Pinderhughes, 1982). As a result, opportunities for education and employment are limited. Under these circumstances, the development of traditional, bicultural, or assimilated cultural/racial identity orientations are not easily accomplished or facilitated by the larger society. Instead, marginality increases the likelihood of stressed or abusive family relationships, poor health, mental illness, development of gangs, criminal behavior, or homicide described in a special journal issue (Williams, 1996).

Pinderhughes (1982) emphasized that marginality is now a subculture with a focus on living/surviving in the present, cooperation and obedience to authority as a source of power, toughness, suppression of feelings, and displacement of feelings to music, as well as belief in luck and magic. Regardless of social-class status, approximately 60% of black children have been exposed to marginality as a result of residence in neighborhoods characterized by high rates of poverty, substandard housing, crime, and inadequate schools. This description of marginality also applies to other urban cultural groups living under similar circumstances.

Most practitioners have had little experience in assessing cultural orientation or any consensual notions regarding base rates for cultural orientation categories. Figure 4.1 presents suggested cultural orientation category base rates for African Americans. It is estimated that about 20% are Afrocentric or traditional, less than 10% are assimilated, 20% are bicultural, and over 50% are marginal in cultural orientation. Although these base rates are inexact, some tentative expectations are needed until more accurate, empirical base lines for cultural orientations by cultural group become available.

As noted earlier, all blacks have some biculturality to function in Anglo American society and marginal cultural orientation implies imperfect biculturality and less than optimal functioning within the larger society. There are probably very few exclusively traditional persons as a result of early fragmentation and dispersal of their original African cultures, required contact with Anglo Americans, and the relatively recent immersion in Afrocentrism.

American Indians/Alaska Natives

Approximately one third of the indigenous persons in the United States are still treated by the government as conquered peoples with quasi-nation

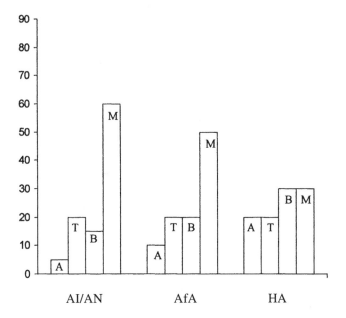

Figure 4.1. Approximations of Cultural Orientation Classification Percentages for American Indians/Alaska Natives (AI/AN), African Americans (AfA), and Hispanic Americans (HA)

status on reservations. Many others lost their official status by detribalization and scattering in urban ghettos. This population of at least 2 million persons has been subjected to a continuous attempt to eradicate their cultures as the price of entry and personal survival within the surrounding society. The price has been too high for many who struggle with personal identity conflicts that almost always include attempts to preserve, restore, and be protected by their group cultural identity.

Worldview. In spite of a time span that parallels the discovery and conquest of the Americas, some American Indians have been able to retain their original worldview relatively intact. This worldview is more different from an Anglo American worldview than almost all other cultural groups and the pressure for assimilation by the dominant society has never taken this fact into consideration. American Indian/Alaska Native group identity has retained a community or tribal focus in which worldview is expressed by spirituality, with intimate ties to a supreme creator, lesser spirit beings, animals, rocks, plants, and natural forces. This spirit world remains relatively intact for many traditional persons and is inseparable from the self, extended family, and community or tribe. The spirit world is invoked by special states of awareness including intuitive perceptions, emotional responsivity to an unseen world in dreams, vision quests, and ceremonies. As a result, the boundaries of the self remain diffuse and permeable. The self still includes an extended family and a tribal community, although, for many persons, the diffuseness of boundaries also permits access to other reality dimensions as well. An extended time dimension provides arenas for positive and negative power transactions.

Health/illness or, more accurately, wellness/unwellness beliefs address a cycle of harmony/disharmony in which harmony between mind and body, person and spirit are essentials. Violations of scared or tribal taboos, and/or witchcraft cause disharmony (Table 4.1). Wellness, or harmony of the mind, body, and spirit, is fostered by a variety of resources (e.g., spirit helpers, protective objects, isolation, healing rituals, medicine people, natural support system). These resources act to counter violations of sacred/tribal taboos or witchcraft. Often, Western medicine is used interchangeably with these cultural resources because a majority of American Indians understand both health/illness conceptions. They also understand the Anglo American health and mental health service delivery systems and are frequently able to present their problems using either idiom to receive whatever services are available.

There has been considerable consistency in expression of group and individual identity through values and belief systems in spite of continued usage of over 100 non-Indo-European languages to shape thought processes and behavioral expression. Their value-orientation structures include a good and evil conception of human nature, preference for harmony with nature, a present-time focus, collateral relationships with others, and being or doing activity orientations (Kluckhohn & Strodtbeck, 1961).

There has been pervasive misunderstanding of the importance of this distinctive worldview as a survival tool and the magnitude of change required for adaptation to an alien educational/occupational system in which American Indians are required to learn new skills and new modes of thinking, learning, coping, and socialization, as well as a new social etiquette for interpersonal relationships. They have been expected to make these assimilative changes in spite of a burden of anger and grief for their loss of sacred land and way of life, the destruction of their culture and traditions, and the dismantling of their history as contained in ancestral burial sites and other sacred places.

Cultural Identity. A description of identity development in American Indians may be helpful to an understanding of their cultural orientations by Anglo American providers, who may feel themselves "outsiders." This developmental process differs from other models by originating not from an inchoate and unverbalized sense of identity, but instead from oral history, particularly in native languages, which has encoded into memory the essence of what it is to be an indigenous person. Moreover, family structure and socialization practices, the forms for expression of spirituality, and some of the languages that formalize thought patterns and information processing have remained relatively intact as descriptions of tribal identities.

Table 4.3 describes my interpretation of American Indian/Alaska Native cultural identity development following a similar format to Tables 4.2 and 4.5, but adds Stages 1 and 2, precontact, and initial contact histories as a basis for Stage 3, an early contact history that resulted in repression of cultural identity. This repression leads to Stage 4, outcomes of History of Contact, and includes assimilation for an unknown number of persons, an assimilation that has sometimes been incomplete and resulted in an individual search for origins. For a majority of American Indians, however, these Stage 4 outcomes include a partial loss of traditional culture. For some of these persons, primarily older individuals usually living on reservations, there has been a tenacious guarding and holding onto what remains of their traditional cultural beliefs and language. For younger persons and those in urban areas, however, a sense of common cause has become a lifelong struggle to recover tribal identities. This struggle leads to identity issues at Stage 5, in which marginal and transitional cultural orientations occur as well as a preoccupation with personal tribal-cultural origins. This intense focus leads toward greater knowledge and understanding of the experiences of all Indian people. At Stage 6, immersion/emersion results in questioning relationships with non-Indians, the beginnings of possible outcomes for this personal struggle. Two possible identity outcomes may occur at Stage 7: a retreat into Indian culture or a continuing process of learning about self and culture in the context of a bicultural lifestyle.

Cultural Orientations. Available cultural orientation information suggests that cultural orientation frequencies depend on the purpose of the research; sampling procedures; measures; and college, urban, or reservation samples. For example, only a small minority—less than 10% in an Oklahoma college population—were assimilated, with approximately equal percentages of traditional, marginal, or bicultural students (Johnson & Lashley, 1989). The presence of very few assimilated individuals in college populations was supported by data from the University of South Dakota, using the Northern

Table 4.3 Stages of American Indian Identity Formation and Transformation

Stage			
1.	*Precontact:* Traditional cultural orientation.		
2.	*Initial contact:* Alcohol, exploration of tribal rivalries, genocide.		
3.	*Early contact history:* Forced reservation residence, often remote from original lands; reliance on commodities for survival; boarding schools; suppression of languages, spirituality-ceremonials; destruction of roles, especially for males. Gradual loss of former traditional cultures. Personal experiences with discrimination/ racism.		
4.	*Outcomes of history of contact*		
	A	B	C
	Complete loss of traditional culture: Adoption by Anglos, assimilated parents; Anglo schools, friends, church.	Partial loss of traditional culture: Some incorporation of Anglo values, behaviors.	Partial loss of traditional culture with reservation residence, isolation from assimilated persons.
5.	*Identity issues*		
	A	B	
	Marginal Transitional	Anger, preoccupation with own culture, denigration of Anglo culture. Contact with persons from other tribes— information/knowledge/understanding. Observation of lives affected by negative experiences with Anglos.	
6.	*Immersion/emersion*		
	Fear/ambivalence in approaching Anglos—cautious, selective overtures, tentative friendships.		
7.	*Identity outcome*		
	A	B	
	Retreat (temporary/permanent) to own culture as reaction to negative experiences, generalization to all Anglos. Look to own culture, tribe, and Indian identity exclusively for emotional security, economic base, and meaning in life.	Continued learning about self and own culture. Discovery of strength in Indian identity. Ability to have sustained relations with some Anglos; be comfortable in some cross-cultural social, occupational, educational settings.	

Plains Biculturalism Immersion Scale (Allen & French, 1994). In this rural setting, 4% of a predominantly Plains Indian population were assimilated, 1% bicultural, 45% traditional, and 50% marginal. Noncollege reservation samples would be expected to include even more persons of marginal orientation. A California urban population study using the above measure described 25% as traditional, 17% marginal, 24% bicultural, and 33% assimilated (Byron, 1995). The percentages of each cultural orientation in the entire American Indian/Alaska Native population have been estimated to be about 20% traditional, with 15% "middle-class"/assimilated in their beliefs, and 65% marginal (French, 1989).

Figure 4.1 presents base rate estimates by cultural orientation category. It is difficult to know how many persons are assimilated, because assimilation implies a denial of cultural origins coupled with an appearance and skin color that does not permit identification. As a result, college student self-reports may underestimate the numbers of persons who have denied cultural origins or are not aware of their own ancestry. There is a large percentage of marginal persons because of persistent obstacles to assimilation or biculturality as cultural orientation alternatives. Moreover, the personal identity conflict experienced by many persons suggests ambivalence and the desire to hold on to some parts of their cultural history and group identities. Many marginal persons may be better described as *transitional* (LaFromboise, Trimble, & Mohatt, 1990), a term that suggests the importance of identifying the components of personal conflict and disorganization, although none of these reported figures/estimates included that categorization.

Asian Americans

There are well over 7 million Asians/Pacific Islanders from 32 distinct cultural groups in the United States, including Vietnamese, Laotians, Cambodians, Hmong, and ethnic Chinese from Southeast Asia. The cultural orientations of all these groups are complex and some examples for specific cultural groups will be used for illustration.

For example, beginning in the 1970s, Japanese Americans of the third (Sansei) and fourth (Yonsi) generations were largely assimilated English speakers. Their second-generation (Nisei) West Coast parents or grandparents had experienced internment during World War II, and this trauma was probably critical in fostering assimilation as the preferred cultural orientation. A majority of Japanese Americans have been assimilated, except in Hawaii where biculturality is common. As a result, most of Japanese Americans are at least third generation. Although there are increasing numbers of Japanese students, tourists, and businesspeople in the United States, there are few recent immigrants.

The Chinese, however, had an early history as immigrants from a country without a strong central government to protect their interests. Discrimination, exploitation, and persecution forced them to live in small town enclaves until a forced retreat to a few urban centers was completed by 1940. Whether new arrivals from Southeast Asia or long-term residents, however, most Chinese Americans have chosen to remain in urban enclaves where Chinese is still spoken, often as a first language. These ghettos were safe havens for preserving traditional culture and language. There was minimal contact with the surrounding culture until recent tourist invasions stimulated economies and created more opportunities to become fluent in English.

Many Chinese who have lived in this country for several generations, as well as Southeast Asian Chinese immigrants, remain traditional in cultural orientation, although the numbers of college-educated, bicultural persons are now increasing. The relative cohesiveness of their society and community social controls have prevented an emergence of large numbers of marginal individuals. More recently, however, probably as a result of limited opportunities in an environment shared with other cultural groups, marginality has become more prevalent among Asian Americans, at least among younger persons and recent immigrants. Many educated, bilingual, bicultural Chinese Americans are now developing a pan-Asian identity.

Other Southeast Asians, depending on their ethnicity, religion, and time of immigration, will vary in the relative frequencies of their cultural orientation categories. For example, the pre-1975 wave of Vietnamese refugees were typically affluent, urban, bilingual, and Catholic. The post-1975 wave contained many Buddhists, ethnic Chinese, rural, and less well-educated persons. Rapid assimilation, biculturality, or both were frequent in the first wave whereas a traditional cultural orientation was more frequent among second-wave persons. In this group, less rapid acculturation occurred, as well as retention of original languages. Because many Asian American immigrant groups also represent intact traditional cultures, they have benefited from viable community structures that assume advocate responsibility for their incoming individuals.

Worldview. The worldviews of Asian Americans are complicated by diverse national origins, religious affiliations, and languages. As a result, there are both culture-specific and developing pan-Asian worldviews. The pan-Asian worldview is a holistic perception of mind/body inseparability and a pluralistic world (Irigon, Claravall, & Christian, 1990).

Chinese worldview will be described as a culture-specific example because historically, Chinese culture influenced the core cultures of Korea, Japan, and Vietnam. A blend of Confucianism, Buddhism, and Taoism emphasized balance with persons and nature maintained by filial piety and an inner focus using meditation and prayer within a hierarchal society. A larger universal context for harmony included ancestors, gods, and spirits in addition to persons and social institutions.

The Chinese recognized an individual self consisting of a "little me" and a "big me" (Dien, 1983). A little me was embodied in the individual and family whereas the big me included the society and culture, and perhaps even a pan-Asian identification for some persons. Big me and little me are not separable within the self-concept. In fact, Hsu (1985) has described the Chinese self as seven irregular, concentric layers from the unconscious to the outer world that have to be in harmony for psychological health.

Asian Americans may accept the entire range of possible causes of illness contained in Table 4.1. For example, different explanations were used to account for bizarre behavior in a 16-year-old Taiwanese girl (Harrell, 1991): naturalistic (fright, low luck, mental illness), supernatural (random attacks from vengeful ghosts, a haunted house, and ghost soldiers all unrelated to the victim), ancestral retribution for moral fault, and malicious attack by a sorcerer. Some traditional persons in the United States continue to share many of these etiological beliefs. Nonetheless, all illness is conceived as physical with multiple causes including lack of will power and morbid thinking.

Health/illness beliefs are embodied in the physiological Yin/Yang. In nature, a balance of forces is required between yin and yang, or male and female, warmth and cold, light and dark, constructive and destructive, active and passive, fullness and emptiness, respectively (Abbott, 1970). Illness is believed to be reversible by exorcism, or with herbs and tonics to strengthen the nervous system to restore balance or harmony. Restoration occurs preferably within the family system as a primary outcome of family harmony and only secondarily within the life of the afflicted individual. There are many restoratives for harmony among components of the self (Table 4.1).

Cultural Identity. Following the conceptualization, models, and measurement of African American racial identity in the form of Nigrescence, attempts were made to generalize identity development to other groups. A Minority Identity Development Model (Atkinson, Morten, & Sue, 1989) defined stages of conformity, dissonance, resistance and immersion, introspection, and synergetic association-awareness (Table 4.4). Conformity is characterized by demeaning and stereotypic attitudes toward the self, their own group, and other groups. Anglo American society and culture is viewed uncritically as the standard for all group comparisons. Dissonance is a process of developing conflict that may be gradual or dramatically responsive to a critical incident. This conflict arises between polar positive attitudes toward Anglo American cultural values and negative attitudes toward self, own group, and other groups. Cycles of pride and pain occur with questioning earlier attitudes on the basis of new experiences and information. Suspicion toward the dominant group becomes stronger. Resistance and immersion attitudes develop as conflict-resolution begins. A greater understanding of having been victimized by oppression, discrimination, and racism leads to anger and guilt. Discovery of a group history and culture reinforces a sense of pride and honor in an emerging personal identity. Other visible racial/ ethnic groups are examined from a personal group perspective and Anglo American society is rejected. A process of introspection leads to discomfort with group-specific attitudes and reevaluation of the dominant society. At the same time, there is greater appreciation and comfort with personal identity. Finally, there are feelings of "self-fulfillment" and a sense of personal liberation that permits both control and flexibility. An examination of culture-specific and dominant cultural values results in selectivity of endorsement. Feelings of self-worth and group pride permit liking and trust on a selective basis for Anglo Americans and greater openness to some attributes of the dominant culture.

Cultural Orientations. It is difficult to suggest cultural orientation base rates for Asian Americans because there are many different Asian groups and there are large within-group differences in cultural orientations. Moreover, most of the research has been with college students who must be proficient in English and actively motivated toward biculturality to succeed academically.

The percentages of college students in three cultural orientation categories for Southeast Asian, Chinese American, Korean American, Filipino American, and Japanese American groups have been reported (Atkinson & Gim, 1989; Atkinson, Whiteley, & Gim, 1990). The Southeast Asians in these studies represented Burma, Cambodia, Indonesia, Laos, Malaysia, Singapore, Thailand, and Vietnam. There may be fewer refugees than would appear in a sample of Southeast Asian persons from Vietnam exclusively. Because all of the individuals in these studies were fluent in English, many traditionally oriented, non-English speakers, or both were omitted from these estimates. These figures were obtained using the Suinn-Lew Self-Identity Acculturation Scale (SL-ASIA; Suinn, Rickard-Figueroa, Lew, & Vigil, 1987), which considers biculturality to be medium acculturation and has no explicit provision for the marginality category.

These groups showed differences in cultural orientation categories by country of origin, and there were some sex differences in each group. This comparative data for Asian American groups is of limited generality. Neither is there any information on length of time, or generation, in the United States, although the SL-ASIA scale has been validated using generation, length of residence, and self-ratings of identity data (Suinn et al., 1987). A trend across all groups toward biculturality and assimilation was noted, except for the

Table 4.4   Minority Identity Development Model

Stage

Conformity
  Negative attitudes toward self, own group, other visible racial/ethnic groups. Positive attitudes toward Anglo Americans.

Dissonance
  Conflict between own positive and negative attitudes based on self/other experiences

Resistance-immersion
  Positive attitudes toward self and own group. Negative attitudes toward Anglo Americans. Conflict.

Introspection
  Awareness of own ethnocentrism as basis for attitudes toward self, own group, other visible racial/ethnic groups, and Anglo Americans.

Synergetic articulation/awareness
  Positive attitudes toward self, own group, other visible racial/ethnic groups, and selectivity in attitudes toward dominant group and individuals.

SOURCE: Adopted from Atkinson, Morten, and Sue (1989).

relatively assimilated Japanese Americans. These studies did not report the numbers of bicultural Hawaii-born Japanese Americans, which may account for the extent of biculturality in these samples. Otherwise, the reported differences across groups may be related to generation or length of residence in the United States.

Hispanic Americans

Over 22 million persons of Hispanic origin are represented by Mexican Americans, Puerto Ricans, and Cuban Americans, as well as immigrants or refugees from Spanish-speaking countries (Chapa & Valencia, 1993).

Worldview. There are major similarities in worldview among Hispanics in the Americas and Europe as a result of shared religion and a common language. Hispanic Americans, however, also have worldview differences due to country of origin, acculturation, and Indian ancestry.

Group identity is shaped by familism as a behavioral-attitudinal referent for obligations and mutual support (Sabogal, Marín, Otero-Sabogal, Vann Oss Marín, & Perez-Sable, 1987). The family is a kinship group typically extending beyond the nuclear family, or *la casa,* to *la familia,* which may include godparents and friends (Sena-Rivera, 1979).

Personal identity is sociocentric with *la casa* and *la familia* often included in a balance of prerogatives between the self and other family members.

Traditional sex roles are very clear and are associated with an inner strength that includes self-control, acceptance of fate, toughness, and will power used directly for problem solving. Values are affected by generation in this country, education/occupation, and retention of traditionality. Value orientations (Kluckhohn and Strodtbeck, 1961) to Hispanics include human nature as both good and evil, subjugation to nature, a present time focus, lineal relationships, and a being activity preference.

Traditional Hispanic Americans perceive mental health in religious and familial terms as balance and harmony. Mental illness has causes related to harmony among these components, and external forces such as witches or hexes remain credible for some traditional persons. Folk healing practices are acceptable when available, although these practitioners often may not be visible in some urban areas.

Cultural Identity. Ruiz (1990) presented a model for the development of Mexican American cultural identity with an emphasis on marginality and ethnocultural strategies for intervention. The model has early causal and cognitive stages during which experiences, feelings, and false beliefs prevent a continued development of an ethnic identity and erode any sense of ethnic self-worth. These early stages foster marginality as a primary outcome of fragmented ethnic identity. For many persons, there can be no movement from a marginal cultural orientation and lifestyle except by culture-specific interventions to refurbish a sense of ethnic identity for personal affirmation and as a coping resource.

This developmental model, presented in Table 4.5, differs from other culture-specific models by not allowing for anger directed toward the Anglo American community during the stage describing Consequences of Alienation. Moreover, it is not explicitly stated in the Working Through Distress stage that the development of biculturality is a bona fide goal for many Mexican Americans. To reach this goal, it would be necessary to recognize anger and deal with it in a treatment process or in life situations with Anglo Americans.

Cultural Orientations. There may be distinct differences among Hispanic subgroups in cultural orientation category distributions, although estimates for all subgroups are contained in Figure 4.1.

Early bilingual immigrants from Cuba experienced opportunities to become bicultural if they wished. Second-generation Cuban Americans are typically assimilated, with English as a first and often only language. These persons tend to have higher educational and socioeconomic status than other Hispanic subgroups. There are relatively fewer traditional persons than

Table 4.5 Mexican American Ethnic Identity Development

Stage

Causal

    Experiential/emotional consequences of racism, ethnocentrism, social class result in ignoring, negating, denigrating heritage and language.

Cognitive

    False beliefs:

    (a) Cause-effect relationships between ethnicity and poverty/racism

    (b) Assimilation and escape from poverty/racism

    (c) Assimilation leads to success

    Conflicts:

    (a) Identity search

    (b) Identity confusion

    (c) Marginality

Consequence

    Fragmentation outcomes of earlier stages: Hurt/shame as result of skin color, name, language, traditional customs. Use of defense mechanisms (Maduro, 1982).

Working through distress

    Ethnocultural assessment. Ethnocultural identification (Cómas-Diaz & Jacobsen, 1987). Ethnography (Cobbs, 1972). Disassimilation (Hayes-Bautista, 1974). Pluralistic counseling (LeVine & Padilla, 1980). Natural support system (Pearson, 1985).

Successful resolution

    Acceptance of ethnicity, culture, self. Ethnicity as source of strength, route to success. Pride in community.

SOURCE: Ruiz (1990).

among Puerto Ricans or Mexican Americans, although marginal and more traditional Cuban Americans came to the United States in the 1980 Mariel boat lift.

A majority of Puerto Ricans have completed high school, speak English, and possess the occupational skills to become assimilated or bicultural. Relatively large numbers, however, also remain traditional or marginal. For different reasons, Mexican American and Puerto Rican populations are dichotomized into either assimilated/bicultural persons or those who are traditional, marginal, or both. Mexican Americans, especially in the younger, more highly educated second or third generations, are frequently bicultural. There are, however, still large numbers of traditional and/or marginal persons who speak little English, are migrants, or are residents of urban barrios employed in the secondary job market.

Marginality appears to be somewhat less frequent for Hispanic Americans than for African Americans as a result of a relatively intact culture with core similarities across different subgroups. After several generations of residency, many families have a worldview that has become less discrepant from the dominant culture due to more educational and middle-class occupational opportunities and because their Catholic religion is shared with many Americans of exclusively European ancestry. The relatively higher percentage of biculturality among Hispanic Americans also reflects a better fit with the larger society.

Hispanic American identity is a mixture of American Indian and African roots in addition to the strong European contribution, depending on their countries of origin in Europe, the Caribbean, South America, and Central America. As a result, many individuals are perceived as belonging to a visible racial/ethnic group. In addition, limiting factors, as with other groups with high marginality rates, include poverty and the effects of prejudice, especially toward readily identifiable individuals, which reduce opportunities for assimilation or biculturality.

Figure 4.1 presents suggested cultural orientation category base rates for Hispanic Americans, although these estimates should be used with caution for Cuban Americans and there are also differences between Mexican Americans and Puerto Ricans. With increasing education and employment opportunities, biculturality and assimilation should increase over time. Marginality remains high and poverty, ageism, sexism, and discrimination have resulted in an underclass that includes persons with these cultural origins.

Anglo American Provider Worldview and Identity Development

Worldview. Table 4.6 presents Anglo American worldview components of personal identity (self), shared group identity, language, beliefs, values, preferred services, and service provider characteristics and behavioral style. All of these components are necessary for understanding Anglo Americans and affect their perceptions of the legitimacy and credibility of services.

Although the group cultural identities of Anglo Americans were originally associated with their countries of origin on the European continent, by the third generation, individuals become sufficiently assimilated to define themselves as American. Early studies examined the shift in culture-specific symptoms of major mental illnesses among Irish and Italians, for example, across generations (Singer & Opler, 1956). Nonetheless, exceptions exist in culturally isolated communities, both urban and rural, where Greeks, Italians, Russians, Norwegians, and others have retained a significant original cultural identity and language fluency for much longer than three generations.

The common language in the United States has been English and there have been intensely negative reactions from the dominant society to sugges-

Table 4.6   Components of Anglo American Worldview

Personal identity
  Self-concept is individualistic.
Group racial identity
  Poorly formed/understood (see Table 3.7, this volume, Stage 1)
Language
  English
Health/illness beliefs
  Health: Absence of disease
  Illness: Organic/psychological causes
Services
  Focus on individual
Service providers
  Objective, rational/sympathetic understanding
  Professional/credentialed/specialized/highly compensated
Service delivery
  Formal/professional relationships without dual roles
Values (Kluckhohn)
  Human nature viewed as evil
  Mastery over nature
  Future time focus
  Individualistic relationships
  Activity: Accomplishing something

---

tions that Spanish, for example, become a second language (see Padilla et al., 1991). In Anglo American society, personal identity is focused on individualism, a self-contained focus primarily or exclusively on each person as a source of power, control, and responsibility. The boundaries of this self are firm to the extent of being relatively impermeable, and function to exclude or minimize the presence of other persons and other external natural or spiritual sources of identity.

Anglo Americans typically believe in organic causes and/or experiential causes for psychological disturbances. These causes may be subdivided into genetic, physiological, social, or psychological. Health is the absence of disease/distress, and interventions are designed to interfere with a physiological condition using medications as well as other physical interventions, or to deal with cognitive and behavioral symptoms by verbal mediation, often involving exploration/manipulation of the personal present or past. The focus of intervention is on the individual client, either alone or in a group/family context, with or without client understanding and compliance or motivation for change.

Kluckhohn-Strodtbeck values associated with a core Anglo American identity include human nature as basically evil, mastery of nature, future time focus, individualistic goals/relationships, and an activity focus on doing in the sense of accomplishment. Most middle-class, educated Anglo Americans expect to be able to exercise self-control and personal efficacy (see Table 4.6) to alter their behaviors, cognitions, or both because of the belief that the locus of such control lies within themselves. Help is, however, acceptable from a variety of expert mental health sources including psychiatrists, psychologists, counselors, social workers, and other specialists. Clients who share the vocabulary and conceptual tools of their providers believe that they will be enabled to cope with everyday living by strengthening their self-boundaries or understanding their memories of past trauma. If they lack these cognitive structures for implementation, however, they may have faith in drug regimens available as an extension of an empirical approach to medicine.

Anglo American health beliefs are now in transition because a positivist, empiricist science is being replaced by a constructionist view. This view suggests an extended range of interacting biopsychosocial causes in a context of an expanding methodological repertoire and an understanding of cultural relativity. The transition to constructionist beliefs is, however, now being expressed by a rapid paradigm shift as a result of sociopolitical forces that favor maintenance of the status quo.

An Anglo American preferred style of service delivery emphasizes a relatively formal, "professional" relationship with providers who are expected to deliberately abstain from dual roles with their clients as an ethical requirement. Providers are socialized to be objective, neutral, rational, and somewhat impersonal but simultaneously sympathetic, warm, and genuine. These contrasting faces of service delivery have occurred, at least partially, as a result of a forced marriage between a medical model approach and the widely accepted research findings of a strong, positive relationship between provider characteristics of warmth, empathy, and genuineness, and positive therapy outcomes (Truax & Carkhuff, 1964). In addition, providers are credentialed, professional, highly compensated, and specialized. They use verbal skills, listening and eye contact; demand self-disclosure; and are expected to understand the subjective experience and overt behaviors of clients who have been characterized as WASP (white, Anglo Saxon, Protestant) and YAVIS (young, attractive, verbal, intelligent, successful) (Katz, 1985). These clients frequently mirror the demographics of their service providers.

Identity Development. Anglo American service providers differ among themselves in identity development, and several models of identity development are available (Bennett, Atkinson, & Rowe, 1993; Helms, 1990b; Ponterotto,

1988; Rowe, Bennett, & Atkinson, 1994; Sabnani, Ponterotto, & Boro-dovsky, 1991). These models are predicated on oppression in the sense of adaptive developmental-stage schemas for racial/cultural groups (e.g., Sabnani et al., 1991) or on the significance of being white as a focus for attitudes toward other groups (e.g., Bennett et al., 1993).

A comparison of these two major approaches is included because providers may want to consider the merits of both formulations. Multicultural competence among Anglo American providers is partially the result of understanding their own identity development, especially their interface with the stage of identity development of a multicultural client.

The stage model of identity development for Anglo Americans is somewhat comparable to the developmental stages of Afrocentrism. For comparisons between racial/cultural groups and Anglo American identity development, see Table 4.2 for African Americans and Table 4.3 for American Indians. In Table 4.7, a lack of Anglo American self-awareness as a cultural being (Stage 1) is a preexposure or preconflict condition. Conflict occurs as a result of expanding knowledge and/or cross-racial interactions or through examination of personal cultural values (Stage 2). A desire to conform to their own Anglo American cultural norms by denying racism is contrasted with humanistic/egalitarian values as a result of confrontation and increased awareness. Anger, anxiety, confusion, and depression are some consequences. These intense emotions may be relieved by a prominority/antiracism stance (Stage 3) or by retreat into Anglo American culture (Stage 4) and withdrawal from multicultural persons. Redefinition/integration (Stage 5) is the hallmark of an increasing balance between acknowledgment of a personal contribution to racism, identification with positive contributions of their own culture, and interest in continued multicultural learning experiences. The stage of Anglo American provider development will influence not only the ability to establish relationships with multicultural clients but also whether or not culturally competent services can be provided.

These approaches to identity development have been criticized as being developmental in nature and predicated on oppression-adaptation group models that focus on non-Anglo American identity attitudes (Bennett et al., 1993; Rowe et al., 1994). A contrasting model from these authors presents Anglo American attitudes toward being white and implications for persons who do not share this group membership. This social learning model is presented as several interrelated clusters of unachieved and achieved racial attitudes (Table 4.8).

Many persons do not achieve racial consciousness as a result of denial (Avoidant type), whereas others may be committed to unquestioned attitudes toward their own racial identity imparted by family members (Dependent

Table 4.7 Racial Identity Developmental Stages for Anglo Americans

Stage
1. *Preexposure/precontact:* Absence of self-awareness as racial being. Acceptance of group stereotypes. No awareness of multicultural issues or personal role in oppressive society. Unquestioned Eurocentric worldview.
2. *Conflict:* Between norms/humanitarian values. Increasing awareness of racism. Exposure to self-examination of assumptions (worldview/group stereotypes) with guilt/anger/depression consequences.
3. *Prominority/antiracism:* Overidentification/paternalism with feedback/information from multicultural persons.
4. *Retreat into white culture:* (permanent/temporary) Result of rejection/defensiveness/fear. Need to work through own feelings.
5. *Redefinition and integration:* White identity internalization/development/ownership/pride. Transform own work to respect/appreciate cultural differences. Culturally transcendent worldview.

SOURCES: Helms (1984); Ponterotto (1988); Sabnani, Ponterotto, and Borodovsky (1991).

Table 4.8 A Developmental Model of Anglo American Unachieved and Achieved Identity Attitudes

Unachieved

Avoidant	*Dissonant*	*Dependent*
No consideration of own identity. Avoid concern for cultural/racial issues.	Uncertain sense of own/others issues.	May reflect family attitudes. Alternative perspectives not considered.

Achieved

Dominative
Ethnocentrism. Anglo American dominance with active (hostile behaviors) or passive (fear, anger, avoidance) expression.

Conflictive
Opposed to discrimination and ameliorative programs

Reactive
Awareness: Anger/shame. Expression: Passive (noninvolvement) or active (paternalistic/overidentification).

Integrative
Value cultural pluralism. Understand sociopolitical issues.

SOURCES: Bennett et al. (1996); Rowe et al. (1994).

type). Still others are uncertain and conflicted about their identity based on their own life experiences (Dissonant type). Dissonance may represent a time of transition. Ethnocentrism as an expression of superiority may be coupled with limited information about persons of color (Dominative type) and expressed actively by hostility or passively by acceptance of their own identity as the standard. Opposition to clear instances of discrimination may occur in concert with unwillingness to support programs to reduce discrimination (Conflictive type). The Conflictive type is poised between the fundamental American values of fairness/justice and personal freedom/ achievement/selfishness. Beliefs that personal benefit accrues from discrimination can produce shame (Reactive type). A passive expression provides an intellectualized approach, a paternalistic approach, or both. An active expression contains anger, which may place the individual in cultural limbo and lead to burnout. A more comfortable pragmatic stance is achieved by the Integrative type, who manages an integration of self-regard with regard for persons who are culturally different.

Clients and Providers

Multicultural clients meet providers in service settings with an expectation of being understood on their own terms. This requires recognition of their cultures, honoring their cultural identities in a context of understanding their personal and group histories of discrimination, and a relationship style during the entire service delivery process that is culturally appropriate and acceptable. Client perceptions of service providers will be described by an brief overview of research.

In 1970, there were only three studies that examined racial effects on psychotherapy (Sattler, 1970), although by 1983 there were over 80 studies (Abramowitz & Murray, 1983). Early studies simply inquired about preferences for counselor characteristics among multicultural college student groups and found preferences for ethnically similar counselors, although within-group differences were usually ignored (Atkinson, 1983).

Three measures of within-group differences were used: paired comparisons, self-reports of racial identity, and specific tests of attitudes or racial identity. The paired comparisons provided an opportunity for choices between two counselors, similar and different from the counselee in education, attitudes and values, personality, ethnicity, socioeconomic status, and religion. Using this technique, preferences for counselors with similar attitudes and personality, but older with more education were found for Anglo American, Asian American, and Mexican American students (Atkinson, Poston, Furlong, & Mercado, 1989). African American students expressed similar preferences, although they included race as well (Atkinson, Furlong, & Poston, 1986). These studies are limited to college students who, with the exception of American Indians, represent skewed distributions of cultural orientations that typically include fewer traditional and marginal persons. In addition, discrepancies in findings may have to do with characteristics of the reported student samples because of extreme within-group differences (Ponterotto, Alexander, & Hinkston, 1988).

Measures of racial/ethnic identity for both clients and counselors were soon incorporated routinely in research with all cultural groups, following Atkinson's conclusion that identity influenced client perceptions of counselor credibility. The use of self-report acculturation measures and self-judgments of strong or weak commitment to their own original culture and Anglo American culture provided self-reports of racial identity as part of survey questionnaires requesting demographic information. Recent studies have compared several cultural groups of college students using similar research designs (e.g., Atkinson, Poston, et al., 1989). Illustrative research for each cultural group will be examined within a historical context suggesting some reasons for the differences in responsivity to Anglo American services and service providers among visible racial/ethnic groups in college settings.

American Indians

American Indians are aware that trust is often not possible with an Anglo American provider or may be illusory or fleeting in nature. The reason for mistrust is simply that the history of intercultural contact has been characterized by the broken promises of Anglo Americans. Indian people typically expect providers to be "white liberals" who want to impose their own values/beliefs, are judgmental, give advice, move too fast, demand change, and are inconsistent in the sense of being "emotional and erratic" (Lockart, 1981, p. 33).

Bennett and BigFoot-Sipes (1991) used a cultural orientation/identification item requiring selection from four descriptors providing combinations of strong-weak involvement with either American Indian or Anglo American culture. A strong involvement with American Indian culture coupled with weak Anglo American cultural involvement is similar to a traditional cultural orientation; a strong-strong involvement is similar to a bicultural orientation; a weak-strong involvement is similar to an assimilation orientation; and a weak-weak involvement describes a marginality orientation. Anglo American subjects responded to racial consciousness descriptors for high/low acceptance of white or "other" cultural values with comparable resulting categorizations for traditional, bicultural, assimilative, and marginal orientations. Their results indicated the type of presenting problem was related to counselor characteristics and similar cultural characteristics required for personal problems but not for academic problems by both American Indian and Anglo students.

African Americans

African Americans also experience problems in trusting Anglo American providers. A variety of tests have been used to examine counselor relationships with African American clients, including the Cultural Mistrust Inventory (Terrell & Terrell, 1981), Attitudes Toward Seeking Professional Psychological Help (Fischer & Turner, 1970), and the Self-Disclosure Scale (Plasky & Lorion, 1984). The Racial Identity Attitude Scale (RIAS; Parham & Helms, 1981), however, is the most widely used test of attitudes regarding racial identity for African Americans. The RIAS has been used to determine high/low acceptance of African American and Anglo American cultures in examining relationships between developmental stages and rankings of counselor characteristics (e.g., Ponterotto et al., 1988). Those students accepting African American culture preferred a racially similar counselor, although age, education, and expertness as well as similar attitudes and personalities were also of importance (Atkinson et al., 1986).

Asian Americans

Most Asian Americans experience discrimination and have no fewer problems during acculturation and psychopathological distress than other cultural groups. Their underuse of services may stem, however, from denial of mental health problems and a compensatory preoccupation with physical symptomatology or somatization. The self-disclosure and emotional expressiveness required by "talking" therapies and counseling are not esteemed because of shame and guilt connected with revealing family problems and an expectation of active, directive problem-solving interventions from the provider. In addition, discouragement and frustration result from lack of English language fluency and confrontation by a therapist who expects involvement and nondefensive responsiveness but does not understand the client's first language, health/illness beliefs, or family structure and obligations of filial piety.

There are, however, notable differences among Asian Americans of different national origins. For example, Filipino American and biracial Asian Americans admitted emotional and personal concerns with greater frequency than other Asian American groups (Tracey, Leong, & Glidden, 1986). Japanese Americans attributed problems to social causes more frequently than Anglo Americans and help was solicited from family members and friends in addition to their own problem-solving behaviors (Narikiyo & Kameoka, 1992).

Another approach to understanding differences lies in the relationship of cultural orientation to acceptable services. A previously described study of Asian Americans included students of Chinese, Korean, and Japanese origins (Atkinson & Gim, 1989). Regardless of national origins, the SL-ASIA acculturation scores of Asian Americans suggested the acculturated Asian American students were more likely to acknowledge their needs for counseling including a willingness to discuss personal problems and a tolerance of stigma associated with receiving such assistance.

Hispanic Americans

Hispanic Americans also may underuse mental health services in spite of psychopathology or exposure to acculturative stress and discrimination. Underuse has been attributed to a paucity of culturally credible services and service providers and to conflict between Hispanic cultural values and Anglo American values inherent in most available services.

Cultural orientation has also been examined as a determinant of acceptability of services. The most widely used measure of acculturation, the Acculturation Rating Scale for Mexican Americans (ARSMA, ARSMA-II; Cuéllar, Arnold, & Maldonado, 1995; Cuéllar, Harris, & Jasso, 1980) has been adapted for Puerto Rican students (Pomales & Williams, 1989). This adaptation found that Anglo-acculturated students perceived counselors as more trustworthy than bicultural or traditional students. Traditional students were responsive to a nondirective counselor style as an indication of counselor understanding. Students with other cultural orientations, however, preferred a more directive style. A second ARSMA study with Mexican American students used tape recordings of nondirective and directive simulated counseling sessions with Hispanic clients and counselors (Ponce & Atkinson, 1989). This study found a strong preference among these students for ethnically similar counselors for personal, social, and academic/career problems and a directive counseling style. There were, however, no differences in preferences among cultural orientation categories. These findings of counselor preferences due to ethnicity alone have been supported using different research procedures (López, López, & Fong, 1991).

In a society increasingly aware of conflict, dissension, and acrimony between and among all cultural groups, ethnicity has greater importance than other provider or service variables. A culturally competent service delivery style performed by an ethnically similar provider has a strong attraction for persons in all racial/cultural groups. Credible style accompanied by ethnic similarity, including first language usage, can resolve issue of trust.

Community Data

College settings, however, are atypical, because any indexes showing distribution of cultural orientation status will be skewed to include greater numbers of assimilated and bicultural persons than exist in the general population. For this reason, it is necessary to examine community data from Los Angeles County where approximately one half of the community mental health center clients in a 5-year period were from visible racial/ethnic groups (Sue, Fujino, Hu, Takeuchi, & Zane, 1991). Comparison of this data with county population statistics showed that Asian Americans and Hispanic Americans underused services while African Americans overused them.

Global Assessment Scale (GAS) scores, drop-out rates, and number of sessions were criterion variables used to assess treatment outcomes. Provider-client ethnic and language matches were examined in terms of these variables. Non-English primary language clients were Asian or Mexican American primarily; matching for these clients included ethnicity, language, or ethnicity plus language because not all racial/ethnic group clients could be matched with providers. Ethnic matching for non-English speaking Asians and Mexican Americans reduced drop-out rates, and resulted in increased numbers of sessions, and better treatment outcomes. Moreover, for non-English speakers, a combination of ethnic and language matching was positively and significantly related to the three criterion values for all groups except Mexican Americans. For non-English speakers, it was particularly helpful to match on both ethnicity and language. The outcome measure most consistent with matching was length of treatment. Outcomes for Asian Americans tended to be favorable whereas those for African Americans were more unfavorable using these criteria.

This study suggests the importance of matching for positive outcomes from brief treatment and also the complexity of relationships including social class, gender, and diagnosis. Nonetheless, there were distinct differences as a function of racial/ethnic group, acculturation status, and English language facility. These findings may be representative only of large urban areas with large, diversified, non-Anglo American populations (55.2% in Los Angeles county) and a mental health service delivery system with a commitment to culturally competent services. Other urban areas may have very small multicultural populations or one large non-Anglo American group, whereas rural areas also vary in population composition. In these instances, although client/provider matching may be the most obvious and effective ingredient in treatment outcome, such matching may be feasible only in culture-specific agencies. In other agency settings, training culturally competent Anglo American providers may be an alternative, using consultants from various racial/ethnic communities whenever necessary. The difficulty is language matching because few Anglo Americans providers are proficient in Asian languages. I recall visiting a San Francisco community mental health center a few years ago in which the stated requirement for all providers was fluency in two Asian languages. Anglo Americans are often proficient in Spanish and some graduate students in clinical psychology now consider fluency in Spanish to be necessary for their future practices.

5

African Americans

Approximately 30 million black persons of African descent were counted in the 1990 census, and an increase to nearly 37 million is anticipated by the year 2000. Within this population, there are large within-group differences in social class, urban/rural residences, and development of racial/cultural identities. There is also a history of three subgroups—free urban blacks, freed slaves, and immigrants from the West Indies—who comprised 14% of the black American population in 1830 (Axelson, 1992).

Fairchild (1985) believed that the term *African American* was less stigmatizing than *black* or *Negro* because it formalized an African connection, avoided ambiguity, and added self-respect and dignity. In 1985, this argument was accurate and convincing, but at present there is a split between Afrocentric African Americans and other middle-class blacks who consider themselves simply Americans. People of African descent use "black," "Black," and "African American" to acknowledge their preferences. This chapter, however, is titled "African Americans" because a major source of problems is the confrontation of African American racial identity by Anglo American racism, which is a continuing experience in the United States (for discussion, see Ghee, 1990). Some of the energy once consumed by depression, despair, violence, and memories of personal and group depredation has been transformed into discovery and affirmation of a racial identity that is believed to be essential for the mental health and well-being of many persons (e.g., Daly, Jennings, Beckett, & Leashore, 1995; Robinson & Howard-Hamilton, 1994).

Use of Services, Providers, and Mainstream or Culture-Specific Programs

In the United States, prior to the 1970s, although there was distrust of Anglo American services based on dissatisfaction with the quality of these services, health and mental health service delivery systems of the larger culture were understood. An absence of provider cultural competence, coupled with racism and stereotyping, resulted in prevalent use of less effective and less costly services. As a result, help-seeking from friends and ministers was followed by frequent recourse in extremis to emergency rooms and hospitalization rather than consultation with mental health service providers. Provider race was not of critical importance during an era when cost and availability were of primary concern, but early terminations of therapy, particularly with white therapists, were frequent in the 1970s and 1980s. With an increasing consciousness of Afrocentric racial identity, many of these clients now strongly prefer providers of color.

At present, before many African American clients are willing to receive mental health services from Anglo American providers, those providers must understand the burden of historic and contemporary oppression faced by African Americans. There are, however, additional complexities for Anglo providers, including extreme diversity in African American communication patterns (Orbe, 1995). These patterns include use of dialect, bidialecticalism, and styles of verbal and nonverbal communication that differ from those of Anglo Americans. Communication issues may either facilitate or inhibit the establishment of trust and task orientation in assessment, which is essential for any subsequent intervention. For example, clients may use Black English Vernacular, and providers should have some familiarity with grammar and meanings (Dillard, 1973). "Street talk" may also occur and providers should ask questions to clarify the meaning of any unfamiliar vocabulary, although, as Paniagua (1994) has suggested, the client must understand that the "correctness" of standard English is not being questioned.

A recent review (Takeuchi & Uehara, 1996) found reduced dropout rates, less recourse to emergency services, and increased use of services in California due to racial matching between client and provider or to services made available within an exclusively culture-specific setting. Nonetheless, a majority of African American women surveyed between 1978 and 1980 did not seek help from private or public sources for adjustment, financial, emotional, and health problems (Mays, Caldwell, & Jackson, 1996). Instead, they relied on their social support networks including church members, family, friends, and significant others, at least until their problems became severe. Younger women used informal network sources more frequently than older women who also sought professional help (Caldwell, 1996). Thus, reliance on informal systems, particularly kin; denial of problems; and self-help/ self-care typically resulted in deferred use of professional services.

Considering the poor quality of mental health services for African Americans in the immediate past, these decisions are prudent and consistent with trying to make the best of an aversive social-professional reality. One partial solution to the poor quality services in mainstream mental health facilities for African Americans, as well as Asian Americans and Hispanic Americans, has been a funneling of referrals away from these facilities and toward ethnic-specific programs (Akutsu, Snowden, & Organista, 1996). Criminal justice and self-referrals are more likely to be made to mainstream services, while referrals from natural help-giving and lay referral sources are much more frequently made to ethnic-specific programs.

Health and Illness Beliefs

Traditional sub-Saharan black Africans conceived of health as a spiritual and societal commitment to a harmonious relationship between a self interpenetrated by others, nature, the spirit world, and the universe. Connections among components of this self were achieved by a group oral tradition. Any disruption of harmony within this self-system resulted in physical expressions of distress, mental expressions of distress, or both, which were inseparable and interchangeable due to a belief in physical monism rather than the Euro-American dualism. Symptomatology and syndromes always reflected cultural infusions (Johnson, 1994) and restoration of harmony in an individual has remained both a family and public concern as well as a community responsibility even during an era of Western-trained physicians and psychiatrists. Because of the partial loss and incomplete recovery of an Afrocentric identity in the United States, this conception of health is no longer completely intact.

In spite of this African heritage, it would be easy to assume that because approximately 25% of African Americans are bicultural, middle class, and college educated, their health and illness beliefs are coextensive with Anglo Americans. Although there is no health/illness belief literature comparable to other cultural groups described in this book, African American college students have group-specific thoughts, feelings, and behaviors pertaining to their own mental health and expectations from providers (Millet, Sullivan, Schwebel, & Myers, 1996). In this study, the students responded to psychopathology vignettes by describing a reliance on beliefs in spirituality, church teachings, and Afrocentrism that were not shared by their Anglo American peers. Furthermore, a study of rural Southern members of fundamental religious groups documented the importance of fate and God control over health and the impact of church teaching for many individuals (Bekhuis, Cook, Holt, & Scott-Lennox, 1995). These findings help to contextualize earlier fears of the mental health system (Homma-True, Greene, Lopez, & Trimble, 1993) and preferences for alternative intervention approaches, including folk healers (Cheung & Snowden, 1990).

Social Class

Social-class distinctions differ between African Americans and Anglo Americans because many more persons are included in impoverished social classes in African American communities. Social classes differ not only in population percentages by race but also by identification of these classes using income, occupation, and educational data (Bass, 1982; Stricker, 1980). Over one half of all African Americans are in three lower subclass divisions of the lower class, including the nonworking poor. Most of these individuals are below the poverty line (Gilbert & Kahl, 1987) with a mixture of lower and middle classes in segregated urban neighborhoods (Myers, 1982).

Lower-class persons are more vulnerable to the aversive impact of particular life events and economic problems (Ulbrich, Warheit, & Zimmerman, 1989). They have difficulty trusting therapists (regardless of their race), relying instead on family and group loyalties, focusing on material pleasures in the present, experiencing feelings of helplessness and little personal control over their living conditions or future events. Initially in an outpatient setting, these persons often fear a mental breakdown and believe they have little to offer to resolving their own problems (Evans, Acosta, Yamamoto, & Hurwicz, 1986). As a consequence, they may require explicit preparation for psychotherapy by educational procedures to reduce fear or discouragement and reduce early termination (Acosta, Yamamoto, Evans, & Skilbeck, 1983).

Middle-class persons, however, may be more similar to their Anglo American middle-class counterparts in expectations and personal resources (Majors & Nikelly, 1983). These persons are relatively verbal and responsive to therapy processes that contain reflection and interpretation. But there are also dissimilarities in family structure, dynamics, and life cycle due to more permeable family boundaries, social system inequities leading to anger and family violence, and keeping up the appearances of middle-class status in integrated neighborhoods and work settings under conditions of external stress from discrimination and in the presence of increased family distress as an outcome (Boyd-Franklin, 1989). Their own children, as well as children in their homes from the extended family, may experience problems in racial identification due to isolation from other black children and may also be under special pressures to achieve from parents who have paid an emotional price for their own advancement. As a result, it is not feasible to compare the experiences within social classes across racial communities. In spite of this fact, the Anglo American class structure and class-related lifestyles have been accepted as applicable for all test standardization purposes and research on group comparisons.

Racial Identity and Cultural Identity

The term *racial identity* is preferred by many African Americans (e.g., Carter, 1990) because racial status is the index for acceptance in white America. Racial identity has been explored and partially understood using the Nigrescence model described in Chapter 4.

This step model also led to a parallel development of Afrocentrism/ Africentrism, a set of shared beliefs, values, behaviors, and standards concerning the social reality and priorities of African Americans in American society. These beliefs are embodied in the African Self-Consciousness Scale (Baldwin & Bell, 1984), a measure of Africentric identity that includes a sense of collective unconsciousness and cultural heritage in self-knowledge as well as active participation in survival priorities and race-specific institutions to oppose oppression and for affirmation of group identity. Racial identity exploration by factor analysis has yielded psychological, physical, cultural, and sociopolitical dimensions described by Thompson-Sanders (1995).

Afrocentrism/Africentrism includes an emphasis on both psychological and sociopolitical dimensions while cultural identity is more focused on cultural dimensions. One measure of cultural or ethnic identity for African Americans includes eight dimensions: religious beliefs/practices, family structure/practices, socialization, preparation/consumption of foods, preferences for things, interracial attitudes, superstitions, and health beliefs/ practices (Landrine & Klonoff, 1996).

This contrast is between group identification/cultural identity and racial identity/racial consciousness. Racial "consciousness is a collective interpretation of personal experience that includes power grievances about a group's relative disadvantaged status, which influences blacks to keep stress external" (Neighbors, Jackson, Broman, & Thompson, 1996, p. 171). Furthermore, such self-consciousness is considered to be critical to health and mental health because it minimizes internalization of stress (Gurin & Hatchett, 1982).

The political issue of Afrocentrism/Africentrism currently dividing the black community has been described by West (1993) as "gallant because it puts black doings and sufferings, not white anxieties and fears, at the center of discussion . . . [and] misguided because—out of fear of cultural hybridization and through silence on the issue of class, retrograde views on black women, gay men, and lesbians, and a reluctance to link race to the common good—it reinforces the narrow discussion about race" (p. 4). An illustration of this split is provided by a 10-year interview study of acculturation stress among black students in a state university (Young, Ekeler, Sawyer, & Prichard, 1994) who lived in an environment polarized by African American or white cultural orientations. Black students who were idealists, upper middle class, or international in origin adapted to a white cultural orientation whereas many of those who were athletes, from working-class families, or black nationalists had roles compatible with Afrocentric values.

Not only is there a prevailing sense of group identification, but personal beliefs concerning life circumstances have been systematized into constructs that do not vary with socioeconomic status and gender (Jackson, McCullough, Gurin, & Broman, 1991). These constructs include an emotional bonding to the racial group by perceiving a common fate, closeness to elite blacks, positive stereotypic beliefs, rejection of negative stereotypes, and black autonomy. Seven factor-analyzed items yielded a two-factor solution for outgroup and ingroup orientations. An outgroup orientation included high positive loadings on "close white friend" and belief that "whites support black interests," and significant negative loadings on items related to system blame and identification as American. Ingroup orientation had high positive loadings on closeness to non-American blacks and a collective orientation with positive loadings on system blame and identification as black. Such research documentation supports Cornel West's (1993) concern that the black community is now divided on the issue of how to react to life in a racist society—by separatism and black nationalism or by integration for the common good.

Psychologists who wish to understand their African American clients need to be aware of what is understood by both racial and cultural identity and to use both kinds of measures in their evaluations of cultural orientation. Racial/cultural orientation status and subsequent identity descriptions provide necessary information for selection of providers and interventions that not only are acceptable to clients but also seek to remediate racial issues more directly, particularly when reactions to oppression are sources of immediate and continuing distress. The availability of racial/cultural information at the onset of services helps to depathologize many problems and thereby prevents unnecessary complications resulting from inappropriate interventions designed for particular pathologies and applied as a consequence of reliability deficiencies and diagnostician bias using *DSM* categories.

Problems-in-Living, Stress and Oppression, Culture-General Disorders, and Culture-Bound Disorders

Problems-in-Living

Any contemporary examination of problems-in-living must begin with the National Survey of Black Americans, which produced *Mental Health in Black America* (Neighbors & Jackson, 1996), *Life in Black America* (Jackson, 1991), and *Aging in Black America* (Jackson, Chatters, & Taylor, 1993). The Neighbors and Jackson book is concerned with "the social and psychological correlates of coping with serious personal problems, the distribution of psychological distress, and help seeking, including the use of specialty mental health care, general medical care, and informal use of social networks" (p. xii). These survey results emphasized that a disproportionate percentage of persons are at high risk for problems-in-living as a result of economic disadvantage, stress due to life events, and chronically high levels of psychological distress that impact negatively on overall health status and morbidity figures. For example, problem drinking (defined as having been told by a physician that drinking has caused a health problem) and chronic diseases are addressed specifically (Obot, 1996). Male drinkers are more prone to arthritis, ulcers, cancer, hypertension, and nervous conditions, whereas women drinkers report ulcers, liver and kidney problems, circulation problems, and nervous conditions.

Stress and Oppression

Anderson (1991) used the Lazarus (1984) model of stress, which separates sources or levels of stress, acculturation factors, mediating factors, and possible outcomes as a framework for evaluation of research. Level I stress is from environmental factors including pollution, noise, overcrowding, poverty, and discrimination that affect a majority of African Americans. Level II includes life transitions (e.g., marriage, divorce, graduation, birth, death) that affect all persons and traumatic events that occur more frequently for African Americans. Life transitions and traumatic events can be assessed using life-event scales, although the traumatic events experienced differ by social class, between cultural groups, and among subgroups within the same culture. For African Americans, these events have been scaled to provide assessment indexes (e.g., Williams & Anderson, 1996; Wyatt, 1977). Level III stress is from daily events, hassles, and repeated conflicts. It is at this level that persistent discrimination is encountered and the effects of oppression are experienced for many persons and there is necessity for constant exercise of effective coping skills to minimize aversive mental health consequences.

Anderson (1991) stated that "although blacks seem to have assimilated completely into American society (sharing a common language, similar behavior patterns, and a set of core values with the majority culture), such acculturative change has not occurred on all levels or in all blacks, and it has not occurred without cost" (p. 696). To the extent that African American and Anglo American worldview and component cultural dimensions differ for individuals, stress is inevitable and often experienced on a daily basis. For this reason, measures of Nigrescence, Africentricity/Afrocentricity, and African American culture/acculturation constitute a necessary part of assessment and evaluation for all subsequent interventions. Anderson cites evidence that cultural estrangement is related to a negative self-image as well as to risk for substance abuse, marital discord, depression, academic difficulty, and low self-esteem.

Experiences of racism provide one form of stress resulting from oppression. One third of an African American nonclinical community-solicited sample reported an experience of racism ("an unfavorable, unfair, or insulting event . . . due to their skin color or group membership") within a 6-month period coinciding with measurable psychological distress in the form of intrusion and denial (Sanders Thompson, 1996, p. 228). Intrusion occurred in the form of thoughts, disturbed dreams, strong feelings, and repetitive behaviors. There was denial of meanings and consequences, constriction, blunted sensation, inhibited behavior, emotional numbness, and avoidance. Racial identification did not moderate these effects.

Culture-General Disorders

Culture-general disorders include schizophrenia, depression, anxiety and panic disorders, and phobias. These disorders occur among African Americans but always have a cultural overlay that should be recognized by a cultural formulation for *DSM* diagnosis and subsequently in planning for introduction of cultural elements into interventions.

Schizophrenia. Schizophrenia, for example, is found in almost all countries but with different prevalence rates, symptom composition, and more favorable prognoses in developing countries than in the United States. The definition of schizophrenia in the United States is a broad-spectrum, inclusive syndrome whereas in Western Europe, Asia, Latin America, Africa and Australia it is conceptualized as a tight, narrow syndrome (Westermeyer, 1985).

As Chapter 2 indicated, African Americans are more frequently diagnosed, misdiagnosed, and hospitalized as schizophrenic with more severe symptomatology than Anglo Americans. These symptoms include anger, impulsivity, hallucinations, dysphoria, and asocial behaviors (Adibimpe, Chung-Chou, Klein, & Lange, 1982). Paranoid symptomatology with a reality basis in life experiences has been frequently accepted as legitimate evidence for a schizophrenia process (Newhill, 1990). African Americans are overdiagnosed as schizophrenic for a variety of reasons. Diagnosis often occurs later in the course of illness with more florid symptoms being present at that time. Diagnosticians often confuse schizophrenia with manic-depressive psychosis (Bell & Mehta, 1979). Misdiagnosis also occurs because hallucinations and delusions are believed to be pathognomonic of schizophrenia, although these symptoms among African Americans also occur in chronic alcoholism, psychotic depression, acute organic brain syndrome, and mania (Adibimpe, 1981).

In addition, misdiagnosis can occur because providers do not understand how to render their services credible by use of appropriate service delivery behaviors and social etiquette. Baffled and alarmed by client reactions to their inappropriate behaviors, they may blame the client's psychopathology for their failure to communicate. An inability to understand Black English Vernacular, or Ebonics, the spoken language of many African Americans (Smitherman, 1973; R. Williams, 1975), particularly in a context of client crisis and agitation, may adversely affect the diagnostic process and outcome.

Misdiagnosis also occurs because social class and schizophrenia are often confounded. Client behaviors always reflect a social class context, but are typically interpreted on the basis of the middle-class standards and expectations of providers. African Americans are at a double disadvantage because culturally normative behaviors, particularly in the dissimilar lower social classes, are also misunderstood by Anglo providers. Considerable disagreement and controversy remain, but socioeconomic variables do account for some unknown portion of the differences between African Americans and other cultural groups in schizophrenia and probably all culture-general psychopathologies as well (Williams, 1986). The effective intervention strategies described subsequently are related to cultural orientation status, social class, and health/illness beliefs.

Depression. High levels of depressive symptomatology have been found in 20% to 30% of African Americans; depressive disorders are diagnosable in

4% to 6%, and prevalence rates for severe depression are higher than for Anglo Americans (Brown, 1990). Major depressive episodes also occur with lower frequency among persons in racially homogeneous urban neighborhoods, suggesting the beneficial effects of buffering and availability of social support (Tweed et al., 1990).

There is controversy over whether the prevalence of depressive symptomatology using the Center for Epidemiologic Studies Depression Scale (CES-D) is higher or lower than among Anglo Americans (Neff, 1984). To clarify these findings, Neff used 21 previously validated psychological distress items from Warheit, Holzer, and Arey (1975) that were analyzed into factors labeled *depressive affect, nervous upset, somatic symptoms, and general psychopathology.* Rural African Americans displayed more depression by somatic symptoms (e.g., heart beat, feel weak, dizzy, tired, with shortness of breath and cold sweats in context with many ailments) and grossly pathologic symptoms (e.g., seems unreal, see things, paranoia, strange thoughts, others argue). Urban residents reported more affective symptoms (e.g., hopeless, no one cares, feel alone). By comparison, Anglo American displayed fewer affective and more somatic symptoms.

These findings were largely substantiated in a Southern state using separate measures of depression, psychophysiologic symptoms, and general well-being (Neff & Husaini, 1987). Race differences were a function of selected dimensions (e.g., urban/rural and specific symptomatology) rather than race per se. As a result, it is necessary to consider not only race but the kinds and intensities of symptoms within a context of residence and overall feelings of well-being. Other relevant demographic variables include separation or divorce, less than a fourth-grade education (Neighbors & Lumpkin, 1990), and lack of employment (Price, Van Ryn, & Vinokur, 1992). Social affiliations patterns, including close family ties, moderate religious involvement, and participation in voluntary associations all contribute to moderation of depressive symptoms (Brown, Gary, Greene, & Milburn, 1992). Moreover, depression in males may be masked as a result of alcohol or substance abuse and cigarette smoking (Brown, 1990).

Anxiety and Panic Disorders. African Americans with 6-month prevalence rates for anxiety and panic disorders in the five-city Epidemiologic Catchment Area (ECA) survey (New Haven, Baltimore, St. Louis, Los Angeles, North Carolina Piedmont area) (Eaton & Kessler, 1985) were higher than for other groups, although panic patients are rare in anxiety disorder clinics. Anxiety disorders were most frequently diagnosed in women and second in men presenting to treatment settings (Neal & Turner, 1991). These authors questioned findings that urban males were more violent, homicidal, suspicious, and unstable in relations and raised issues pertinent to nonparticipation in research studies and differences among investigators.

Panic disorders among African Americans include isolated sleep paralysis, or inability to move accompanied by feelings of acute danger and hallucinations on awakening or falling asleep with panic-like symptoms, fear, and hyperventilation in the aftermath of paralysis (Bell et al., 1984). Moreover, panic disorder has been reported with high frequency in hypertensives (Neal, Rich, & Smucker, 1994) and with secondary symptoms of impairment in attention and registration (Griffith & Baker, 1993). It should be noted that blacks with panic disorder, although equivalent in numbers and symptoms to whites, have histories with considerably greater childhood trauma and frequent separations in homes with substance-abusing parents and more current life stressors (Friedman, Paradis, & Hatch, 1994).

Phobias. African Americans endorsed more phobia items than whites in an early study (Warheit et al., 1975). This finding has persisted over time for simple phobia and agoraphobia at four ECA sites (Eaton & Kessler, 1985), although ECA sampling may have been biased (Neal & Turner, 1991). Urban/rural differences would also be anticipated due to scarcity of treatment resources in rural areas (Griffith & Baker, 1993). Phobic disorders among African Americans include specific fears in different urban settings and greater fear in some cities, using individual indicators (i.e., bugs, closed places, harmless animals, heights, storms, water) (Neighbors & Lumpkin, 1990).

Posttraumatic Stress Disorder (PTSD). PTSD has emerged as a major reaction to stress. The higher incidence among African American Vietnam veterans has been attributed to conflict over fighting a similarly oppressed people and returning home to face not only discrimination but accusations of having fought the wrong war (Neal & Turner, 1991). Parson (1985) adds to the Vietnam trauma the burden of dual identity in the United States and being a survivor/descendent/kin of slavery victims in a context of continuing stress in a racist society. The most recent review examined the PTSD effects of natural disasters and violence on victims, observers, and perpetrators as well as the consequences for interpersonal relationships (I. M. Allen, 1996).

Culture-Bound Disorders

African Americans from West Africa or the Caribbean, particularly Haiti, may present culture-specific syndromes, or *culture-bound disorders* in *DSM-IV* terminology. There are still some rural areas in the southern United States, however, notably islands off the South Carolina coast, Miami, and the New Orleans area, where these syndromes may still be found.

For example, "falling out/blacking out" is a sudden collapse into semiconsciousness, with or without warning, but with immobility accompanied by understanding and inability to see. This syndrome occurred in 19% of Miami Fire Department emergency "run reports" and is generally an unrecognized and untreated reaction to stress among blacks (Lefley, 1979b). Occurring primarily among women who live with characterological depression, sexual problems, relative isolation, and constant economic and psychological stress, projective assessment suggested immaturity, disturbed sexuality, denial of affectional needs, and few effective mechanisms for coping with stress or conflict (Lefley, 1979a). Falling-out episodes are reactive to a low tolerance for situational stress and are typically treated ineffectively with medications. This condition has also been called *indisposition* in Haiti and further information is available elsewhere (Charles, 1979; Philippe & Romain, 1979; Weidman, 1979).

"Rootwork" (sorcery/witchcraft) also occurs in these same black populations with unknown frequency, sometimes leading to death. Rootwork has been associated with Voodoo death, called *hex, embrujeria,* and *mal puesto,* referring in Spanish to "belief in witchcraft—the putative power of other people to bring about misfortune, disability, and death through "spiritual" (psychological) means" (Hughes & Wintrob, 1995, p. 571). Prevention and treatment of illnesses believed to be of occult or spiritual origin remain the domain of folk practitioners in Brazil, Haiti, Jamaica, and other Caribbean Islands as well as in some rural areas of the United States.

Interventions

Following the theme introduced earlier in this chapter, black Americans differ from other cultural/racial groups described in this book by the presence of salient or underlying racial issues in their various forms of distress and by extreme within-group variability in how these racial issues are addressed and responded to in their everyday lives. It is desirable to have information on the effects of racism at the onset of any assessment and prior to initiating an intervention; the Perceived Racism Scale has been developed for this purpose (McNeilly et al., 1996).

African American psychologists have also suggested that interventions must always acknowledge these racial issues. For example, Jones (1985, 1989) has provided a model in which reactions to oppression, African American culture, majority culture, and personal experiences/endowments contribute to presenting problems and can be represented by circles that vary in size or relative importance for all individuals. An identification of the modes of dealing with racial issues and encounters can increase options and facilitate conscious choices. Similarly, Watkins-Duncan (1992) elaborated a set of principles for formulating treatment. Ethnic/racial background should be explored, any reports of real or imagined prejudice must be examined, experiences within black culture should be evaluated, and a healthy self-concept/pride always is fostered. In addition to cultural issues, countertransference issues can interfere with therapy. Self-evaluation through relevant reading, supervisory sessions, and a racially/culturally mixed peer group can be helpful in this process. Finally, avoiding the derogatory stereotyping of considering blacks as "minority" patients must be accomplished through recognition of their heterogeneity.

A basic dimension of this heterogeneity is exposed by the contemporary dichotomy described earlier in this chapter between beliefs, behaviors, and consciousness among more Afrocentric/Africentric persons and their less racially conscious counterparts who may be similar in other characteristics such as social class and educational status. Carter, Sbrocco, and Carter (1996) suggested a rationale for selection of relevant interventions that underscores this dichotomy by describing orthogonal dimensions of acculturation and racial identity paralleling measures developed for other groups, including the Acculturation Rating Scale for Mexican Americans-II (Cuéllar, Arnold, & Maldonado, 1995) and the Northern Plains Bicultural Immersion Scale (Allen & French, 1996).

These cultural identity scales are analogous to measures of racial identity, or the extent an individual belonging to African American group culture may be contrasted with acculturation to the normative expectations and individuality of the white community. A 2×2 interaction of high and low racial identity and acculturation separates persons who are high in both dimensions from those who are high in one dimension but not the other (i.e., high racial identity and low acculturation or low racial identity and high acculturation) (Carter et al., 1996). Few individuals are low on both dimensions. Acculturation to white normative standards has not been measured using separate orthogonal scales for African Americans, however, although low scores on the African American Acculturation Scale represent immersion in white culture (Landrine & Klonoff, 1994) whereas high scores indicate a traditional orientation and moderate scores suggest biculturality. Nonetheless, within-group differences in racial identity components measured by existing scales can provide a rationale for choice of culture-general, combined, or culture-specific interventions.

This formulation is complicated by moderator variables, which include socioeconomic status, age, stress, client-provider matching, provider cultural sensitivity, and service delivery style. These variables interact with the racial identity and acculturation dimensions to provide additional information for selection of acceptable providers and interventions likely to have beneficial effects (Table 5.1).

Culture-General Interventions

Culture-general interventions are most appropriate for persons who are low in racial identification but high in acculturation. These individuals may be expected to have similar symptoms, willingness to receive treatment, and are likely to remain in treatment until some benefit is obtained. Interventions for these persons may require some modification by recognition of racial issues, incorporation of them, or both in the treatment process. These interventions include psychoanalysis (Leary, 1995), behavior modification (Turner & Jones, 1982), cognitive behavioral therapy for a variety of problems (Hays, 1995; Randall, 1994; Sapp, Farrell, & Durand, 1995) as well as other standard interventions.

Individuals who are high in both racial identity and acculturation may also be amenable to culture-general interventions because there is some symptom similarity, treatment is voluntary, and there is a moderate likelihood that they will remain in treatment until some benefit is obtained. These persons, however, are able to make informed choices on the basis of their presenting problems whether or not they wish to participate in culture-general interventions or prefer to have cultural issues and elements present in combined or culture-specific interventions, although some cultural elements and recognition of racial issues will always be present.

Combined Interventions

Combined interventions are most useful for persons high in racial identity and low in acculturation to white society. These interventions can be focused on development of social skills, social assertiveness, and problem solving to augment acculturation and general competence or can foster parenting and relationships skills. In either context, cultural elements such as the family and social support network, including the church, can be used for empowerment.

A second area in which combined interventions are useful is family therapy. Examples are described for multiple problems, teaching parenting,

Table 5.1   Racial Identity (RI), Acculturation Status (A) Dimensions, and Moderators
Suggesting Efficacy of Culture-General Interventions

Low RI-High A	
Moderators	No modification of intervention
	No modification of service delivery
	No modification of *DSM* use
	Racial match not required
	Older provider may be helpful
	Gender match important for some problems
	Provider cultural sensitivity helpful for awareness and articulation of additional or unrecognized problems
High RI-High A	
Moderators	Possible modifications of intervention
	Provider recognition-ability to use credible service delivery style
	DSM use modified by cultural formulation
	Gender match critical for some problems
	Age of provider may be relevant
	Racial match helpful but not mandatory
	Provider cultural competence mandatory

and for alcoholism. Boyd-Franklin (1989) has advocated use of a comprehensive model combining several family therapy strategies into a multisystems approach for African American families. This model recognizes and takes into account the cultural ingredients of extended families, role flexibility, and complex role relationships including secrets of informal adoptions and parentage, spirituality/religion, and empowerment applied in treatment formulations for single-parent, middle-class, and poor families as well as couples. This multisystems approach has two axes to describe the treatment process and the multisystem levels. The process begins with joining and engaging new subsystems, an initial assessment, problem solving to establish credibility, use of family tasks/prescriptions, information gathering using the genogram, and restructuring the family and the multisystems. Intervention at each of identified multisystem levels is emphasized. These levels include the individual, subsystems within the family, the family household, extended family, nonblood kin and friends, church and community resources, and social service agencies and other outside systems. This approach is especially applicable to poor families who often live in constant fear for their children and themselves and who feel rage over their life predicament that cannot be vented except by domestic violence and child abuse. These families have histories of contact with welfare agencies and experience with foster care dilemmas. Boyd-Franklin emphasizes the importance of therapist values and assumptions, becoming a system guide and facilitator, and legitimizing concrete problems by using case examples.

One case history will be included here for illustration of the process with an inner-city family with a schizophrenic mother (Boyd-Franklin & Shenouda, 1990). This family consisted of a 30-year old mother with a history of psychiatric treatment; a 40-year old father who abused his wife after losing a job; an 8-year-old, developmentally delayed boy and an 11-year-old girl, a "parentified" child who acted as spokesperson and caretaker but had not accepted her mother's illness and the parental separation; a 58-year-old physically handicapped maternal grandmother who was the primary family caretaker and legal guardian of the children for 6 months; and the 63-year-old maternal grandfather described as an abusive alcoholic. A custody battle between the parents and grandparents resulted in return of legal custody to the mother.

Treatment issues are described at individual, nuclear family, marital dyad, extended family, and outside systems levels. At the individual level, relationship is established with each family member using meetings and telephone contact. The mother's medication stabilization and involvement in day treatment was an immediate goal. Psychological examinations of the children identified intervention areas and subsequent individual and family sessions occurred concurrently to emphasize individual issues. The father was initially highly resistant to treatment and home visits were required to enlist his participation. At the nuclear family level, an initial focus on parenting and communication skills began with the mother and eventually included the father. Subsequently, the mother/daughter reversal of roles was addressed by an agency homemaker who undertook household chores that gradually involved the mother and increased her ability to regain control over her family. Education for a family approach to treatment of schizophrenia was provided.

At the marital dyad level, the initial focus was on relationship issues to strengthen bonds between mother and father and define their boundaries with the children. Subsequently, communication difficulties became the focus because noncommunication had been responsible for the severe physical abuse and both partners used denial. At the extended family level, family supports were refurbished by maintaining therapeutic contact with the grandparents and demonstrating that neither couple could provide adequate care for the children alone. Healing the breach between parents and grandparents required renegotiation of the grandparents' role. At the outside systems level, school contact was maintained and services were coordinated between the extended care and day treatment units for the mother and, for the children, between the child welfare agency as agent for the court and the children's case worker. All of these linkages between systems and providers were crucial to a continuing benefit for each family member following a year of intensive treatment.

A second example initiated by the Center for the Improvement of Child Care used parental skills training to reduce known risk factors for mental illness, drug abuse, and delinquency (Myers et al., 1992). This program combined a cognitive-behavioral approach originally designed for middle-class white parents with culture-specific elements of pride in race, reducing self-disparagement, helping children cope with racism, and group-specific environmental issues—coping with drugs, gangs, and life in the inner-city—implemented by black professionals.

Using 13 schools, all parents with children in first or second grade were contacted in two cohorts, and treatment and control groups were formed with parents who were paid a token amount or given a gift for participating in 15 group sessions. These parents were primarily high school graduates in family-based social networks of regular churchgoers with relatively uninvolved fathers, but the percentages of the total parent populations in these cohorts were relatively low. The program focused on replacing traditional black family physical punishments with modern discipline by encouraging an examination of the reasons for parental rules, teaching parents to describe and count child behaviors and to provide behavioral consequences for respectful and disrespectful child behaviors.

A variety of relevant measures of parental acceptance/rejection, parenting practices, quality of parent-child relations, and child behaviors were used. Initially the program resulted in less parental rejection and hostility/aggression toward children and more positive feelings, with some improved child behaviors. A one-year follow-up indicated a continuation of positive parent-child communication with lessened rejection, but somewhat more delinquency among girls. Although these results may seem meager and disappointing, it must be recognized that unless environmental and economic conditions are also substantially improved simultaneously, the interventions themselves are less able to impact overall quality of life.

Family therapy for alcoholism has applied Problem-Centered Systems Therapy (PCST) to focus on specific family problems in 6 to 12 sessions, using active collaboration between family members and providers (Epstein & Bishop, 1981). PCST is used with culture-specific components suggested by Ziter (1987) for incorporation into existing interventions to foster empowerment using bicultural counseling and a dual perspective. Empowerment is an antidote for powerlessness, the inability to manage personal resources, developed from power blocks that limit development of these resources within the family and denial of subsequent opportunities in the larger society

(Solomon, 1976). Bicultural counseling emphasizes maintaining continuity of physical/psychological ties with the black community, isolating survival-enhancing behavioral components, and addressing the implications of successful adaptation to a racist society (Beverly, 1975). The dual perspective implies the ability to understand the values, attitudes, and behaviors of both black and white societies simultaneously from both perspectives (Norton, 1978).

These culture-specific components form a context for using PCST stages of assessment, contracting, treatment, and closure. Empowerment in the first meeting, the orientation phase of assessment, is created by a partnership with the family in which the clients have the responsibility for recovery and the provider has the skills and knowledge to be helpful. Provider and family members' expectations are stated explicitly as well as use of community supports for referral. An agreed-on contract helps to indicate the power the family must assert and is a prerequisite for the data gathering phase of assessment in which PCST is modified by the provider's dual perspective to include the family's broader social system by means of an ecomap using a multigenerational family genogram, the McMaster Model of Family Functioning (Epstein & Bishop, 1981), and the McMaster Family Assessment Device (Epstein, Baldwin, & Bishop, 1983).

This ecomap is used to illustrate the dual perspective by labeling important parts of life in the black, interracial, and white worlds at increasing distances from the family. The influence of racial/cultural issues on the quality of relationships in these worlds are examined for evidences of biculturalism. The support of an alcoholic family member, for example, is perceived differently in both worlds. The purpose of the ecomap is to improve problem solving, increase ties to the black community, and identify results of indirect and direct power blocks. Family and environmental foci for interventions are determined by this process and disrupted family roles are resumed or developed. Additional understanding of family relationships is provided by the family's interactions, the modifications of the McMaster Model of Family Functioning to encompass problems outside the family boundaries, and genogram study.

The treatment stage includes orientation to structure treatment as rational problem solving, defining the beginning of treatment, clarifying priorities within the family, setting tasks by negotiation within the family for individual responsibilities and a designated mentor, and evaluating whether tasks were accomplished. Unfortunately, there is no data on the efficacy of this method with black families. Nonetheless, there is no more compelling illustration in the literature of how culture-specific components may be used to alter a standard intervention.

Culture-Specific Interventions

Culture-specific interventions for African Americans originated in an African worldview and belief system that dictated the development and use of effective healing practices. This perspective and some of the practices have been applied in the United States. Culture-specific interventions are often relevant and necessary to initiate, foster, or nourish racial identity, and they can be used with persons low in racial identity or who experience identity issues as a major concern.

Culture-specific interventions have their origins in Africa. More than 75% of the rural African population use traditional healing specialists exclusively, while all persons, urban and rural, seek out these healers for their problems before and after consultations with Western-trained providers (Johnson, 1994). The roles and practices of these traditional healers have been described by Vontress (1991). Initially, healing is accomplished by herbalists using a lexicon of 350,000 plants and herbs. A second line of restoration to health is provided by fetish men, mediums, healers, and sorcerers. Fetish men or *juju* men combine roles of priest, physician, and teacher to manipulate powers inherent in objects. Mediums are women whose power permits transmission of messages between the dead and the living. Healers are used to cure mental disorders among many other problems and ailments. For the 40 million Muslims in black Africa, an Islamic cleric, or *marabout,* specializes in healing. Sorcerers use power to inflict psychological or physical harm by mental suggestions, hexes, or spells, and can cause suicides or kill from a distance. A wide variety of African interventions are received from these healers with faith and hope within a familiar treatment setting in the presence of family members (Laosebikan, 1973). At present, these interventions include abreaction in various cult forms (e.g., rituals, symbolic sacrifices, suggestions, dancing), detoxification, dream interpretation, exorcism, music, oral legends, pharmacology, possession, and shock by immersion in cold water (Awanbor, 1982; Vontress, 1991).

The Bantu concept NTU refers to a universal, unifying force believed to be the essence of life. The term *NTU* makes the cultural connection explicit and applicable to African Americans in the United States (Phillips, 1990). NTU specifies a universal unifying force for human existence, and this therapy was designed to restore harmony and balance within a natural order of mind-body-spirit unity. A healthy black self is aware of extended, permeable boundaries that include community needs and social priorities for affirmation, enhancement, survival, positive development, and fulfillment (Baldwin & Bell, 1984). NTU psychotherapy assists individuals, families, and communities in restoration of harmonious functioning and authenticity in accord with the natural laws of African healing. This intervention is applied within Kwanzaa principles of unity, self-determination, collective work/responsibility, cooperative economics, purpose, creativity, and faith (Karenga, 1977). The techniques for implementation of NTU psychotherapy represent both African origins and mainstream Anglo American derivations and borrowings. For example, the techniques used in the service of the unity principle are genograms, humor, reenergizing spirituality, reframing, rituals, self-disclosure, and being real. Other techniques are specified for each of the other Kwanzaa principles as well. NTU uses a spiritual/sacred relationship between two black persons as a delivery mode and the healing occurs through the therapist who lives according to Kwanzaa principles. This process serves to illuminate the client's past, present, and future path and to encourage problem-solving skills during nonlinear phases of holistic design that emphasize harmony, awareness, alignment, actualization, and synthesis.

In the United States, the cultural connection to Africa is embodied in traditions essential to identity, in recognition of affect and cognition as equally important, and by sponsoring interventions for the person that prioritize not only group survival, group self-actualization of interests, aspirations, and goals, but the exercise of authority by the group rather than reason or free choice by the individual (Jackson, 1976).

6

American Indians/Alaska Natives

The major mental health problems experienced by American Indians/ Alaska Natives have been described in epidemiological studies. These *DSM*-diagnosed disorders have, however, been reported primarily by non-Indian "outside" observers and omit the more frequently occurring culture-specific conditions and problems-in-living. Service use patterns suggest that these conditions and problems assume at least as much importance as psychiatric illnesses. Culture-specific conditions, or *DSM-IV* glossary designated culture-bound disorders, are generally not diagnosed. The syndromes described here include soul loss, spirit intrusion, taboo breaking, and ghost sickness or rootwork. Behavioral and symptomatic residues of these disorders still permeate everyday life, particularly on reservations, although their original descriptions have been altered by psychiatric terminology. Culture-specific problems-in-living include marginal cultural orientation status, damaged sense of self, relationship problems, chronic alcohol/drug abuse, and lack of skills.

In addition to diagnoses originating in mainstream American society, standard interventions have also been imposed on Indian people. Some of these interventions are appropriate and potentially beneficial for assimilated and bicultural individuals who are often able to use these interventions because of their familiarity with both idioms of distress. Acceptance of these interventions may be facilitated by a culture-specific style of service delivery.

Interventions that combine dominant society methods with traditional culture elements are particularly applicable to marginal persons because they have superimposed some of the values and beliefs of Anglo American society on American Indian identity structures. These combinations include use of standard interventions in traditional settings with locally developed modifications for particular American Indian communities. Traditional persons and others wishing to recover a more traditional worldview may be uncomfortable with mainstream interventions but find more credible avenues toward balance/harmony using culture-specific interventions within the American Indian community.

Culture-specific intervention settings can provide interventions in the form of modified services that parallel those available in the larger society, or new services available exclusively in tribal settings. Healing practices within traditional American Indian communities emphasize the role of traditional healers and the tribal community as a necessary social support system. Eastern Cherokee, Washo, Sioux, and Navajo tribal examples illustrate the range of practices and kinds of practitioners and provide a context for considering the role of healing among American Indians.

Finally, a model for culture-specific interventions for American Indians/Alaska Natives is applicable to individuals representing all cultural orientations. This model includes linkages between traditional practices/practitioners and the mental health service delivery system of the dominant society. The dimensions of this model come from current literature, particularly in material provided by American Indian social scientists, educators, and mental health professionals.

Psychopathology, Culture-Bound Disorders, and Problems-in-Living

Psychopathology in Epidemiological Studies

Three early epidemiological studies of traditional communities reported high rates of *DSM* psychopathology among Baffin Island Eskimos (Sampath, 1974); Pacific Northwest Coast villagers (Shore, Kinzie, Hampson, & Pattison, 1973), including a 19-year follow up (Kinzie et al., 1992); and Saskatchewan Indians living on reserves (Roy, Choudhuri, & Irvine, 1970).

The retrospective and case-finding Saskatchewan study found prevalence rates for psychopathology in the Indian population to be twice as high as for neighboring non-Indians. In the Eskimo settlement, "at-risk" adults were interviewed through an interpreter. Ratings of diagnosable mental disorders of *severe* or *moderate* were found in 37% while 58% were *mild* on a sickness/wellness continuum obtained by categorization of Health Opinion Survey (HOS) scores (MacMillan, 1957; Murphy & Hughes, 1965). The Schedule for Affective Disorders and Schizophrenia (SAD-L) was used in the replication (Boehnlein et al., 1992/1993), but comparisons are difficult due to changes in instruments, *DSM* criteria, and village economy-living conditions. The Pacific Northwest Coast village yielded a 54% rate of *definite psychiatric disturbance* and 15% *probable,* with 27% of villagers having *no psychiatric disturbance.*

Data collection methods, sampling strategies, criteria for judgments of disturbance, and instruments varied across these studies, but the lack of comparability cannot be accounted for simply by methodology differences or the history of only mediocre agreement among experts using diagnostic systems for classification. These three groups have experienced differences in contact and degrees of acculturation with the surrounding society. The Eskimos were probably least acculturated, although any assumption of relationship between high prevalence rates and modernization (Sampath, 1974) should be tempered by the fact that this group also has the greatest difference in worldview from Western societies leading to possible over-representation and misinterpretation of personality disorders and consistent confounding between culture and symptomatology. O'Nell (1989) suggested the personality disorder rate (18%) may have reflected "the ability of an individual to be an adequate Eskimo" (p. 68).

The tests and measures used in these studies were predominantly pseudo-etics developed using Eurocentric psychometric methodology on Anglo American populations (see Dana, 1993a, chap. 9). By contrast, emic methods are locally developed using community vocabulary for description and community standards for identification of abnormal behaviors and the severity of these behaviors as evidenced by departure from community standards. Assessment instruments and interview procedures used for American Indian/Alaska Native populations are always suspect unless they have been developed within the specific culture using emic methodologies employed by culturally competent persons, preferably local residents including traditional healers, community elders, and health care providers. Emic methods are useful for the development of test items by identifying culture-specific disorders and providing local vocabulary for descriptive concepts or evaluative dimensions (Manson & Shore, 1981).

Psychopathology in Service Settings. The service use patterns among reservation and urban area residents complement and update the epidemiological studies as indicated by a comparison of Indian Health Service (IHS) (Neligh,

1988) and community mental health center data from 17 agencies (Sue, 1977; Sue, Allen, & Conway, 1978). Neligh (1988) provided information from the Billings, Montana, IHS based on expanded *DSM* diagnostic categories used by providers for the 2% of all patient visits for mental health needs. The 1983 sample indicated that less than one half (41%) of the total numbers of visits were given psychiatric diagnoses whereas 48% received other diagnoses, and 8% received medical diagnoses. The most frequent psychiatric diagnoses were alcohol dependence syndrome (18%), major depressive disorders (14%), adjustment reaction (10%), personality disorders (10%), anxiety (8%), and nondependent use of drugs (8%). These four areas—with alcohol and drugs combined—accounted for 68% of diagnosed visits.

Approximately one half (49%) of all mental health visits received no diagnostic code whatsoever, but did receive codes for family/psychosocial circumstances, unspecified administrative purposes, or consultation without complaint. Finally, 9% of all visits were tabularized as having specific medical disorders, primarily physiological complaints. Many of these complaints were essentially psychological in nature with physiological expressions of symptomatology.

A failure to diagnose in over one half of visits suggests that the diagnostic system was considered by these providers/diagnosticians to be incomplete or not relevant. Providers may also have been reluctant to assign diagnoses of severe or stigmatic psychopathology and made frequent use of neutral codes for "adjustment reaction" or "unspecified administrative purpose" instead. Whenever there is a confounding with culture, symptoms often may not fit the *DSM* classification system for mental illness.

By contrast, 17 community mental health clinics collected information on nearly 14,000 urban clients over a 3-year period (Sue, 1977). The major reported intake diagnoses were personality disorder (19%), psychosis (18%), transient situational disorders (18%), and neurosis (12%). Only a small number of American Indians/Alaska Natives made use of these agencies, however, and a majority did not return for a second visit (55%). As a result, these percentages may not have been representative of the urban Indian population in this community.

Comparisons of these urban community mental health centers with rural IHS figures are hazardous due to differences in personnel training, the categories used for diagnosis, and the mental health settings. More urban psychoses or severe mental disorders are suggested, however, because the IHS rate for schizophrenia and bipolar disorders combined is only 7%. The high combined urban rates for personality disorders and transient situational disorders (37%) suggest a failure to diagnose perhaps because diagnosticians lacked cultural competence. These categories represent behaviors that may be more adequately described as problems-in-living and also suggest confounding of culture and psychopathology.

Culture-Bound Disorders

A number of culture-bound disorders have been reported historically using case studies. *Windigo*—a transformation experience—and *pibloktoq*—stages of withdrawal, excitement, convulsions/stupor, recovery—are of disputed etiologies (Dick, 1995; Marano, 1982). Soul loss, spirit intrusion, taboo breaking, and ghost sickness, however, are clusters of behaviors/symptoms that occur across many tribes (Trimble, Manson, Dinges, & Medicine, 1984). Soul loss describes an absence/weakness of soul that has been reported among the Assinboine, Dakota, and Ogalala Sioux; Cheyenne; Eskimo; Haida; Kwakiutl; Mohave; Paiute; Pomo; Seminole; Tenino; Tsimshian; and Winnebago. Spirit intrusion, or being made sick by spirit power, has been reported among the Eskimo, Ojibwa, Salish, and Tenino. Taboo breaking, a violation of norms, usually for sexual behaviors but also including social obligations and murder, has been reported among the Dakota, Ojibwa, Mohave, and Navajo. Ghost sickness, or being made sick by witchcraft, has been reported among the Navajo (Table 6.1).

This literature has been criticized for reinterpretation of a small number of first-hand accounts, translation errors, erroneous attribution of psychopathology to normal behaviors, and failure to separate different causes from similar behavioral expressions (Trimble et al., 1984). Nonetheless, depression and physical symptomatology are characteristics of all four conditions whereas hallucinations/delusions may be inferred from three descriptions. Tribe-specific differences in reported behaviors suggest that residuals of conditions, which were separate historically, appear to be still present.

Some of these behavioral manifestations have become diagnostic signs for depressive syndromes variously labeled as "feeling worthless" (O'Nell, 1992/1993), "totally discouraged" (Johnson & Johnson, 1965), or "one is being killed by melancholy" (Topper & Curtis, 1987); and *wacinko*, "mild to severe reactive depression," with symptoms of anger, immobility, mutism, psychomotor retardation, and withdrawal as described by Lewis (1975) in Western psychiatric terminology. It is probably erroneous to expect that either symptomatology or effective interventions can be generalized across tribes.

As a reminder to be cautious in creating new psychopathologies, Trimble et al. (1984) have retranslated *totally discouraged* as "tiredness" or "approaching with dread" and have translated *wacinko* as "to pout" in Lakota reservation vernacular. These terms have been divested of any inevitable

Table 6.1 Symptomatic Behaviors Associated with Soul Loss, Spirit Intrusion, Taboo Breaking, and Ghost Sickness

Soul loss:	Sudden, repeated faints; withdrawal; self-deprivation; dream adventures: preoccupation with death/dead kindred/ghosts/spirits; suicide threats/alcohol.
Spirit intrusion:	Somatization and vague, spastic pains; hallucinations; passivity/apathy coupled with restlessness/agitation; crying; feelings of despondency/discouragement/defeat.
Taboo breaking:	Psychophysiological: Mild weight loss; sleep loss; fatigue; tissue edema; headaches; heavy, irregular menstruation; mood variations; paranoia; seizures.
Ghost sickness:	Confusion, loss of mental control, fear, feelings of helplessness, futility, suffocation; weakness, dizziness/fainting, loss of appetite, nightmares; hallucinations, delusions.

synonymity with psychopathology as a result. Moreover, Trimble et al. (1984) suggested that privacy in tepees was minimal and that, historically, *wacinko* may have referred to timeout periods. Contemporary instances of decision-making autonomy lend credibility to this alternative interpretation. For example, babies may express *wacinko* by throwing themselves on the ground; children temporally *wacinko* to distance themselves from siblings-parents; teenagers *wacinko* by moving into the home of members of their extended family; males *wacinko* to be away from their wives with male peers and alcohol; women can *wacinko* from a husband following a quarrel; grandparents express *wacinko* by moving from the home of one child to another.

Well-meaning professionals pathologize behaviors by minimizing differences between groups whenever a traditional culture is markedly different from Anglo American middle-class society. The use of psychiatric language can also pathologize behavioral descriptions. As a result, the original cultural meanings of these behaviors become obscured by translation and jargon. Such distortions can result in culturally inappropriate interventions such as individual psychotherapy rather than strengthening community structures to improve quality of life.

Problems-in-Living

To depathologize behavioral descriptions, the term *problems-in-living* is substituted for a variety of descriptions found in psychiatric nomenclature. Rodger Hornby (1992a, 1992b) described five specific human problems characteristic of American Indian communities: (a) fragmented and confused lifestyles, (b) cultural confusion, (c) damaged sense of self, (d) relationship problems, and (e) lack of skills. I have collapsed (a) and (b) into marginal cultural orientation status, retained (c) and (e), but added chronic alcohol/ drug abuse and tribe-specific syndromes as indicated in Table 6.1. Definitions for this suggested nomenclature of problems-in-living follow.

Marginal Cultural Orientation Status. This results from fragmented and confused lifestyles, coerced assimilation, lack of clarity on what it is to be Indian due to internalization of racism/discrimination, crisis-driven use of limited resources, spiritual confusion, and disillusion with the dominant society.

Damaged Sense of Self. This results from inadequate/inconsistent child care/parenting, developmental disruptions, fragmented/dysfunctional family life, boarding school effects, physical/sexual abuse, constant confrontations with loss/death of significant others. These experiences are compounded by arbitrary governmental programs, unemployment/underemployment, and a relatively unresponsive health/mental health service delivery system.

Relationship Problems. This includes family discord, dysfunctional relationships, jealousy/envy, and distrust/possessiveness leading to compulsive monitoring of other persons, violence, conditional respect, and impaired spontaneity. These chronic behaviors interfere with the stability, security, and safety of family life.

Chronic Alcohol/Drug Abuse. Alcohol and drug-related mental and physical health problems are the single most frequent and destructive social issue. These problems are coextensive with and exacerbate all other problems-in-living. May and Moran (1995) found that American Indians began drinking at an earlier age, drank more frequently, consumed more alcohol, and experienced more negative consequences than non-Indians.

Lack of Skills. This includes inadequate development of academic and life skills required for adequate functioning in the dominant society. Negative (aversive/punitive/dehumanizing) educational experiences have resulted in low expectations, diminished academic performances, and unsatisfactory job training outcomes.

Many of these problems-in-living and culture-bound disorders appear to be derived from a sense of overarching sadness and grief for loss of identity, a meaningful way of life, the lives of millions of forebears, and coercive attempts to obliterate American Indian cultures and spirituality. This historic presence is coupled with contemporary life in which early deaths are commonplace due to accidents, injuries, homicide, and suicide (frequently alcohol-related) in a larger context of inadequate medical and psychological services, especially preventive care for women and children. These human losses are an oppressive burden and this legacy of genocide diminishes the quality of life for all persons. This cumulative trauma has recently been labeled as PTSD and related disorders (S. Manson et al., 1996; Robin, Chester, & Goldman, 1996) and specific intervention strategies have been recommended, particularly for children (Long, 1983).

Culture-General Interventions

There has been widespread use and misuse of Eurocentric intervention models with American Indians/Alaska Natives, especially one-on-one techniques in counseling, psychotherapy, or psychoanalysis. Self-disclosure, particularly in response to confrontation, is a requirement for many of these techniques but was never part of any traditional American Indian intervention ideology.

Several assumptions undergird the use of standard psychological interventions with American Indians/Alaska Natives. First, the symptomatic expression of problems is believed to be similar across all cultural groups. This ostensible similarity has been used to justify application of the *DSM* to these populations. Second, the available Anglo American intervention resources are believed to be applicable to all groups. Third, the within-group or tribal and urban/rural differences are often minimized by Anglo American providers (Trimble & Medicine, 1993). The effect of not recognizing either the magnitude or importance of these differences has been to generalize inappropriately across different tribal settings and to ignore the vital contribution of tribal identity and culture to any intervention. Furthermore, all members of any particular group are believed to desire assimilation to become part of a homogeneous North American population. For American Indians/Alaska Natives, these assumptions have questionable merit. There has been a continued resistance to assimilation among traditional persons and a conscious attempt to mobilize unique tribal and pan-Indian cultural resources to prevent either assimilation or genocide.

Dominant culture interventions have been largely unacceptable because of conflicting health/illness beliefs, a cultural history of prevention rituals, and the practice of specific ceremonial interventions for a wide range of human problems (Trimble, 1992; Trimble & Fleming, 1989). Traditional health/illness beliefs are typically present in persons whose first language is not English; who are bicultural in orientation; or who live in isolated, rural settings in which traditional values are accepted. Traditional intervention measures have always had contexts in the spiritual, natural, and tribal communities. Often, the individual interventions used in the surrounding society have focused on helping an individual client exclusively and had no community context whatsoever. As a result, the beneficial impact on American Indian clients has been diluted and minimized.

Combined Interventions

Culture-general intervention technologies have been modified, altered, and redesigned for use in culture-specific settings and presented using culture-specific styles of service delivery. Most major methods can be adapted for setting-specific applications including psychoanalysis, person-centered counseling, gestalt therapy, existential therapy, transactional analysis, traditional behaviorism, operant strategies, rational-emotive therapy, reality therapy, marital therapy, and family therapy (Hornby, 1992b).

A potentially more powerful use of culture-general interventions occurs whenever the methods themselves are given careful local consideration and modified by consumers and culturally competent professionals prior to application. The local community should decide on consensual definition of problems and prioritize all interventions and remediations. The combined interventions can then be applied by tribal personnel, including indigenous healers, or by culturally competent, locally respected Anglo providers, preferably cooperatively, but always with community oversight.

The following examples of combinations include (a) culture-general methods applied in reservation service-delivery settings (e.g., cognitive-behavioral, family therapy, and Alcoholics Anonymous [AA]), (b) the use of local responsibility/authority for developing services (e.g., suicide prevention, alcohol abuse prevention/intervention, and a community mental health center), and (c) a consulting relationship that emphasizes style of service delivery and training of providers in an urban area.

Setting-Specific Applications of Culture-General Methods

Trimble (1992) recommended a cognitive-behavioral approach to the development of bicultural competency for problems of adolescent drug abuse. Life skills training components developed in the dominant society were blended by American Indian professionals/paraprofessionals in concert with local cultural lifeways. This program emerged from an American Indian Advisory Committee review, critique, modification, and approval of plans, curriculum, and materials. After collaborative relationships were established in the community, an intervention curriculum was designed to reflect traditional values and lifeways. Local paraprofessionals were then invited to be leaders of small groups and received 16, 2-hour training sessions. Youth groups met twice weekly for 15 2-hour sessions with these trained leaders for orientation to history, incidence, prevalence of drug use generally, and linkages between American Indian drug use and social learning principles. Strategies for decision making and problem solving were emphasized. Self-instruction using "inner speech" became a basis for personal coping and were linked with the development of communication skills. Homework provided practice in learning these skills. An acronym—S.O.D.A.S.—stands for Stop!, Options?, Decision?, decision-based Acts followed by Self-praise. Overlearning this acronym was facilitated by buttons, posters, leaflets, and cards emblazoned with the acronym. Three intervention sites were used with 102 youths, and a 6-month follow-up suggested lower rates for alcohol, marijuana, and inhalant use for participants compared with nonparticipant peers (Gilchrist, Schinke, Trimble, & Cvetkovich, 1987).

The second example—family therapy and family system models—can be applied in a variety of tribal settings. Problem families are identified by resident mental health technicians and services are provided by IHS consultants and traditional healers. These services combine modified culture-general interventions with traditional American Indian ceremonies and rituals. Topper and Curtis (1987) used family therapy with adolescent male Navajos who were unable to obtain livestock permits and grazing land or nontraditional jobs. This blocking of both traditional and assimilated economic lifestyles produced a reservation-specific depressive syndrome complicated by alcohol, suicide attempts, anger, and sporadic violence. A Navajo medicine man focused on the individual and the entire extended family simultaneously in a context of healing ceremonies. Directives to the family during this process were used to alter behaviors and relationships among family members. This particular combination was orchestrated by an Anglo American therapist who was known socially, respected, and trusted as an exemplary human being.

The third example is a modified AA program used by the Indian Shaker Church in three Northern California counties (Slagle & Weibel-Orlando, 1986). This church is part of an intertribal religious movement/curing cult with historic origins in the nativistic movement. Shake membership/treatment is considered to be a "last resort" when conventional alcoholism interventions have been ineffective. The Shake is a personal conversion experience analagous to AA. Consecration occurs during three consecutive church healing services. The components of this experience are participation by meditation (AA Steps 2, 3, 6, 7, 11), sanctification by means of confession (AA Steps 4, 5, 8, 10), and glorification as a result (AA Steps 9, 12). The spiritual component of the Indian Shaker Church combines Judeo-Christian doctrine with Indian beliefs in supernatural forces and shamanism.

Local Responsibility for Services

Local responsibility always involves cooperative efforts to plan community action for solving immediate problems. These initiatives ordinarily require a deliberate reordering of priorities for crisis intervention. Examples include the development of a suicide prevention center on a reservation, a social/cognitive developmental suicide prevention intervention, a program for alcohol abuse, and a community service facility.

Suicide Prevention Center. Shore et al. (1973) described the steps in developing a suicide prevention center on a reservation for several Plateau Indian bands. During a 7-year period, the 24 suicides were primarily by young males with arrest records and did not include other violent deaths, which may have been suicidal in intent or victim precipitated. The suicides were associated with alcohol abuse, inhalant sniffing, or both and typically accomplished by hanging while in jail. The tribal council met with personnel from the IHS, Bureau of Indian Affairs, and National Institutes of Mental Health over a 2-year initial period. Characteristics of self-destructive individuals were examined and a reservation-based medical holding center for detention and emergency intervention was planned. In 3 years, this tribally controlled center was developed with published guidelines, and community volunteers were recruited as counselor-attendants. Thirty patients were admitted for 24 hours or less during the first 13 months. Evaluation by a physician and social worker was followed by conversations about the current crisis with a volunteer counselor-attendant and the parents/grandparents while inpatient care and supervision were coordinated by community health representatives. This holding period provided an opportunity for self-control to be regained in familiar surroundings. Before the 24-hour time period had elapsed, there was a conference with the patient, a social worker, a consulting psychiatrist, and tribal police (if involved) to develop a treatment plan.

Developmental Intervention for Suicide Prevention. Suicide vulnerability among high school students in the Zuni pueblo was related to suicidal ideation, previous suicide attempts, to drug/alcohol abuse, and a depression/

hopelessness/stress syndrome in a context of little social support, limited inter-personal communication, and dislike of school (Howard-Pitney, LaFromboise, Basil, September, & Johnson, 1992). Suicidal behavior was understood as direct learning by modeling coupled with social support for substance abuse and individual characteristics such as hopelessness mediating decisions (Bandura, 1986).

Zuni leaders initiated a high school life skills training curriculum to develop social cognitive skills that would reduce the persuasiveness of these influ-ences. This curriculum included units to rebuild self-esteem, identify emotions/ stress, increase communication/problem solving, recognize/eliminate self-destructive behavior, receive suicide intervention information/ training, and personal/community goal setting (LaFromboise, 1991). LaFromboise and Howard-Pitney (1995) used four required classes in intervention and non-intervention conditions. Curriculum evaluation included self-reports of risk factors, behavioral observations of targeted intervention skills, and peer ratings of these skills. Postprogram problem-solving and suicide intervention skills increased for the intervention students. Although cultural tailoring and a life skills approach had merit, earlier implementation by the school system and follow-up or booster sessions were also believed to be necessary.

Alcohol Abuse Prevention/Intervention. A mother's realization in 1971 that family alcoholism was driving her daughter away from their Alkali Lake Shuswap community led to a sobriety commitment by both parents (Willie, 1989). Moral suasion to promote AA in the community failed until the father was elected Chief. He then arrested bootleggers, outlawed public drinking, withheld welfare checks from drinkers, encouraged a renewal of traditional customs, and provided community aftercare support for recovering alcohol-ics. Within 15 years, 97% of the tribal members were sober. A message of hope and community power was communicated using videotaped documen-taries and presentations at national Indian conventions.

Unfortunately, specific community interventions usually do not generalize to other settings, although some of the conditions for possible generalizabil-ity are suggested in this example. After a review of prevention efforts, May and Moran (1995) recommended a comprehensive approach to investigate the sequelae of related health problems, injury, deaths, and accidents result-ing from heavy drinking. The heterogeneity of this population should be recognized by local community empowerment that includes planning and monitoring of culturally relevant interventions.

Community Mental Health Center Services. The Tohono O'odhan (literally, *Desert People* or *Papago* as named by Spanish explorers) have had an indigenous facility for many years (Kahn, Lejero, Antone, Francisco, & Manual, 1988; Kahn et al., 1975). This tribe is located in a south central desert area of Arizona, bordering on Mexico. The tribe controls, funds, and staffs their facility with tribal members. A "cooking pot" model includes mental health problems with alcohol, nutrition, infant mortality, disease control, and other problems. The community determines priorities for using resources. Medicine persons with diagnostic and healing specialities cooperate on an equal basis with tribal mental health technicians, physicians, and consultants. Most services, however, have been provided by consultant-trained tribal mental health technicians who train their consultants simultaneously (Kahn & Delk, 1973). The training of these technicians fuses tribal and Anglo skills and focuses on how and when to use both indigenous and professional consultants. A formal training program has been sponsored by the IHS.

Although reservation unemployment has remained constant at approximately 50%, there has been gradual improvement of educational outcomes, quality of housing, and roads/transportation with a stronger, more integrated tribal government. The available services have changed with changing problems resulting from modernization. Television viewing has increased the willingness to recognize child sexual abuse. Half of the persons treated suffer from depression and suicide potential. Alcohol/drug problems are addressed in a special program that focuses on school-based preventive education. These problems-in-living rather than psychopathology receive priority attention.

There is explicit use of a culture-specific service delivery style. The acceptable style of service delivery avoids eye contact, and confrontation, and recognizes that respect for age and social status may be expressed by silence. Caution is used in addressing personal issues and directive techniques and clear interpretation are provided. Differences in perception of time necessitate flexible, informal sessions. Secrecy in personal matters, avoidance of affect in interpersonal situations, and a continuing mental illness stigma influence the tempo of individual sessions.

Crisis intervention is available on a 24-hour, 7-day-a-week basis, using two-way radios for immediate contact. Referrals to psychiatrists-clinical psychologists and medicine persons are dependent on the perceived nature of the problem. Noncrisis interventions include a tribal adaptation of group therapy for adolescents, who are paid an hourly wage, tribal and professional cotherapists, an educational format with topics of interest, and a third-person focus in discussion (Kahn, Lewis, & Galvez, 1974). In one year, this process resulted in an 85% reduction in arrests and fewer absent days from school for participants.

Consultation and Training
for Urban Areas

Urban programs generally provide services to American Indians who compose a sizable and significant cultural community. Many cities, however, have small numbers of persons in each ethnic/racial community. Under these conditions, a consultation/training model is necessary to provide culturally competent services. For example, the Spokane Community Mental Health Center served a 1% American Indian population with a six-person part-time bicultural consultant staff for all ethnic/racial/refugee groups (Dana & Matheson, 1992). A group intervention was designed to deal with major potential problems-in-living, child-rearing relationships, and issues of grief, loss, anger, frustration, and self-esteem. Lou Matheson, a traditional American Indian, served as facilitator using informal, "open door," food sharing, and voluntary participation in recounting problems and successful solutions. In addition, most American Indian clients working with Anglo American providers had case management services provided by these consultants. The formal in-service training included courses in minority mental health including how to use an interpreter, family structures in different cultural groups, culture-specific profiles, and a bicultural referral form.

Culture-Specific Interventions

Sue (1977) suggested the development of new models to provide parallel services as well as new services for cultural groups in this country. To some extent, both of these suggestions have been followed by traditional communities in developing culturally competent services. A Child and Adolescent Service System Program (CASSP) report described 11 culturally competent service delivery settings selected from a pool of 136 nominated settings in 35 states (Issacs & Benjamin, 1991). Increased use of available services by visible racial/ethnic groups has occurred largely as a result of culturally competent services provided by culture-specific agencies (e.g., Bui & Takeuchi, 1992; O'Sullivan, Peterson, Cox, & Kirkeby, 1989; Sue, Fujino, Hu, Takeuchi, & Zane, 1991).

Two urban and two rural programs illustrate use of parallel new services for American Indian populations. Urban and rural programs are presented separately not because the problems faced by individuals are dissimilar in kind or intensity but because of differences in available support systems, potential community resources, and social/professional pressures for use of specific interventions.

The Indian Health Board of Minneapolis and Yakima Indian Reservation IHS were included among CASSP settings (Issacs & Benjamin, 1991). Two other programs in Washington State also provide new services: the Seattle Indian Health Board Mental Health Program (Culturally Relevant Ethnic Minority Services Coalition [CREMS], 1989a), and the Skagit Community Mental Health Program (CREMS, 1989b; Swinomish Tribal Mental Health Project, 1991).

Urban Programs

Seattle Indian Health Board. The Leschi and Thunderbird treatment centers serve approximately 18,000 Indian persons with medical, dental, mental health, and optometric services. This population has a 52% unemployment rate, 68% have no health insurance, and their educational level is low. Mental health services are provided for persons suffering from "isolation, culture shock, alienation, and identity confusion in the impersonal, confusing, and white-dominated urban environment" (CREMS, 1989a, p. 14). These problems are often compounded by alcoholism, which affects 80% to 85% of men and 35% to 55% of women, contributing to 75% of deaths, 80% of suicides, and a homicide rate that is triple the national average (CREMS, 1989a).

The services include inpatient and outpatient alcoholism treatment; family services (e.g., family planning, family therapy, domestic violence counseling, referral, and outreach); and individual and group therapy. Outpatient services provide psychological assessment and medication. An evaluation process for each client includes an assessment of cultural background and degree of traditionalism prior to individual, group, marital, and family therapy. In addition to group psychotherapy per se, group therapy encompasses cultural classes, living skills classes, socialization and communication, anger management, groups for women, and Talking Circle. The Talking Circle uses community or spiritual leaders and mental health workers in the informal support network of Indian communities. Traditional activities include arts and crafts, field trips to cultural events and sites, visits with spiritual leaders, and dinners with food giveaways, storytelling, and traditional healing ceremonies. Some transportation is provided for clients, and services are immediate for crises either by walk-in or outreach. Indigenous healers, other leaders, and culturally competent mental health workers are employed to provide treatment following a holistic evaluation of social, cultural, and spiritual needs designed to provide safe and culturally appropriate settings for identity-affirming services congruent with traditional values. Tribal support networks are fostered and enriched by these services. Desired outcomes of treatment include an increased ability to deal with presenting problems and maximizing potentials for vocation, interpersonal relationships, and cultural identification/reintegration. For chronically ill and seriously disturbed persons, the desired outcome is to make community living feasible under conditions of minimal danger to self and others and without dependence on acute care facilities.

Soaring Eagles Program. The Indian Health Board of Minneapolis (Issacs & Benjamin, 1991) is the second culture-specific urban agency example. Their services began in the 1970s with a dental clinic, medical services, and mental health services. An American Indian client population of over 17,000 included 69 different tribes. Half of this population was below poverty level with an 80% illegitimacy rate, predominantly female-headed households, and high mobility. Alcohol abuse, fetal alcohol syndrome, domestic violence, and child abuse/neglect were major problems.

The Soaring Eagles Program for youths aged 3-20 began in 1985 and focused on prevention by using cultural values to stimulate leadership potential and reduce alcohol/chemical dependence in approximately 200 youths who had *not* been previously identified as having problems. Cultural identity was fostered by means of community support, an emphasis on education, and parent education/training. Recreational activities and mental health services were available. The primary accomplishments have been low attrition from the program, maintenance of school-grade placement, decreased juvenile court incidents, and minimal alcohol/drug usage and teenage pregnancies.

All interventions were guided by their cultural relevance and employed community helpers to socialize children in an Indian way of life. Weekly age-related peer group meetings were held to design activities including reservation tours, teaching fishing/farming, pow wow participation, sweats, and a drum and bugle corps. Medicine people, tribal leaders, natural helpers, and artists focused cultural experiences. Academic achievement received support by tutoring, study periods and a reading program, as well as individualized improvement activity and didactic lessons on AIDS, teenage pregnancy, and chemical dependence. Full-time American Indian college student staff members were role models. The mental health unit services, however, had an Anglo American staff who were primarily dominant culture in orientation. As a result, the potential for cultural conflict between units had to be examined in group meetings/training.

Rural Programs

Coast Salish Tribes. Served by the Skagit Community Mental Health Center, these Swinomish and Upper Skagit tribe members live on small northwest Washington State reservations (Swinomish Tribal Mental Health Project, 1991). The tribal-based mental health program started in 1984 with a conventional array of services, but the uniqueness of this program is an interface with tribal resources and local nontribal agencies, including a Job Corps facility, state institutional programs, and a Community Alcohol Center. Adapting dominant culture mental health services to the specific Indian culture has always been central to policy. Tribal resources included employment/training of natural helpers and cooperation with the traditional healing system to develop a culture-specific model of service delivery for traditional and "hard to reach" or marginal clients. Initially, these services were provided only to clients described by state criteria for acute or chronic mental illness. During the first 4 years of operation, over 165 clients received services for problems-in-living (e.g., suicide attempts, domestic violence, social withdrawal, family crises, child abuse, runaway teens, unresolved grief), diagnosable psychopathology (e.g., conduct and somatoform disorders), and spiritual problems.

The tribal orientation is reflected in the primary value of improving mental health on a community basis. Offices/services are physically located on the reservation with organizational ties to tribal social services. Tribal support counselors are Indian tribal members with training in Tribal Mental Health from the Skagit Valley College. A tribal orientation strengthens positive cultural identity by emphasizing issues of sovereignty, extended family relationships, spirituality, role of elders, unverbalized social etiquette, attitudes toward time, and distrust of Anglo American society.

Yakima Tribe. The Yakima Reservation program originated in the 1960s with social work family services (Issacs & Benjamin, 1991). This large reservation has 13,000 residents with nearly half under 20 years of age. Alcohol/substance abuse is the primary personal difficulty leading to community disruption and individual death. Chronic unemployment (80%) and poverty provide constant economic stressors typical of reservation communities.

The treatment philosophy includes problem definition by families, use of brief interventions that are relatively nonintrusive, and a fostering of family cultural strengths. The professional and support/administrative staff are Indian, including one speaker fluent in the Yakima language. A full range of medical/dental services in addition to mental health are offered. Services for youth include group treatment for sexually abused preadolescent girls, a substance abuse program, and child protection team services. These services occur within a framework explicitly acknowledging the necessity of a traditional cultural milieu for clients. A holistic approach to individuals increases native language skills, tribal values, and traditional group problem-solving approaches. All services network into formal and informal tribal structures providing an integrated support and communication system. The extended family is the primary support system sharing resources as well as responsibilities.

An evaluation process for cultural ties of clients includes questions regarding feelings about Indianness, how identity is perceived, and discussion of needs within the traditional belief system, child-rearing practices, language fluency, preferred use of medical doctors-healers, kinds of social activities, and informal-personal associations are also available.

Traditional Healing Practices

American Indian/Alaska Native philosophy is essentially preventive in nature to provide guidance for living in harmony with the human community, the natural environment, and a spirit world. Ceremony, ritual, and self-explanation in dreams form a significant portion of everyday experience for traditional persons. Traditional medicine has persisted, although the extent of current practices and numbers of practitioners now varies considerably across tribes. For example, it was recently stated by Peterson Zah, Nation President, that roughly 36 to 50 shamans were practicing with 175,000 reservation Navajos (Korte, 1993), and there are no remaining shamans among the Washo (Siskin, 1983).

In the early 1970s, traditional Indian medicine was practiced in San Francisco where bilingual or English-speaking clients used both Anglo and traditional healing systems for different ailments (Fuchs & Bashshur, 1975), although some other urban areas (e.g., Vancouver, British Columbia and Tacoma, Washington) have either not retained these resources or they were never available (Waldram, 1990). Saskatoon, Saskatchewan, however, apparently still retains traditional Indian medicine, and members of the 10% Indian population were interviewed to obtain information on services they used. Although both systems were used, bilinguals were more likely to use traditional healing services, especially herbs or sweetgrass, and these services were preferred by persons for whom English was not a first language.

Traditional medicine practices differ not only in kind but in their availability across tribes. Examples from Lakota and Ogalala Sioux (Mohatt, 1985), Eastern Cherokee (Irwin, 1992), Navajo (Kahn et al., 1975), and Washo

(Siskin, 1983) are illustrative. The Cherokee and Washo examples are described first to represent historic differences in health/illness beliefs and generalist-specialist traditions, whereas the Sioux and Navajo examples are somewhat more contemporary.

Eastern Cherokee

Irwin (1992) described the complex mythic world and shamanic resources of the Eastern Cherokee. Seven levels of this world extended above the horizon, including the "seventh height," a sacred realm of vaulted stone above the day and night. In this sacred realm, great celestial powers and Thunder powers lived with the ancestors of each animal clan. A lower world existed below the horizon populated by material and mythic beings. Tension existed between humans and the celestial prototypes of animals. Plants were allies, or spirits who helped to protect humans from punishment by the animals who resented being killed. The punishments devised by animals were believed to be known to their animal enemies and to the plants. Shamans could evoke sacred powers in plants or animals to restore health. Other causes for illness were also recognized as ghosts of humans or animals, insects/worms or their ghosts, and recently deceased relatives were also responsible for illnesses.

There were three categories of Eastern Cherokee shamans in the 19th century. First were the men and women specialist healers/curers, who used medicinal plants; these included midwives, clairvoyants who provided diagnostic/referral advice, and priests specializing in prayer and invocation to address the sacred powers. A second category of shamans were "night goers," who might take the form of night creatures to induce physical symptoms, draw life forces from sick persons, or use their knowledge to harm persons by producing illnesses. A third category of master shamans had an identity with the sacred and were revered for knowledge of healing and witchcraft. All of these shamans existed on a developmental continuum of transformations due to increasing absorption and identification with sacred powers and were categorized by what they chose to do in their practices.

Dreams were vehicles for presenting shamanic acts of power understood by means of a sign-based and indexical interpretation. Illness was seldom named directly because of the amplifying power of labels but was instead made real in patients' dreams. Healing involved recitations of sacred formulas and other rituals, tobacco to aid in sucking out an intrusive object and for smoking, and other plants. A final ritual involved seven entrances into a stream by the patient to carry away the illness while the shaman incanted formulas in the "old language." These formulas were a verbal counterpart to the dream and provided a link to the healing powers. The result was a restoration of health, or balance, by establishing reciprocal relations between supportive sacred powers.

Washo

In contrast to this complex and elaborate system, the Washo experienced a worldview of vague, inchoate forces with power embodied in supernatural helpers, the spirits of birds, animals, reptiles, and water babies (Siskin, 1983). Water babies were believed to be miniaturized human counterparts of males and females who lived in water but traveled from place to place and spoke Washo.

Disease was believed to originate in supernatural causes and to become materialized as an object lodged in the body. Disease was caused by sorcery/witchcraft, soul loss, and ghosts. Washo ritual ceremonies for curing were determined by the shaman's dream and the severity of illness. Brief treatments using smoke and cold water were used for snakebite, wounds, or to take precautions against dangers resulting from having walked in the abandoned camp of a dead person, but a 4-night ceremony in the home of the afflicted person was characteristic for more serious ailments. The shaman would sing, dance, smoke, pray, wash the patient, make an offering, and suck out the object. Payment for services was a basket or a shell necklace. The shaman was a generalist and drew power from involuntary dreams.

Future shamans (equally men or women) would have a dream early in life followed by sickness. Dreaming was cultivated, especially during a 3- to 5-year apprenticeship with a shaman, followed by 32 days of ritual procedures using dream-related paraphernalia including eagle feathers, rattles, pipe, tobacco, headdress, and miniature baskets.

The power and credibility of these shamans began to be challenged in 1936 by the Peyote Cult associated with the Native American Church. Ingestion of peyote cactus caused general euphoria followed by depression, nausea, and visual hallucinations. All-night ceremonial meetings would focus on an earth altar containing a large peyote button while everyone smoked cigarettes, ate peyote, sang, and drummed, with water provided at midnight and special foods at dawn. The healing process occurred as a result of a physical/spiritual purging with accompanying ceremonies to unite the participants. A peyote chief, a chief drummer, cedar man, and fire chief were present.

Peyote ceremonies were largely determined by the personality of the leader and there were conspicuous differences among tribes in details. The Washo cult leaders, however, were motivated to sell the peyote and to use their power for personal reasons, including sexualizing women participants.

As a result, the presence of this cult helped to destroy what remained of traditional Washo culture by pitting family members against one another, diminishing the earlier power of the medicine men and creating a new order of shamans who were neither trusted nor respected many traditional persons. Although peyotists still practice among the Washo, traditional shamans now have to be called from other tribes.

This tribe-specific description of peyotism is not included to minimize the therapeutic value of peyote, but to suggest effects of misuse in one setting. Although peyotism is controversial, there are no reports of dependency (Pascarosa, Futterman, & Halsweig, 1976) or serious emotional disturbance (Bergman, 1971; LaBarre, 1941). There is one positive report of peyote use in an alcohol treatment program for Southern Cheyenne and Arapahoe, which included participation in the Native American Church (Albaugh & Anderson, 1974).

Sioux

Mohatt (1985) persuaded nine medicine men on the Rosebud Sioux reservation in South Dakota to provide biweekly reports of their ceremonial activities including *yuiwipi,* sweat lodge, vision quest, and sun dance. *Yuiwipi* are night ceremonies for healing, seeking help for interpersonal psychological problems, thanksgiving, and marking birthdays and other celebrations. A sweat lodge may be held daily as preparation for other ceremonies, for diagnosis, and for health maintenance through personal prayer, purification, and strength. The vision quest involves a fast for as long as four days and nights in a remote power spot selected by the medicine man. The sun dance is a 4-day summer ceremonial led by a medicine man, which provides a ritual focus on individual sacrifice through fasting and dancing designed to help the entire tribe.

These medicine men performed an average of seven healing ceremonials per week (Mohatt, 1985). Their healing ceremonials comprised less than one half of all ceremonies and were conducted for a variety of physical ailments, psychiatrically diagnosable conditions (e.g., anxiety states, alcohol/drug abuse, depression, psychosis), and problems-in-living (e.g., marital/family relationship issues). Medicines for continued ritual treatment were frequently recommended. The patients generally came from within a 20-mile radius of the medicine man's home. All ceremonials were voluntary and involved gift giving, which symbolized the continuity of these ceremonials with traditional values. Additional information on Sioux practices are available elsewhere (see Jilek, 1975; Powers, 1982).

Navajo

Jilek (1975) has described the ceremonialism of Navajo healing to restore an order necessary for harmonious living with self, fellow men, nature, and universe. Curing rites, or "sings," were myth-based recitations that embraced a designated client and the extended family and friends in ceremonies lasting for as long as nine days and nights. These sings/chants were used for psychopathology but also had particular purposes for prevention (e.g., Blessing Way); accidental injury (e.g., Life Way); ghost sickness (e.g., Evil Way); alleviation of anxiety/guilt (e.g., Enemy Way); and thunder, lightening, or sacred animal influences (e.g., Holy Way).

The therapies were developed from concepts (Luckert, 1972) shared with Salish and Eskimo cultures, among others (Jilek, 1975). For example, in transformation/retransformation therapies, deities made an offender sick whereas ritual appeasement restored health.

Fragmentation/reassemblage provided therapy for traumatic injury by a symbolic reconnection. For intrusion, the pathogenic agent was removed by purification, exorcism, or Sucking Way. A Ghost Way trance ceremony was used to retrieve a lost or abducted soul from the underworld.

Navajo shamans included herbalists using medicinal plants; seers with supernatural powers for divining; and singers, the ceremonial therapists who learned exact texts and intoned archaic chants for curing. The herbalists provided a Life Way curing using herbs as analgesics, purification with emetics, and hydrotherapy or balneotherapy using sweats and yucca root baths. The seers, or diagnosticians, typically divined by hand trembling while in an autohypnotic trance but also used star-gazing, listening to the wind, or reading in a quartz crystal. Singers, as a result of long apprenticeship, choreographed tribal mythology into ceremonial rituals, which included dry or sand painting among other curing paraphernalia. Navajo healing thus included ceremonial rituals for purification, invocation of the deities, and a channeling of powers into patients. To increase the numbers of Navajo practitioners, Bergman (1973) helped to develop a school for Medicine Men at Rough Rock, Arizona.

Three examples of traditional Navajo cases illustrate applications (Coulehan, 1980). Traditional Navajo healing is analagous to psychotherapy with effectiveness for depression, for perceived relief from the discomfort of gallstones, and for demonstrable improvement in the quality of life with a metastatic carcinoma. Healing also implies removing obstacles at several levels—emotional, social, and spiritual—simultaneously to enable healing to occur and counter the personal experience of illness as loss through the restorative consequences of intervention.

A Model for Culturally
Competent Intervention

American Indians/Alaska Natives have lost much of their original self-sufficient heritage without any satisfactory discovery of new roles to replace their historic activities. They were rendered increasingly dependent on the government and this learned helplessness, as well as a modicum of acculturation, became necessary for economic survival. Their religion as an overarching philosophy of life has been sundered, partially replaced by Christianity, and partially reconstrued. Although American Indian/Alaska Native children no longer experience isolation and victimization in boarding schools that at one time vigorously denied use of traditional languages, the intergenerational residues of this trauma persist. Language renewal has been a recent accompaniment of reinvestment in traditional culture. Ceremonies requiring active participation in which an appearance of Indianness is defined by shared behaviors are used to reinvoke the spirituality that provides strength, fortitude, and meaningful beliefs.

Major American Indian problems-in-living are overlapping and interpenetrating expressions of an uneasy juxtaposition with Anglo American society. Dreams of middle-class comforts stimulated by television are simultaneously frustrated by stereotyping, discrimination, and racism. Tafoya (1990) suggests there are polarity flips among Anglo Americans between Indians as "romantic mysteries . . . and drunken savages" (p. 92). The occasional adulation of idealized Indian virtues by the larger society created a popular culture status of Indians as "pets" who receive protection in exchange for entertainment and docile acceptance of a limited freedom. Mixed messages from the surrounding culture have aided an erosion of some significant traditional values and facilitated adoption of some dominant society values in a very personalized way for individuals. Many American Indians/Alaska Natives have conflicted identities and identifications as a consequence, often without the ideological coherence or substance provided by either system of values or a meaningful integration of both systems.

Toward Culturally Competent Interventions:
Steps, Procedures, and Resources

The American Indian self is a context that embeds, encapsulates, nurtures, and sustains a sense of integumentation within a larger social and spiritual context. This contextualization and submergence of individuality within an infinitely larger whole provides the possibility for restorative balance and continuing interconnectiveness of person and community necessary to endow an individual life with meaning.

Prior to application of any intervention an exploration of cultural identity, or cultural orientation evaluation, should occur preferably during an interview. Knowledge of cultural orientation categories (i.e., traditional, marginal, transitional, bicultural, or assimilated) is essential for a description of cultural identity. Only on the basis of information about the cultural self can different intervention resources be mobilized for the same problems within varied cultural contexts.

This exploration should be done using a culturally acceptable service-delivery style that is tailored to be tribe-specific by knowledge of tribal nonverbal communication content and style. This style is difficult for Anglo American providers who will not be familiar with appropriate behaviors or affect unless they have lived in the Indian community for a long time.

Trust will not materialize from a simple application of provider presence or good intentions, regardless of relationship skills. Trust develops slowly, if at all, with an outsider in the shadow of genocide, and is based on a longstanding social relationship and a positive provider reputation in the Indian community. In developing any relationship with Indian persons, it is helpful to use "common basing," or referring to persons that both provider and client know, and talking about local issues, concerns, and history (Hornby, 1992b).

For these reasons, interventions have the greatest likelihood of success when applied within the local Indian community, preferably by tribal members, unless the client is assimilated or bicultural in orientation and prefers the dominant culture technology and style of service delivery. Although use of Anglo American cotherapists or consultants may often be appropriate and necessary, particularly as a "last resort," the context in which referrals are made and subsequent services provided should affirm tribal identity and the priority of traditional values expressed by means of specific interventions. Anglo American providers can become a part of a reservation community, or can become known by reputation in an urban setting. Lou Matheson (1986) has suggested that respect and knowledge are essential for an Indian to feel wanted with an Anglo provider. Respect is a deeply internalized process based on nourishment of "a personal and satisfying relationship within the self and with all other living forms" (p. 116).

A description of problems-in-living, psychopathology, or both should follow the assessment of cultural orientation. Culture-specific syndromes, marginal cultural orientation status, damaged sense of self, relationship problems, and lack of skills—the major problems-in-living—may have to be arbitrarily demarcated and taken out of their life contexts in order to apply some therapies. It is always preferable, however, to develop intervention plans to work with all of these problems simultaneously using intervention criteria including symptom relief for immediate stress, crisis, or problems-in-living, and strengthening identity-affirming resources within the individual for continued coping over the long term. The involvement of community as therapist is essential for development of skills, an internalization of resolve, and a sense of group identity as a source of motivation and strength. The effectiveness of interventions will be determined by the acceptability of the person or persons who provide the intervention, the choice of an intervention, how it is accomplished, and an accurate assessment of the client as a cultural being.

The choice of an intervention to fit criteria of symptom relief and cultural rejuvenation at the same time is complicated by the treatment setting. In culture-specific reservation or urban settings, there is always recognition of these criteria and selection among services will follow this awareness. In settings that are not culturally competent, the focus will usually be on intervention for cost-effective symptom relief using dominant society technologies and a modified medical model service delivery stance. For traditional, transitional, and many marginal individuals, such interventions will be ineffective and may even increase resistance to subsequent interventions leading to a downward spiral into lifestyle marginality, deteriorating health, or early and often inadvertent and accidental death.

The most successful interventions to date for persons who retain significant traditionality have been combined interventions in which technology from the dominant society is modified by the tribal community and applied in a local Indian setting. Because these interventions are embodied within a tribal social context, the option for traditional services by a shaman should always be present either on the basis of individual preference or because of the nature of the affliction and availability of these providers.

Relocation of all services in the local community not only mandates cultural competence in service delivery but also fosters vital linkages to natural support systems and community therapeutic resources (Biegel & Naparstek, 1982; Katz & Rohde, 1981) and sanctions role shifts by providers that can have enabling consequences (Rappaport & Rappaport, 1981). A separation of treatment roles into symptom alleviation and management of anxiety/values issues is facilitated. These linkages are necessary for individuals to be able to experience "self as embedded in and expressive of community" (LaFromboise, 1988, p. 392) because the supportive community resources provide the means for continuing and augmenting the treatment process in everyday life. As a consequence, it is necessary to evaluate the natural support system as a precursor to using established linkages, or establishing new linkages between this system and the professional caregiving system (LaFromboise, 1988). Furthermore, opportunities for referral to culturally sanctioned healers must be available whenever desired by patients or considered helpful by other providers (Attneave, 1974).

An adequate selection of individual interventions is based on an ability to mix traditional and modern approaches (Meyer, 1974) with a recognized reliance on adaptations of group intervention processes. Guidelines for group services are available (see Dufrene & Coleman, 1992; Edwards & Edwards, 1984). Specifically, family therapy in the form of network therapy may be used for retribalization in urban settings (Speck & Attneave, 1973). Family therapy has been adapted for American Indians by recognition of traditional healing approaches, incorporation of these approaches, or both, including ordeal therapy, humor, rituals, altered states of consciousness, paradoxical interventions, directive therapy, and insight (Tafoya, 1990). A family-systems model has examined American Indian families within their unique community settings to provide child-rearing information and alternatives for the development of their handicapped children (O'Connell, 1985). Home-based therapy for families has been described as a necessary application of family therapy (Schacht, Tafoya, & Mirabela, 1989). Group therapy for alcoholism among marginal individuals has been modified to embody American Indian values using structures for confidence development, problem exploration and identification, specification of group tasks or task centering, as well as for individualized tasks with group support (Nofz, 1988).

Individual therapy by Anglo American providers has been appropriately criticized from the perspective of culture-specific health/illness beliefs, which shape expectations for process and outcome (Trimble & Fleming, 1989). Some additional Anglo American provider pitfalls include patronizing behaviors; missionary zeal; a gratuitous, subversive, and alienating focus on traditional Indian values; and inadvertent or well-meaning behavior shaping toward lifestyles acceptable in the dominant society (LaFromboise, Trimble, & Mohatt, 1990). These criticisms of non-Indian providers are coupled with a perception of public-sector services as deficient or lacking in confidentiality and potentially reinforcing community stigma. Nonetheless, these criticisms notwithstanding, some Anglo American providers have been able to provide acceptable services. For example, Mohatt (1988) applied Lacanian psychoanalysis, with the understanding of local medicine men that he was not infringing on their prerogatives, by using what they referred to as power coming from within his own psyche rather than from the spirit world. LaFromboise and colleagues (LaFromboise et al., 1990) provide evidence that adolescents, at least, look toward providers as knowledgeable experts who can address their problems in concrete and practical terms.

Anglo American providers may often anticipate personal rewards for professional services in the form of verbal responsiveness and expressions of gratitude that are not forthcoming. What may be forthcoming instead is an attempt to override boundaries of a professional relationship by seeking to involve the provider as friend or guardian, as a condition for continuation of services. These client tactics may reflect a fear of vanishing (i.e., soul loss) and a need for identification with a provider as member of a powerful group (Gustafson, 1976), or, more simply, may be an expectation that the provider should become part of the cultural group with provision for other concomitant roles and relationships with the client. Mail, McKay, and Katz (1989) suggest that teaching clients and learning from clients is essential to providing acceptable services for American Indian people, a model endorsed by Kahn and Delk (1973).

This discussion has suggested an awareness of cultural contributions to health/illness beliefs and a necessary interface between available traditional and modern interventions. For individual Anglo American providers, such knowledge, although necessary, is not sufficient. An openness to new experience, curiosity, and a willingness by providers to question Anglo European emic assumptions, research methods, and intervention technologies as legacies of their own professional training are also required. Such questioning is facilitated by an ongoing confrontation between American Indian service providers and social scientists. Openness, curiosity, and the ability to question their own professional training must combine with in-depth knowledge of their specific practice settings and client populations, including understanding the social behaviors/affect required for delivery of acceptable services. Cultural competence includes these ingredients in addition to an awareness of available intervention technologies and how to adapt them for practice with American Indians/Alaska Natives. Anglo American students and practitioners should be aware of culturally relevant intervention approaches, primarily by American Indian professionals (Dinges, Trimble, Manson, & Pasquale, 1981; Jordan, 1988; LaFromboise et al., 1990; Trimble, Fleming, Beauvais, & Jumper-Thurman, 1996).

7

Asians and Asian Americans

Prior to 1980, Chinese Americans and Japanese Americans, respectively, were the largest Asian groups in the United States. By 1990, however, there were almost as many Filipinos as Chinese Americans, and Koreans, Asian Indians, and Vietnamese were almost as numerous as Japanese Americans in the United States. The 1990 census reported 7.3 million Asians/Pacific Islanders from 32 different cultural groups with separate enumerations for 21 groups, including Southeast Asians, Vietnamese, Cambodian, Hmong, Laotian, and Thai (U.S. Bureau of the Census, 1990a, 1990b). Other Southeast Asian groups—including Chams and Montagnards from Vietnam; ethnic Chinese from Vietnam, Laos, and Cambodia; and Mien from the highlands of Laos—did not have separate census enumeration. More than one million Indochinese are now in the United States as part of a refugee population of well over 2 million documented and undocumented persons (Loescher & Scanlan, 1986). The Asian American population is expected to double by the year 2005 (U.S. Bureau of the Census, 1993).

The majority of these Asians are immigrants and refugees with problems of acculturation and often with histories of trauma and minimal English-language facility. Southeast Asians bring with them more traditional symptomatologies and culture-specific idioms for the expression of problems than Asians who have a history of several generations in this country. Each Asian group in this country is culturally distinctive with a history of antagonisms and conflict toward other groups, and great differences exist in their familiarity with Western mental health service delivery systems available to them in their countries of origin.

This chapter will present material for Chinese, Japanese, and Indochinese separately. For these groups, the status of mental health service delivery systems, health/illness beliefs, and frequently used interventions in each country are described and relevant interventions for these Asian populations in the United States are examined.

Chinese and Chinese Americans

Many Southern Chinese migrated to Southeast Asia for economic reasons beginning in the 14th century, although they maintained their own culture, language, and residential communities (Rin, 1975). Chinese immigration to the United States began in the 1840s. These first immigrants, male railroad laborers, experienced violent racism accompanied by restrictive immigration legislation, continuous harassment, and victimization. Migration of intellectuals began in the 1920s, but by 1940, there had been a rapid decline in the Chinese American population due to continued racism. In the 1960s, immigration "hemisphere quotas" replaced the national origins system and most immigrants were women and family members. By this time, the effects of discrimination had, however, concentrated 60% of the Chinese American population on the West Coast; over 90% of this population were in only 13 states and the District of Columbia. All of these groups were strongly motivated to remain Chinese in identity, language, and beliefs (Dana, 1993, pp. 48-50; Wong, 1992).

Mental Health Services in China

To provide information and perspective on mental health services, various professional groups and individuals visited China and reported their observations. A group of psychoanalysts examined the mental health system during 1988-1989 (Chang, 1989; Halberstadt-Freud, 1991) and described a somatic approach with traditional healing, suggestion, and reeducation. They found that there was an increasing use of imported Western behavior therapy, including token economies and social skills training, cognitive-behavioral therapy, and pharmacology, although psychodynamic psychotherapies were not used in China until relatively recently (Muensterberger, 1984; Ng, 1985).

China and the United States use somewhat different diagnostic systems. Chinese psychiatric nomenclature differs from *DSM* and World Health Organization (WHO) systems as well as from local folk systems. When Chinese and American psychiatrists use these systems there is profound disagreement, particularly on depression, neurasthenia, paranoid states, and affective disorders (Altschuler, Xida, Haiging, & Qiang, 1988). Schizophrenia is diagnosed by Chinese psychiatrists whereas affective disorders or atypical psychoses were perceived in the same patients by Western psychiatrists (Wilson & Young, 1988).

Mental health care differs in urban and rural areas. In urban centers, which include approximately 20% of the population, psychiatric services are integrated into primary care medicine in centralized hospitals (Lieberman, 1994). These are long-term facilities to help prevent homelessness due to housing shortages and the scarcity of community aftercare treatment services. Therapeutic resources include calligraphy, creative art (i.e., occupational therapy), hospital work assignments (i.e., industrial therapy), music therapy, and exercise. These facilities serve as training sites, particularly for retirees who serve as volunteers for medication supervision, support, and counseling for crisis management.

These urban center hospitals are insufficient for the psychiatric patient population. As a consequence, community mental health care is increasingly promoted with prevention and health promotion as priorities (McClure, 1988; Yucun, 1989; Zuoning, 1987) and with an emphasis on the use of available resources and existing social structures (Pearson, 1992). Liaisons between factories and clinics are established by small neighborhood work stations and care units as well as home beds. There is reliance on the extended family (with emphasis on the cultural values of filial piety and avoiding loss of face), centrality of the government, as well as laws and prescriptions for moral and ethical behavior (i.e., heavenly way) (Domino, Affonso, & Slobin, 1987).

Folk healing practices by part-time "witch doctors," although illegal, still flourish in rural areas. Two thirds of one sample had consulted these healers prior to becoming psychiatric hospital outpatients (Li & Phillips, 1990). In Okinawa, there were five times as many practicing shamans as medical practitioners prior to 1966 (Lebra, 1969) and in China, culture-specific interventions by shamans are also still widely used. Although these culture-specific interventions have been viewed negatively by the postrevolutionary government and the medical profession, there has been a deliberate attempt to integrate Western medicine with culture-specific techniques, particularly acupuncture, balance-inducing therapy, herbalism, meditation, Morita therapy, music therapy, and supportive therapy (Lieberman, 1994).

As a consequence, traditional healing practices still prosper for treatment of chronic conditions and shamanism continues a primary source for interventions, especially in rural areas. These interventions include medication in the form of sedatives; charms; attempts to threaten, scare, or cajole the victim; and offerings to gods, ghosts, ghost soldiers, and ancestors. Shamanism has also persisted because of the multiple explanations for illness among Chinese.

Interventions in China are eclectic, a combination of historical and modern techniques with an infusion of Western technologies. The variety of interventions for specific problems in particular populations has been perpetuated by accepting competing diagnostic systems representing different health/ illness belief systems.

Health/Illness Beliefs

As indicated in Chapter 4, contemporary beliefs in causation are multifaceted with moral, religious, genetic, physiological, social, psychological, and genetic explanations (see Table 4.1, this volume) and yin-yang physiological theory provides a basis for understanding physical symptoms and psychopathology. Yin-yang imbalance is believed to result in anger, insanity, numbness, speech disturbances, or wildness. Any physiological excess can lead to physical exhaustion, or dysfunctions in bowel function, breathing, eating, or sexual activity. Figure 7.1 presents some of these health and illness imbalance beliefs among traditional Chinese and restorative interventions to implement these beliefs.

In China, health was traditionally conceived as balance or harmony among physical, social, and spiritual aspects of life. Health maintenance was achieved primarily by self-discipline, the will power necessary to be stoic and endure distress, and by avoidance of morbid thinking (Lee, 1982). A loss of the balance/harmony that constituted health resulted from imbalances at different levels: (a) inner state (yin-yang), (b) physical/physiological, or (c) social. Imbalances could be expressed by symptoms, culture-general, and culture-bound syndromes. A variety of interventions applied by oneself or others were used to alleviate distress, remove symptoms, or treat these disorders.

Culture-Specific Interventions/
Traditional Healing

The 11 specific interventions listed in Figure 7.1 will be briefly described (Leung, 1993; Lieberman, 1994; Wang, 1993). Acupuncture has a history of

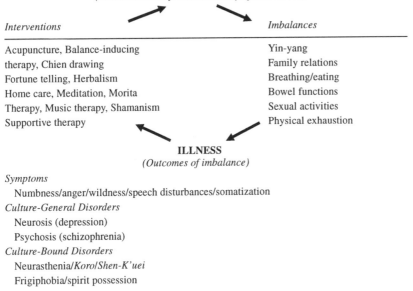

HEALTH
(Balance/harmony: Alleviation, symptom removal)

Interventions   *Imbalances*

Acupuncture, Balance-inducing   Yin-yang
therapy, Chien drawing   Family relations
Fortune telling, Herbalism   Breathing/eating
Home care, Meditation, Morita   Bowel functions
Therapy, Music therapy, Shamanism   Sexual activities
Supportive therapy   Physical exhaustion

ILLNESS
(Outcomes of imbalance)

Symptoms
  Numbness/anger/wildness/speech disturbances/somatization
Culture-General Disorders
  Neurosis (depression)
  Psychosis (schizophrenia)
Culture-Bound Disorders
  Neurasthenia/*Koro*/*Shen-K'uei*
  Frigiphobia/spirit possession

Figure 7.1. Traditional Chinese Health/Illness Beliefs

use for surgical anesthesia and for its effects on blood pressure, breathing, and heart rate; its effects on subjective feelings and emotional states are recognized; and it is used routinely in mental hospitals to reduce symptoms of auditory hallucinations and agitation. Enhanced compliance with medical regimens often results. Balance-inducing therapy is induced by application of low-voltage electrical current to the 12 channels of energy surrounding the extremities and trunk of the body.

Chien-drawing literally means "pleading for a divine stick" (Leung, 1993, p. 26) and this form of divination is practiced in Chinese temples. Kneeling before the altar, the problem is related to God. A fallen stick is then selected after shaking a vase containing 100 sticks. Bean-shaped divine blocks with flat and rounded sides are then cast and must land with different sides up to indicate consent to the drawing. This consent permits a *chien* paper containing a Chinese poem corresponding to the number on the *chien* stick to be provided. This paper also includes specific problem interpretations that can be supplemented from a divination book. An aged, respected interpreter assists in making concrete sense of the abstract poem and providing conservative advice. Positive outcomes of using *chien* sticks occur twice as frequently as negative outcomes and thus stimulate optimism and hope for good problem solving.

Fortune telling, or *Suang-Ming,* literally means "calculation of one's fate" (Leung, 1993, p. 25). I Ching yin-yang principles and the five elements composing the universe and their interrelations are invoked on the basis of historical wisdom by fortune tellers. In marketplace stalls or in their homes, fortune tellers combine a problem statement with client birth information to provide guidance for a fee.

Herbalists work either independently or in cooperation with pharmacologists in hospitals to combine their herbs with antipsychotic drugs. Herbs are often used to reduce agitation and excitement.

Home care has always been the intervention of choice for severe mental illness because the family assumes responsibility for all family members. Recourse to isolation at home for protracted time periods is the customary intervention (Lin, 1982). Denial, intense shame, and guilt are experienced as a result of mental illness in any family member. Eventually, trusted nonfamily members—the family physician, herbalists, religious healers— might be enlisted to provide treatment and eventually to hospitalize the afflicted individual when the family becomes unable to cope with care and stigma.

Meditation, also called Chinese psychotherapy or *quigong,* is used to achieve a quiet state for stress reduction. Wang (1993) reported research from Chinese language sources suggesting that use of this form of meditation reduces neuroticism on the Eysenck Personality Questionnaire and Type A behavior on the Type A Behavior Pattern Questionnaire (Wang, 1993). Morita therapy is used in China for obsessive-compulsive and anxiety disorders (see p. 155). Supportive therapy is provided on an individual basis. Music therapy has been provided in passive and active forms for chronic schizophrenics in mental hospitals. Passive music therapy for stress reduction in groups is synchronized with brightly colored ceiling lights. Active music therapy is used to permit individuals with florid symptoms to play instruments in groups to stimulate social responsiveness.

Shamans, or "witch doctors," are believed to have special powers of communication with the gods. Shamanism is conducted within a ritual format during which the client presents a problem that is then responded to with interpretation by the shaman while in a trance state. The clients are primarily women and services include diagnosis, explanation, and suggestion for remediation of a variety of conditions.

Chinese spirit medium cults form a social counterpart to altered states of consciousness among shamans (Seaman, 1981). Religious cults provide a medium for communication between living individuals and souls of ancestors. Incense provides symbolic recognition with ancestral spirits. Moonstones or coins provide a potential communication medium with spirits who have power over the living in accord with their status in a social hierarchy. Guest shamans are paid for house calls used to provide seances for the household cult head and the supplicant with a presenting problem.

Interventions for Chinese Americans

Chinese American communities developed their own distinct services as a consequence of segregation and racism (Chin, 1984); to preserve traditional cultural beliefs and practices; and to establish rules for community governance to settle clan, family, and business disputes. These services were developed initially by local family organizations and secret societies. By the 1950s, Protestant church and missionary organizations had supplemented many of these community structures. A third wave of services was provided by social agencies staffed by professionals from outside the community. These services were often alien to community residents because they were superimposed on existing cultural institutions, traditional health/illness beliefs, and a history of discrimination.

Intervention services now need to recognize and encompass at least four groups of Chinese and Chinese Americans: (a) individuals with a family history of two or more generations in the United States; (b) immigrants and their children; (c) migrant students, sojourners, and others who have chosen not to return to their countries of origin; and (d) recent refugees from many different countries including Vietnam, Hong Kong, Malaysia, and Singapore (Chin, 1984).

What is unique about Chinese American clients is the degree to which Chinese culture and the Chinese language have been retained. Because these clients come from many countries of origin in addition to China, they differ from persons in established Chinese communities in the United States. These four groups have within-group and between-group variations in cultural orientation status. As a result, a determination of cultural orientation status is always needed to suggest interventions that are likely to be acceptable and ultimately beneficial. Due, however, to a relatively high frequency of traditionally oriented persons in all groups, especially among recent immigrants and sojourners, consideration should always be given to interventions that combine culturally acceptable elements with Western technologies.

Family-Centered Interventions. A first consideration is the mode of service delivery. Due to the omnipresent family role in decision making, the entire family is the client regardless of which family member presents with a problem. The general family practitioner and family therapy models provide family-oriented services.

Hong (1988) described a practice model for psychologists that can meet client expectations for credible services and can be used with all Asian Americans. This model focuses attention on one family member while recognizing the subordination of that individual to family interests, family authority, and decision-making prerogatives. Ground rules for ethical relationships can be established at the onset of treatment. Therapist tact and discretion concerning disclosures can implement these rules throughout the entire process. Because family members may be reluctant to disclose or discuss personal problems in the presence of other family members, one therapist can see one or more family members in multiple roles of advocate, consultant, parent, and teacher with a variety of directive activities for advising and guiding the client. Because of within-family differences in cultural orientation status especially by generation, family members may need to be seen only separately, or separately and together in response to specific problems. Knowledge of the entire family constellation of interrelationships can then be used for individual members.

Using this practice format, interruptions can readily occur, especially after immediate symptomatic relief has been experienced or a crisis resolved. The flexibility and brevity of the method is cost-effective and may compensate somewhat for the small numbers of culturally and linguistically competent service providers. Responsible use of this intervention requires a high degree of general clinical skill to provide services for clients in different age groups with age-specific problems or diagnoses. In addition, the practitioner must have detailed knowledge of the specific culture and language as well as cultural competence in using a credible service delivery style with combined or culture-specific intervention techniques.

Family therapy for Chinese Americans and other Asian Americans has been described in a number of sources (Ho, 1987, chap. 2; Jung, 1984; Kim, 1985; Lee, 1982). Family therapy differs from the family practitioner model primarily by a conceptual shift in the importance of the intervention locus toward the family rather than individual family members within a family context. An implicit assumption is made that the particular family may be more homogeneous and traditional than families in which individuals are singled out for treatment. The power structure in the family needs to be identified and alliances made to address different members within the social and power hierarchy.

A goal-oriented and symptom-relieving problem focus using a directive approach that is highly structured, especially at the onset, has been recommended. Problem definition is focused on the designated client but seeks to engage the entire family in a process of problem solving that can occur without loss of "face." Reframing can minimize shame and provides empathy and respect for the family. The therapist can serve as intermediary for communication between family members and negotiate differences in perceptions. The cultural expectation of an immediate and tangible outcome from consultation should be honored in setting goals and by the content within each session.

Group-Focused Interventions. Group interventions for Asians have been underreported in the literature (Chu & Sue, 1984; Ho, 1984; Lee, Juan, & Hom, 1984) and underused by practitioners (Leong, 1992). Historically, the cultural uniformity assumption among many Anglo American providers provided a rationale for using the same technologies for all clients. In group settings, Asians are typically less disclosing and forthcoming with regard to personal and family problems than Anglo Americans. Providers complain that this lack of spontaneity inhibits direct feedback concerning the group process from participants. Probing by the provider to elicit personal problem-laden content is viewed not merely as an intrusion but as an unhealthy undermining of self-control and self-discipline. Verbal assertiveness, including confrontation, challenges to authority, and interruptions, are deemed rude and demeaning.

Culturally credible forms of subtle and indirect communication should be used to avoid loss of face and preserve honor. How a question is phrased often determines whether or not a response can be made, particularly whenever a negative response is required. Responses will be muted or withheld to avoid loss of face or shame to others to maintain harmony. Nonverbal cues and how they are presented are part of the communication format in societies where hierarchical status is very important and that employ elaborate forms of courtesy to mark these distinctions. Anglo Americans have forgotten their own pre-immigration history of formal etiquette in social relationships as a result of a blurred social class distinctions based on speech and nonverbal communication patterns. Indirect communication is often necessary for retention of Asian clients and Leong (1992) has provided guidelines that are essential for their providers.

Individual-Focused Interventions. There have been many informed discussions of underuse of services by Asian Americans as a result of provider cultural incompetence (Chan, Lam, Wong, Leung, & Fang, 1988; Leong, 1986; Root, 1985; Ryan, 1985; Sue & Sue, 1972; S. Sue & Zane, 1987; Tsui

& Schultz, 1985; Yamamoto, 1978). Moreover, individually focused interventions are more likely to be vulnerable to criticism because the family
context for problems and potential problem solving may be omitted.

Regardless of intervention focus, however, this literature contains the
following consensual recommendations: (a) the role of culture should be
understood for describing cultural orientation status and as part of any intervention; (b) there should be a focus on immediate symptom relief; (c) there
should be examination of the role of symptomatology in problem expression
including recognition of a somatization preference with group differences in
symptom clusters, which may merit the same diagnostic label (e.g., depression); (d) there should be cautious and slow-paced demands for any personal
disclosure or amplification of disclosed materials; and (e) provider roles should
be structured, directive, educational, and often multifaceted with the same client.

There is ongoing discussion of the applicability of insight-oriented individual psychotherapy with Chinese Americans. Tung (1991) believes that
this therapy must always be adapted because the enlarged boundary of the
self always includes the family. Uncovering suppressed material can diminish somatic symptoms and is conducive to improved psychological functioning. Such intervention is a luxury, however, when compared with a five or
six session average in outpatient mental health centers. Chinese Americans
who are bicultural may desire and choose interventions tailored to their own
personal problems whenever their insurance or personal income permits and
this choice may include an individually focused intervention.

In addition, Chinese immigrants may not necessarily be vocal concerning
their personal and group histories of racism. Asamen and Berry (1987)
suggested that although they experience alienation, powerlessness, and social isolation, these individuals may simply have an untarnished idealism
concerning American social doctrines that is not shared by Asian American
peers with three or more generations of residence.

Toupin (1981) examined effects of racism on Asian American psychotherapy clients. She indicated that therapy goals for these clients must incorporate (a) knowledge of the migration history, reasons for migration, and
settlement area in the United States; (b) extent of public education; and (c)
experiences with conflicting cultural norms during acculturation. Anglo
American providers should understand the history of contact experienced by
clients and their forebears, including the effects of restrictive legislation,
exploitation, and violence.

Community-Sponsored Interventions. All visible racial/ethnic groups in the
United States now believe that the community must assess its own needs for

services by problem identification and case finding and be responsible for developing credible interventions consistent with their own resources. In this generation, however, community movements are pan-Asian, often student initiated, and committed to helping the disadvantaged, including recent immigrants, the aged and poor, especially by direct confrontation of racism (Sue, 1973; Wei, 1993).

Community mental health centers provide a contemporary locus for services to members of all groups. Murase (1992) described available services in 49 Asian community-based West Coast agencies. Direct services included information/referral, case advocacy/management/networking, counseling, health, drug abuse, protection for abused children/battered women, youth services, vocational rehabilitation, employment, housing, immigration/legal assistance, and refugee resettlement.

These services were provided using four patterns: (a) single-ethnic, single-service; (b) single-ethnic, multiservice; (c) multiethnic, single-service; (d) multiethnic, multiservice. Successful services recognized similarities across various Asian groups in the primacy of the collectivity that includes strength of family relationships, and respect for authority, traditional values and practices. These similarities were translated into programs that included family members on therapy teams and a modified group approach with structured, concrete goals in conformity with family/friendship arrangements. A medical model integration of physical health and mental health services focused on symptom reduction using time-limited therapy (i.e., 2 to 3 months), although use of this model was related to the extent of acculturation.

For an example, Lorenzo and Adler (1984) described these integrated services in the South Cove Community Mental Health Center in a Boston Chinese community with a high percentage of recent immigrants. A majority of clients spoke Chinese as their primary language (83.5%); 8% spoke other Southeast Asian languages, and only 8.5% were English speaking. Initially, this facility was a community information resource for health services, crisis intervention, and education for social and mental health using bilingual, culturally competent professional staff whenever feasible. Over time, it became a full service facility including individual, family, and group therapy; early intervention for children; psychological assessment; psychiatric consultation; and medication supervision. Primary client diagnoses were child-adolescent behavior problems (36%), psychosis (28.3%), and adjustment disorders (18.3%). Almost all psychotic clients remained in the community with only occasional and intermittent hospitalization. Close contact and support for clients and their families was maintained during rehabilitation with intense efforts to improve English language skills and secure gainful employment. Children were often referred for "depression, passivity, anxiety, phobic behavior, poor communication, social withdrawal, poor self-esteem, frequent illness, disturbed sleep patterns, and parent-child conflicts" (p. 603). These problems were related to stress in families alienated from Anglo American society or lifelong residuals of discrimination. Staff members believed the frequent intake complaints by adults of "insomnia, headaches, inability to concentrate, difficulty with memory, palpitations, and nervousness" (p. 603) were related to changes in immigration policies from restrictive to more relaxed for recent immigrants. Many of these clients were willing to receive Western medications or consider separation, divorce, or both for marital problems. Long-term residents often presented with "identity problems, conversion, and psychosexual disorders, and antisocial behavior" (Lorenzo & Adler, 1984, p. 604).

The Center complex included an elementary school, swimming pool, gymnasium, auditorium, city hall, day care center, and a 160-unit apartment for seniors (Gaw, 1975). More recently, curriculum development was initiated to develop a nationwide interactive forum for discussion of Asian American clinical issues by Asian American professionals. A staff exchange program with the Los Angeles Chinatown Service Center has contributed to this continuing education process (Chin, 1991).

A second community intervention locus uses the school and school-based models for dealing with depressive symptomatology (Land & Levy, 1992; Shon & Ja, 1982). Asian youths have specific vulnerability to depression because they often act as family interpreter/culture broker to reconcile differences between traditional and host cultures. Role ambiguity may result from two sets of conflicting behavioral expectations. Stereotyping of Asians as model citizens, overt racism, high family achievement expectations, and control of emotionality also contribute to risk for depression. The depression may appear primarily as somatic complaints with differences in symptoms among Asian groups.

A school-based prevention model should identify the target population and find an acceptable idiom for framing help giving. Second, the methods used should be culture compatible. For example, cognitive intervention methods have aided Anglo Americans to reevaluate and modify distorted thoughts and misperceptions of the self. Such methods often fail with Asian Americans because these clients may be unable to identify these cognitions in themselves as a consequence of valuing suppression. Furthermore, the method itself may be construed as blaming because it relies on self-insight and affect abreaction and any increase in feelings of self-blame and family shame would also be counterproductive.

Instead of cognitive interventions, competence building and social support strengthening are recommended for school programs. Competence building augments self-esteem by bridging the gap between hope and the available opportunity structure. For Asian adolescents, feelings of learned helplessness, inadequacy, and incompetence often result from the conviction of having failed their families' achievement expectations and fear of public shame as a consequence. These feelings may be exacerbated by war traumas and lack of family support in their new cultural context.

Competence building using decision-making and problem-solving skills may be accomplished within the existing curricula. Parents give informed consent to course descriptions and are asked to be supportive figures or consultants. Self-identification of strengths and areas in need of support are coupled with coping strategies for resolving conflicts and solving problems. Active, participatory methods encourage provider-student partnerships and help to develop or increase an internal locus of control. Using these methods, interpersonal conflicts and social stressors can be identified either by students or providers. The range of problem solving includes finding alternatives to somatization or drugs, dealing with prejudice, building friendships outside of gangs, practicing interviewing skills for job seeking, negotiating family conflicts due to role reversals, and working through memories of trauma and survivor guilt.

A variety of active, participatory problem-solving methods may then be used, including role play, behavioral rehearsal, modeling, and psychodrama. These approaches encourage problem sharing and problem solving with providers, other school personnel, and family or community members. The outcomes can increase the use of effective coping skills to diminish the sense of helplessness, isolation, and burden that often leads to depression by internalizing shame, guilt, and unexpressed feelings.

Social support strengthening can be provided in school settings by maximizing student potentials for achievement. Linkages with family and mentors provide community involvement in these programs. Peer counseling can be helpful to both students and student helpers from the same culture, particularly for augmenting positive ethnic identification.

In addition to competence building and strengthening social supports, services for crisis intervention and optional referral to community agencies should be available. A school-based drop-in center or crisis hot line can be staffed by peers, parents, or community volunteers who have received appropriate training. School-based personnel can also act supportively with depressed students who have received treatment or who have left school (e.g., dropped out, attempted suicide, required hospitalization). Rapid reentry to school should be facilitated in concert with both the family and the individual student to minimize stigma and shame. All of these services can inadvertently increase stigma and must be handled with tact and sensitivity.

Japanese and Japanese Americans

Mental Health Care in Japan

Care for the mentally ill, handicapped, and elderly in Japan has been primarily a family responsibility with legislation to enforce family compliance. The prevalence of mental disorders in Japan, however, has been increasing rapidly since 1955, particularly among the aged. Simultaneously, international pressures and critical local incidents resulted in legislation to provide new day care facilities to help patients become reintegrated into their communities or to reinstitutionalize patients not responding to community interventions. Community-based facilities included supervised residential care hostels, group homes, and sheltered workshops, although many psychiatrists continued to feel that hospitals were a preferred locus for community mental health programming in Asian countries (Mandiberg, 1993).

Health is considered a unitary phenomenon, but mental illness/mental health has been ritualized for protection of the patients' inner feelings as well as to preserve social controls over negative feelings toward the family, intimates, and authorities. Outside of caregiving in the family context, psychiatrists in Japan care for mentally ill persons and serve families as technicians. Psychiatrists are often trained in psychoanalysis in Europe or the United States. Immersion in Euro-American personality theory and psychotherapeutic technology led to incorporation and modification of theory and technique for application in Japan. There are relatively few clinical psychologists who typically practice under the supervision of psychiatrists. Most primary care physicians continue to be disinterested in mentally ill persons and treat them in a discriminatory manner.

During 1987, schizophrenia accounted for 61% of the psychiatric hospitalizations with an average hospitalization of 496 days. Outpatient treatment is also provided for schizophrenics, who constitute 18% of outpatients; of these, 33% are classified as neurotics and 13% as manic-depressives (Koizumi & Harris, 1992). Until the 1970s, schizophrenia was not considered to be a "real illness," but an inherited weakness providing stigma for the family and prejudice toward the afflicted, and physicians often used the disguised diagnosis of neurasthenia, which was less stigmatizing (Munakata, 1986). The term *neurasthenia* has been largely replaced by the term *psycho-*

somatic disorders due to public preference for disorders believed to be physical in nature.

Since 1988, day or night care centers have been increasingly available to provide multidisciplinary treatment; today Japan has more rehabilitation centers than mental hospitals (Koizumi & Harris, 1992), although there are psychiatric units in many general medical hospitals, largely in the private sector (Takasashi, 1993). In traditional hospitals, a family representative shares a room with the family member and prepares meals to maintain continuity with the family (Yamamoto, 1977). There are smaller numbers of halfway houses, training centers for pregnant mentally ill women, and occupational training facilities.

Problems-in-living among Japanese have rarely been catalogued or compared with these problems in the United States. Taki (1985) had three judges reliably abstract the concerns of letter writers to advice-giving columnists Jinsei Annai in Japan and Dear Abby in the United States. In Japan, the primary concern was with conflicted family obligations (95%) whereas the major concerns for Americans were with relationships with nonfamily members (48%) or with themselves (25%). Neuroticism, old age, and debt were prominent in the Japanese sample, but there was silence on major contemporary social problems of parent battering by teenagers and juvenile delinquency.

Psychiatric illness is experienced in Japan as a loss of mental self-control (e.g., psychosis and neurosis), loss of physical homeostasis (e.g., heart disease and diabetes), and loss of behavioral self-control (e.g., sexual deviance and drug/alcohol dependence) (Munakata, 1986). Interventions seek to be restorative and to control symptomatology by using an interpersonal relationship and a variety of different techniques requiring introspection, following directions, and clearly specifying both expectations and outcome (Doi, 1984). These therapies have origins in Zen Buddhism, Japanese medical/correctional practices, and cultural conventions (Murase & Johnson, 1974).

Medically Supervised Interventions

Morita Therapy. This cognitive-behavioral therapy was developed prior to 1920 for patients with *shinkeishitsu,* a culture-specific condition comparable to *DSM* phobias, anxiety disorders, and somatoform disorders. Morita suggested three symptom types: neurasthenia (psychosomatic symptoms), phobic obsessions (fears of fainting, heights, meeting another person's eyes, not being able to be perfect, and inner conflicts), and paroxymal anxiety (seizures or fits) (Ishiyama, 1986). Four inpatient treatment periods are recognized that require from 3 to 9 weeks to implement (Kondo, 1953; Miura & Usa, 1974; Murase & Johnson, 1974): (a) bed rest/social isolation (4 days to over a week) with instructions for peaceful restfulness; (b) occupational therapy or light work outside the room (3 days to one week) with continued rest, contemplation, and ignoring complaints. During this time, the patient keeps observations on daily life in a supervised diary that is read and annotated by staff; (c) manual labor is accompanied by directions and permission to read selected books and have contact with other patients (7 to 20 days); (d) this "life training period" (one to 4 weeks) provides a gradual resumption of normal occupation/school/life outside of the hospital.

Morita therapy recognizes that thought and fact may be dissimilar and does not use intellectual means to change thought into fact. The body is not controlled artificially by thinking processes, and attention is directed away from the body in obedience to nature. Instead, a focus on concrete experiences is used to increase self-consciousness. Attitude changes restore normal activities and lead to acceptance of things as they are (Ishiyama, 1990; Miura & Usa, 1974).

Naikan therapy. Naikan therapy was developed in the 1930s for correctional institution inmates as an introspective process to relieve guilt over innate selfishness (Murase & Johnson, 1974). The term means looking inside or within one's experience (Murase, 1974). Naikan is a routine of supervised, private meditation applied with neurotic disorders, personality disorders, and psychosomatic illnesses.

Naikan counselors come from a variety of disciplines, and there is training only in procedures to be used for directing the process and providing a positive, supportive, empathic, benign presence. A 7-day, 100-hour period includes consecutive meditation periods in a semienclosed and screened area. A counselor visits for 5 minutes at 90-minute intervals for an account of what is being examined and to provide meditation themes of major interpersonal relationships, beginning with mother. A chronological but flexible review follows to include relationships with father, siblings, spouse, teachers, employer, employees, and friends.

Naikan therapy seeks to rediscover personal guilt for ungrateful and irresponsible past behaviors and to develop positive attitudes of gratitude toward those who are helpful, or have "extended themselves" (Murase & Johnson, 1974, p. 124). Memories of having been loved and cared for permit security and satisfaction to be reexperienced. This therapy reaffirms the patient's social position, roles, and required behaviors toward other persons.

Nonmedical Religious Healing: Shamans and Cults

Shamans. Japanese forms of shamanic trances include the ecstatic (spirit leaves shaman's body, flies, discourses with gods/spirits in heavens), possession (gods/spirits enter shaman's body), and dreamlike (gods/spirits encounter shaman's spirit via hallucinations) (Nishimura, 1987). During the 1970s, prior to being hospitalized, most hospitalized patients visited shamans for possession by a deity or spirit, especially the spirit of a fox, and received treatment in the form of ecstatic, dreamlike, and possession trances. Many shamans practice in the southern Aomori Prefecture and contribute to treatment for deity/spirit possession or possession in the form of schizophrenia prior to hospitalization. These shamanic practices still remain, although use of shamans for fox possession is now infrequent (Fujii, Fukushima, & Yamamoto, 1993). Some 30% of Japanese are believed to still use some form of religious healing (Sasaki, 1986).

Cult Therapy. Therapies generated by new religions, for example, the Salvation Cult (Lebra, 1986), advocate self-reconstruction using self-accusation to discover the locus of difficulty in deficient virtue or negligence of familial/ social obligations. Acknowledgment of control over a self containing both guardian spirits and human kin sensitizes the cult member to the necessity for increasing passivity to facilitate spirit possession. Spirit possession provides explorations of an enlarged personal identity leading to an apology ritual for redemption of sins. An aftermath of spirit nurturance by food and special tea permits the sinner to become caretaker for the spirit. Finally, expurgation or purification of the spirits permits restoration of harmony with nature.

Doi's Imported/Adapted Mental Illness Explanation

Japan has always been ambivalent toward Western ideas/technologies considered to be potentially dangerous and disruptive. Locke (1983) called this process "making the strange familiar" to solidify a sense of coherence in which dissimilarity to Western societies remains in spite of borrowed and adapted technologies. The Japanese style of dealing with the outside world has been to avoid feelings of helplessness through identification, consumption, and incorporation (Doi, 1973). In this process of ingesting foreign ideas-technologies, there have been alterations for compatibility with the Japanese psyche and behavioral codes for living.

Doi (1973) observed differences in dependency between Japanese and Euro-American personality structures that he believed were caused by societal differences in the bond between children and mother/family. Believing that Freudian psychoanalysis was a European emic in its assumptions and conceptualization, Doi (1990) looked at differences between Indo-European languages and Japanese for an explanation and found that the noun *amae,* unique to Japan, was defined as "to depend and presume on another's benevolence" (Doi, 1962) and included the feelings of an infant toward mother, dependency, being passively loved, and an unwillingness to separate. The verb form *amaeru* was defined as to snuggle up, be enveloped by indulgent love. The expression of *amae* in *amaeru* has a complementarity of acceptance of another's *amae* in *amayakasu,* and both *amaeru* and *amayakasu* have connotations that are active and passive (Fujii et al., 1993). The constellation of family and social events during child rearing resulted not only in an extraordinary intensity of familial relationships based on *amae* but in the continuation throughout life of this profound attachment to family and society expressed by *amaeru* and *amayakasu.*

In essence, Doi rewrote Freud for Japan and thereby provided a basis for understanding health/illness relationships. He not only used the cultural idiom of distress, or symptomatology, and associated syndromes or disorders, but also provided a rationale for the effectiveness of culture-specific intervention strategies. Doi's work has resulted in applications (Popp & Takemoto, 1993) as well as criticism (Takemoto, 1984). Doi's paradigm offered one partial explanation for the losses of mental self-control described as psychopathology in Japan. Some outcomes of Doi's thinking in terms of individual distress (symptoms) and potential psychopathology will be described.

Doi's version of Japanese symptomatology, eventual psychopathology, or both includes three major categories: (a) inability to *amaeru,* with symptoms translated as sulky, defiant, resentful, irresponsible, suspicious, and perverse; (b) improper use of *amae* in social situations, which are highly structured and dichotomous (family/close friends vs. strangers/others) with symptoms of pessimism, embarrassment/shame at revelation of self-indulgence, indifference concealing resentment; and (c) inability to be certain that the understandings of other persons in everyday life are accurate. These inferences are derived primarily from nonverbal cues and must be used as the basis for subsequent behaviors.

Figure 7.2 suggests some relationships between a culture-specific, socially structured developmental humanization represented by *amae* and the resultant personal distress/psychopathology whenever this process goes awry for an individual.

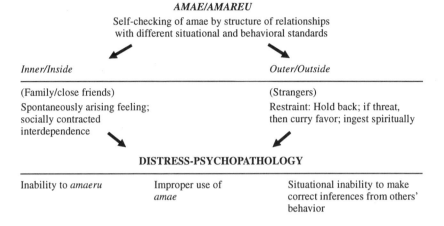

AMAE/AMAREU
Self-checking of amae by structure of relationships
with different situational and behavioral standards

Inner/Inside	*Outer/Outside*
(Family/close friends)	(Strangers)
Spontaneously arising feeling; socially contracted interdependence	Restraint: Hold back; if threat, then curry favor; ingest spiritually

DISTRESS-PSYCHOPATHOLOGY

Inability to *amaeru*	Improper use of *amae*	Situational inability to make correct inferences from others' behavior

Figure 7.2. Health/Illness Relationships: *Amae* and *Amareu* (noun and verb)

Interventions for Japanese Americans

There has been some weakening of *amae* over time among Japanese, not only in the United States but also in Japan. The acculturation of Japanese in this country, excluding Hawaii, has resulted in fewer Japanese speakers and a sharing of many middle-class values in the host culture. For example, Sansei, or third-generation Japanese Americans, appear more anxious and introverted than their Anglo American peers (Meredith, 1966). When these behaviors are construed in nonpathological *amae* terms, turning inward with guilt is an outcome of family and peer socialization experience that can become major therapeutic issues.

Most traditional Japanese interventions, except for Morita and Naikan, are unlikely to be useful except for sojourners. Individual insight-oriented therapies including psychoanalysis, counseling, and feminist therapy (Bradshaw, 1990), can be useful for Japanese Americans. The use of existential/humanistic therapies has been documented by an unpublished report cited in Leong (1986) that Japanese American clients entered therapy for personal growth with twice the frequency of Japanese clients.

Although there has been controversy regarding counseling as a uniquely Anglo American phenomenon, high structure with clear explanation of process, explicit counselor and client roles, patience with regard to self-disclosure, and assurances of confidentiality are suggested modifications (Henkin, 1985). Behavioral and cognitive therapies have the advantages of being directive, requiring compliance to stated regimens, and being amenable to family, school, and community participation or direction; however, they should also incorporate an acceptable service delivery style as well. A family practitioner model and family therapy are useful with careful modifications for culture analagous to what has been described earlier for Chinese Americans.

The persistence of culture-specific experience and behaviors suggests that interventions adapted to account for residuals of cultural psychodynamics are most likely to be beneficial. In this regard, Doi (1984) stated that "psychotherapy is indicated . . . when the internalization of the conflicting cultural values disturbs one's familiar world, making one part of the self strange to another, thus leading to alienation from the self" (p. 272). In addition to a supportive function, the main task of psychotherapy for Doi is to identify the conflict, isolate it, and to heal the schism within the client.

Another example of perdurable culture-specific experience is found in the 2- to 3-year trauma of internment of 120,000 Nisei families during World War II. The transgenerational impact has been studied for 742 children from these families in the Sansei Research Project (Nagata, 1990). Parental secrecy concerning these experiences inhibited family communication within a climate of foreboding. Children of interned parents felt more vulnerable than children whose parents were not interned, and their self-esteem and identity issues were exacerbated by parental internment. This vulnerability extended to their perceptions of possible future violations of their rights by the U.S. government and preferences for relationships with Japanese Americans instead of Anglo Americans. For many Sansei, family communication experiences contributed to therapeutic issues even when the presenting problems were different (Nagata, 1991).

Family therapy and individual therapy using narratives, dreams, imagery, and videotaped stimuli address these issues. Narrative therapy examines actions by focusing on personal myths, fairy tales, and novels (Polkinghorne, 1988). Sharing these narratives can facilitate a more coherent understanding of past events and be related to future endeavors. "What if?" narratives are used frequently by Sansei and can also be used in therapy. Similarly, dreams and videotapes can recreate internment experiences and address the unfinished and incomplete family communication.

Southeast Asians and Southeast Asian Americans

The Indochina peninsula has a diverse cultural population in Vietnam (North and South), Cambodia, and Laos; it includes ethnic Vietnamese,

Khmer in Vietnam and Cambodia, ethnic Laotians, Hmong and Yiu Mien largely from Laos, and ethnic Chinese from all these countries.

There are differences between these groups in ethnic identities, religion, history, language, and cultural traditions. These groups came to the United States at different times from 1975 to the present, with different resources, under conditions of forced emigration, and frequently with histories of trauma, torture, and experience in refugee camps during the process of escape to neighboring countries by boat or on foot.

Many of these persons were in acute need of mental health care for preacculturation stress residuals and later in response to new stressors during the acculturation process. Approximately two thirds of all Indochinese refugees during this period were ethnic Vietnamese (Hung, 1985).

Vietnamese

Synopses of the history and culture of Vietnam, including the refugee exodus, have been abstracted here from Hung (1985), Montero (1979), and Rutledge (1992) to provide an introduction. Vietnam has nearly a 2,000-year history of unremitting struggle against domination by other countries. Chinese rule for 1,000 years ended with independence from China in 939 A.D. and lasted with only one 10-year interruption until Europeans began to exploit and colonize. Finally the French were successful in establishing dominance, although it was not the French merchants but the Catholic church that provided an impetus for sustained pressure and eventual encroachment on the Vietnamese government. The French colonized Vietnam in 1844 and imposed heavy taxation, brutality, and rampant political imprisonment, which fueled rival nationalist movements that eventually included Communists and non-Communists espousing different political ideologies.

The Japanese invasion in 1945 resulted in a short-lived provisional government in Hanoi with Ho Chi Minh as president. Returning in 1946, the French were forced to recognize the legitimacy of the Vietminh political regime, but this was not acceptable to Ho Chi Minh. The ensuing French-Indochina War lasted until 1954 when the 17th parallel became the boundary between North and South Vietnam. One million refugees from North Vietnam subsequently resettled in South Vietnam.

Premier Ngo Dinh Diem made a futile attempt to reunite South Vietnam but was overthrown in 1963 and replaced by a series of governments. From 1962 until 1966, the United States began active aid to the South Vietnam government, matching the escalation by North Vietnam until full-scale military operations were undertaken from 1966 to April 1975 when Saigon fell to the North Vietnamese.

The first major immigration of ethnic Vietnamese refugees in 1975 included approximately 132,000 persons, many of whom were government officials, military personnel, and professionals and their families. Many of these skilled and educated persons were aided by Americans they had known in Vietnam and also received cash assistance for 3 years during resettlement throughout the United States as part of a moral obligation (Rutledge, 1992). Many of these refugees came to the United States because they were not welcome in neighboring Asian countries and had to depart under duress and in crisis. Refugees were exempt from immigration quotas and could apply for citizenship after 12-months residence in the United States. Meanwhile, hundreds of thousands of persons also remained in South Vietnam in concentration camps.

In 1977, a second emigration wave included approximately 127,000 Vietnamese citizens who were largely ethnic Chinese. From 1979 through the mid-1980s, a third-wave program provided safer, legal departure from Vietnam for ethnic Vietnamese. A fourth wave in the late 1980s included many former Vietnamese soldiers imprisoned for protracted reeducational periods and Amerasians (Freeman, 1989). Subsequent waves of Vietnamese peoples continued the exodus into the 1980s and included many Cham, Khmer, and Montagnards (Rutledge, 1992).

The 30,000 Chams in south-central Vietnam were isolated, and their culture contained Hindu and Islamic elements. Ethnic Vietnamese associated them with the Malays whom they disliked, and prejudice against the Chams continues in the United States. The 500,000 Khmer, or ethnic Cambodians, in Vietnam had their own culture, religion, and language, although they intermarried with ethnic Vietnamese and were living in the South around the Mekong Delta. Because many Khmer had acquired Vietnamese citizenship and cultural characteristics, they were more accepted into Vietnamese society than other minority groups. The 800,000 Montagnards were migratory hunters and occasional rice farmers in the northern and central mountains. Their apparent cooperation with the Central Intelligence Agency during the war marked them for extermination by the North Vietnamese.

Cambodians

Cambodian history and the Khmer refugee process has been described in detail by Ebihara (1985). Cambodia, a Theravada Buddhist agricultural country of over 7 million persons, had an 85% to 90% Khmer population and a history from before 800 A.D. to 1431 A.D., when it had been a powerful, regional country, rich in art and architecture. Cambodia became a French protectorate in 1863 and formed the Union of French Indochina with Laos and Vietnam in 1887. Occupation by Japanese forces during World War II was followed by independence in 1954 when Prince Sihanouk established a constitutional monarchy, the Republic of Kampuchea. The monarchy was replaced after the 1970 Khmer Rouge coup by Democratic Kampuchea from 1975 to 1978. Pol Pot collectivized the economy, dissolved families in favor of work teams, and replaced Buddhism with a secular political ideology. Factional disputes within the communist party and infractions of the new rule structure led to large-scale executions. Malnutrition, debilitation, and illness among soldiers and civilians resulted in 1 million to 3 million deaths. In late 1978, the Vietnamese invaded and occupied the country, capturing Phnom Penh early in 1979 and calling the new regime the People's Republic of Kampuchea.

An exodus began in 1979 with about 40,000 persons going to Thailand and at least 150,000 going to Vietnam. These groups included government officials, affluent Khmer, ethnic Chinese, and rural persons. A second departure in 1978 of 100,000 persons to the Thai border included surviving military, professional, and business persons as well as rural peasants. Some refugees were forced out of Thailand while others perished in mine fields or died of illness and starvation. Wars, forced migrations, labor camps, purges, famine, and annihilation of the intelligentsia by the Khmer Rouge were responsible for as many as 3 million deaths and 2 million refugees. Famine and continuing war created a third exodus in late 1979 and early 1980 of a half million persons in holding centers and border "village-camps." Many Khmer refugees who came to the United States from 1975 to 1984 had been in Thai holding centers for 5 years. By 1984, approximately 98,000 Cambodians had been to Indochinese Refugee Processing Centers for English language instruction and cultural orientation. These refugees were mostly young persons or school-age children without kin in the United States.

Laotians

Laos has contributed refugees from both lowland ethnic Lao, ethnic Chinese, and highland tribesmen, including Hmong, Mien, and some members of other tribes. The Lao accounted for 83,000 persons, or 13% of the Southeast Asian resettlement population between 1975 and 1983. Details of Laotian history and the refugee process appear in another source (Van Esterik, 1985) and are summarized here. The Lao nation dates from the acceptance of Buddhism in the 14th century by speakers of the Thai language and long-term South Chinese residents. Upland populations were non-Buddhists including Thai, Hmong, and Yao.

Historic Laos had three levels of inhabitants: rulers, commoners, and slaves who were non-Buddhist highlanders. Originally, one large kingdom included parts of modern Vietnam, Cambodia, Thailand, and China but was weakened and divided into three kingdoms after the 16th century with the capital at Vietane on the Mekong River. When French colonialists took Laos in 1893, the Mekong River became the boundary with Siam, thus arbitrarily dividing the ethnic Lao and reducing their control of highland groups because of relatively equal numbers. The French weakened the Buddhist moral order by separating the government, the French-language educational system, and religion. During World War II, the Japanese were the major power in Lao until independence in 1954. The Pathet Lao originated with North Vietnamese troops aiding one of two rival Lao Princes in northeastern provinces and the Lao People's Democratic Republic was the result in 1975. More than 40,000 Lao officials were sent to reeducation camps, and approximately 175,000 Lao went to Thailand between 1975 and 1984 as illegal immigrants and were maintained in refugee camps for 2 to 5 years. In 1984, only 20,000 Lao remained in camps while 2,397 had been repatriated and over 75,000 came to the United States.

A majority of the 5 million Hmong still live in south and southwest China and others have scattered throughout Indochina (Schein, 1983). They were typically autonomous, subsistence farmers who raised poppies and destroyed timber, acts resulting in a history of conflict with several national governments. Many Hmong males had militia or army service. Wars with the Manchu government from 1850 to 1880 resulted in a mass migration of Hmong to Laos (Cooper, 1983). Approximately 10% of the Laotian population, or 300,000, were Hmong (Olney, 1993). They practiced animism, although some were Christians as a means to strengthen Hmong cultural identity and group unity. Their religious beliefs defined relationships with ancestors memorialized by sacred rituals that also strengthened group identity (Dunnigan, 1983).

Over 100,000 Hmong left Laos beginning as early as 1950, then later on because of drought in 1977, floods in 1978, and fear of persecution. Nonetheless, economic reasons may have been of major importance in the decision to leave their homes (Cooper, 1983). More than half of the 65,000 Hmong in the United States by 1983 came during 1978 and 1980 while an equivalent number of Hmong were unwilling to resettle and remained in refugee camps. On arrival, a majority had no formal education or English-language facility. They settled in Fresno, California, composing a Hmong community of over

35,000 persons by 1993 (Ng, 1993) and in several other locations, especially in Minneapolis and Portland where sponsorship by other Hmong was available. It has been estimated that by 1988 there were over 105,000 Hmong in the United States as well as approximately 13,000 other Laotian tribal highlanders (i.e., Mien or Yao, and Khmu, Lahu, Loa Lue, Lao Tinh) (Moore & Boehnlein, 1991; Yang & North, 1988).

Ethnic Chinese

The ethnic Chinese in South Vietnam numbered about 745,000 whereas those in Cambodia numbered approximately 400,000 (Whitmore, 1985). They lived primarily in urban areas and ports such as Saigon and Cholon in South Vietnam, Haiphong and Hanoi in North Vietnam, Phnom Pehn in Cambodia, and Vietiane in Laos. These Chinese, a privileged and protected group during the French occupation, controlled production and trade with a superb internal organization and an informal network both locally and internationally. They predominated in "shopkeeping, the rice trade, fish, tea, soy, transportation, scrap iron, textiles, and general dealings, among other fields" (Whitmore, 1985, p. 65).

This protected status diminished with restrictions by the Vietnamese and Cambodian governments with the end of French occupation. The Vietnam War resulted in even greater restrictions on economic activities, travel, immigration, schools, and the practice of Western medicine. This earlier history of government harassment was coupled with people's awareness that their properties would be confiscated following the fall of Saigon to North Vietnam in 1975. After the fall of Phnom Penh to the Khmer Rouge, the ethnic Chinese in Cambodian cities were removed to rural areas from which they fled by land to the Saigon-Cholon area or to Thailand. Whitmore (1985) suggested that 15% of the first wave of immigrants in 1975 were ethnic Chinese merchants from Vietnam. In 1978 and 1979, a second exodus took place in direct response to discrimination and persecution in both South and North Vietnam. Many thousands escaped from South Vietnam by boat to Hong Kong and Filipine refugee camps and to Thailand, Malaysia, and Singapore with an estimated 50% loss of life.

The ethnic Chinese in North Vietnam maintained Chinese citizenship prior to 1979, but were exempt from military service, although otherwise they had the same rights as Vietnamese citizens. The invasion of North Vietnam by China, however, resulted in expulsion of all ethnic Chinese, with about 150,000 going by land north to China and another very large number escaping by sea to the countries listed previously and to Indonesia and Macao as well. Many of these refugees have been reluctant to reestablish themselves in primarily Vietnamese communities in host countries.

Health Care in Vietnam

Prior to 1976 Vietnam had only limited mental health resources for diagnosis and intervention services. In the early 1980s, for example, there were only three psychiatric facilities in South Vietnam (Bowman & Edwards, 1984). Moreover, there were no distinct and available professional cadres to deal with mental health problems because Vietnamese cultural values and health/illness beliefs provided no separation between mind and body. Feelings and emotions, or what would be called mental health issues, were not sufficient reason for complaint or help seeking but were instead considered an inevitable part of life and in which "lamenting is simply a sign of weakness and denotes a lack of character" (Tung, 1985, p. 11).

As self-sufficient social units, Indochinese families were expected to exercise primary responsibility for home care during protracted time periods (Tung, 1972). When home care proved insufficient and family shame and stigma became unbearable, traditional healers exorcised and propitiated spirits, sometimes spitting a ball of flame at the patient or threatening him or her with knives, or Buddhist monks listened, explained, and prescribed pharmaceutical nostrums (Bowman & Edwards, 1984). Help seeking from Western medicine was a last resort in cases of severe symptomatology, incapacitation, or potential for violence. Western medicine was associated with hospitalization and was reserved for violent and uncared-for persons because hospitals were considered a last residence before death.

Health care became a governmental responsibility after reunification of North and South Vietnam in 1976. The health care system is centralized in Hanoi with an extension to the southern provinces. Service delivery is highly structured and accomplished by specialty institutes in which Eastern and Western medicine have equal status in training and practice (Ladinsky, Volk, & Robinson, 1987). Two kinds of Eastern medicine are used: an empirically based Chinese herbal pharmacopia and a more theoretical Vietnamese medical tradition. An Institute for Traditional Medicine and 17 hospitals are devoted exclusively to research and practice with Eastern medicine. Traditional medicine continues to be available from healers and spiritualists throughout Vietnam, especially in rural areas.

Large numbers of Southeast Asian refugees were surveyed by Chung and Lin (1994) and asked to specify the kinds of practitioners from whom they sought help prior to coming to the United States. These practitioners were found primarily to be healers and spiritualists (traditional), herbalists and accupuncturists (Eastern medicine), or physicians (Western medicine) (Chung & Lin, 1994). Western medicine was used in their countries of origin by 50% of all Southeast Asians, Eastern medicine by 9%, and traditional practitioners by 8%, whereas 30% used some combination. Persons using Western medicine were proficient in English, had received a formal education, and were younger. Vietnamese were most likely to use Western medicine (68%), followed by Laotians (53%), Cambodians and ethnic Chinese (44%), and Hmong (11%). Moreover, there were relatively small numbers of physicians practicing Western medicine outside of major cities prior to 1975. As a consequence, there was greater reliance on traditional medicine by Hmong (85%), Chinese Vietnamese (53%), Cambodians (48%), and ethnic Laotians (41%) than by Vietnamese (29%). Rural residence, increased age, low literacy-formal education, and absence of English-language skills made use of traditional medicine more likely (Chung & Lin, 1994).

Health/Illness Beliefs

Vietnamese health/illness beliefs include natural, supernatural, and metaphysical causes (see Table 4.1, this volume). Illnesses from natural causes (i.e., trauma or food poisoning) are treated using Western medicine. Metaphysical causation is premised on the Taoist necessity for balance within the body to ensure harmony, particularly between "hot" and "cold." The Vietnamese share with the Chinese a yin-yang disease concept that posits imbalance of male and female, lightness and darkness, warmth and cold, wetness and dryness, fullness and emptiness in bodily functions (Ladinsky et al., 1987). An imbalance of the Vietnamese yin-yang equivalents, *am* and *dong,* requires its opposite element for restoration of balance. Any imbalance may produce symptoms, illness, and feeling a lack of well-being. Foods classified into hot, cold, and neutral are used as restoratives. A complaint of "hot" can mean constipation or hoarseness (Eyton & Neuwirth, 1984).

An ill or bad wind, or *phong,* however, is the most prevalent supernatural causal belief and can result from certain foods, hunger, breach of custom, alcoholism, or spirit possession. Being "hit by the wind" leaves the person feeling unwell or debilitated (Eyton & Neuwirth, 1984) with a range of resultant symptoms including fatigue, stomachache, general malaise, fainting, and seizure. Self-treatment often consists of *Cao Gio,* a bruising of the skin either with a small coin (i.e., "coining") (Yeatman & Dang, 1980), or a spoon used to "rub out the wind," or extracting blood by suction from "cupping" (Eyton & Neuwirth, 1984).

There are some differences among health/illness beliefs in various Southeast Asian cultural populations. For example, the ethnic Chinese in Vietnam have health/illness beliefs from both their ancestral origins in China and their long-term residence in Vietnam (Crissman, 1991). The Cambodian Khmer are Buddhist (with Brahmanistic concepts of life cycle and rebirth) (Boehnlein, 1987), but with traditional beliefs in the supernatural and ancestor spirits or ghosts as well. The ethnic Laotians are also Buddhist and they have many explanations for mental illness including physical, social, and psychological causes (Westermeyer, 1988; Westermeyer & Wintrob, 1988).

The Hmong have similar but less complex beliefs than ethnic Laotians. The primary cause of disease for the Hmong is loss of soul and cure involves attempts by the family to call back the soul (Thao, 1986). When frightened, alone in a dark place, or depressed and lonely as a result of separation/loss of loved ones, the soul may leave the body. Secondary causes of illness are magical spells and spirit intrusion by illness, plague, or catastrophe because the person is not living in harmony with the spirits. The Mien also believe in animism and ancestor worship. Problems are believed to be caused by feared evil spirits. There is exclusive reliance on shamans to propitiate these spirits by rituals and ceremonies. Physicians in lowland Lao cities are a last recourse when shamanistic rituals and herbalism have been unsuccessful (Moore & Boehnlein, 1991). Compliance by Hmong, Mien, and other highland peoples with Western medicine and psychiatry in the United States has been minimal (Kinzie, Leung, & Boehnlein, 1987).

Interventions in the
United States

Southeast Asians in the United States continue to believe that mind and body are inseparable. Their mental health problems are presented in medical settings as somatic complaints by a majority of clients (Nishio & Bilmes, 1987). Like other Asians, they believe mental illness brings shame, stigma, and social disgrace to the family for being unable to deal effectively with problems of their members. As a result, families are reluctant to bring their members to mental health settings for psychological interventions. As in their home countries, they prefer to meet problems-in-living and psychiatric disorders with stoicism and endurance.

There is procrastination in seeking outside assistance and distrust of services and service providers. When outside assistance is desired, often as a last resort, help seeking is similar to customary patterns in the country of origin. These groups have had differing opportunities and degrees of willingness to use either Western medicine or traditional medicine, which continues to be evident in choice of practitioners and kinds of services in the United States. For example, the reported usage of Western medicine in the United States is 88% for Cambodians, 86% for ethnic Lao, 65% for ethnic Vietnamese, 69% for ethnic Chinese, and 56% for Hmong (Nishio & Bilmes, 1987). The reported usage of traditional healers in the United States remains high for the Hmong (39%) and ethnic Chinese from Vietnam (25%), moderate for Vietnamese (16%), and low for Lao (7%) and Cambodians (5%) (Chung & Lin, 1994).

As first-generation immigrants from Indochina, many of these persons bring with them histories of personal trauma, including war-related trauma, separation from loved ones, sudden relocation, traumatic escapes, Pol Pot concentration camps, reeducation internment, refugee camp experiences, and physical abuse, rape, or torture. Moreover, some groups (e.g., Hmong; Mien) have had very limited English language proficiency or exposure to Western culture and technology. These ingredients created additional problems in service delivery because immediate crisis intervention has often been necessary as well as long-term, multifaceted interventions for a variety of problems.

Service delivery in refugee camps and after resettlement in the United States also has been complicated and attenuated by language barriers and services that ignored relevant cultural considerations, particularly health/illness beliefs. Instead, a primary focus on emotional/psychological issues neglected more pragmatic concerns (Gong-Guy, Cravens, & Patterson, 1991). Psychological problems, including depression and anxiety, are perceived by clients as secondary to unemployment and limited funds, family problems, and the mechanics of interfacing on a daily basis with a new and often hostile or unresponsive society.

In addition, there is typically a scarcity of providers who speak the same first language and share the same culture as the client. Westermeyer (1986) reported some of his own early experiences with recruiting translators for Indochinese clinics. Chinese Americans and Japanese Americans were often unsatisfactory translators or service providers due to cultural differences and histories of antagonism toward wealthy ethnic Chinese or Japanese invaders in the refugees' countries of origin. Anglo Americans, however, were acceptable service providers whenever they had appropriate language skills and cultural knowledge based on living in the countries of origin of their Southeast Asian refugee clients.

Much of what has previously been described for Chinese Americans and Japanese Americans may be applied to Vietnamese with alterations or modifications for culture of origin. Such changes may affect the service delivery style and the likelihood that the particular intervention will be effective. Similarly, the culture of origin will suggest the relative importance of approaching the family directly or providing services in modified group contexts by imposition of structure and use of direct leadership style to foster indirect communication. One major difference in the kinds of services for Southeast Asians is the high percentage of persons who were exposed to severe trauma in their countries of origin or during the relocation process.

In Search of an Intervention Lexicon

There have been many surveys of the adjustment status of Southeast Asians in the United States, Canada, and Australia conducted over a 20-year period. These studies provide a basis for characterizing psychopathologies and problems-in-living necessitating interventions for Vietnamese (e.g., Berry & Blondel, 1982; Hinton et al., 1993; Matsuoka, 1993; Meinhardt, Tom, Tse, & Yu, 1985/1986; Tran, 1993), ethnic Cambodians (Boehnlein, 1987; Carlson & Rosser-Hogan, 1993; Meinhardt et al., 1985/1986), Hmong from Laos (Westermeyer, 1986; Westermeyer, Neider, & Callies, 1989), and ethnic Chinese (Hinton et al., 1993; Meinhardt et al., 1985-1986; Yamamoto, Lam, Fung, Tan, & Iga, 1977).

There is no clear intervention lexicon by group or by country of origin. Instead, generic interventions have been used for frequently occurring conditions; these include trauma-induced symptomatology occurring immediately or later in the resettlement process, depression, and somatization in response to problems-in-living, including psychosocial disorders due to stressors during acculturation at any time during resettlement. These conditions differ in their severity and reliability of diagnostic labeling. Interventions will be described for all conditions rather than separately by condition because reduction of immediate suffering due to symptomatology and maintenance of psychosocial functioning in the community are the goals.

Trauma-induced symptomatology, particularly as a consequence of torture, has been estimated to affect between 20% and 30% of refugees may require a multidisciplinary approach (Bojholm & Vesti, 1992). Counseling and therapy is complex and extraordinarily difficult; few specialty texts are available (see Basoglu, 1992; Benjamin & Morgan, 1989; Owan, 1985a; van der Veer, 1992). Moreover, there are many therapeutic impasses or treatment traps that require understanding of dynamics for thoughtful decision making, particularly for inexperienced therapists (Chu, 1988). These traps stem from the intensity of the therapeutic relationship and issues of trust. Resistances occur in the form of memory difficulties and reluctance to deal with abusive events. An adequate clinical response requires interventions to be supplemented by research, practice, and education (Pope & Garcia-Peltoniemi, 1991).

PTSD is an anxiety disorder with an array of symptoms produced by unusually stressful psychosocial events that induced terror and helplessness. The *DSM-IV* diagnostic criteria include the event, disorganized/agitated behavior, persistent reexperience of this event, either an avoidance of trauma-associated stimuli or a generalized numbing of responsiveness, and persistent symptoms of increased arousal (American Psychiatric Association, 1994, pp. 424-429). These symptoms include sleep difficulties, irritability or anger outbursts, concentration difficulties, hypervigilance, startle response, and physiological reactivity to trauma-associated events. Traumatic events will produce some symptoms in most persons with increases in the intensity, severity, and number of symptoms as the trauma becomes more severe or prolonged. A diagnosis of PTSD is made on the basis of symptomatology occurring within three months following the trauma. Recovery occurs for some persons whereas others develop chronic or delayed onset PTSD. Often, PTSD is presented with other disorders, notably depression, in Southeast Asians.

Studies of PTSD in traumatized groups of World War II prisoners of war (POWs), Vietnam veterans, Israeli Lebanon War veterans, rape victims, and California school children on a playground during a sniper attack, have been compared and reviewed (McNally, 1992). These studies suggest an immediate effect on high percentages of victims (i.e., 39% combat veterans, 67% POWs, 77% children, 95% rape victims), prolonged effects from 6 to 14 months on approximately two thirds of victims, and effects after as many as 40 years on appreciable percentages of POWs (20% to 32%) and Vietnam combat veterans (2.2% to 17.5%). These figures suggest that PTSD is an anticipated aftermath of trauma for many but not all survivors.

High PTSD rates have been reported among all Southeast Asian refugee groups in specialty clinics at St. Elizabeth's Hospital (Boston) and the Oregon Health Sciences University (Portland) (Kinzie et al., 1990; Mollica, Wyshak, & Lavelle, 1987) with different rates for various subgroups, including Mien (93%), Cambodians (92%), Laotians (68%), and Vietnamese (54%). These subgroup rates are consistent with studies in other geographical locations (e.g., Chung & Kagawa-Singer, 1993). Moreover, the psychological effects of premigration trauma and refugee camp experiences are known to persist for 5 years or more.

For example, treatment of Mien with PTSD and major depressive disorder has separate group socialization processes for men and women every 2 weeks with individual sessions every 6 to 8 weeks and an available Mien telephone counselor. A psychiatrist coordinates all medical care and shares group facilitation with Mien and Lao counselors and an occupational therapist.

There is an open agenda and the focus is on validating autonomy using support and education within a context where cultural beliefs are respected and understood.

An Intervention Model for Refugees

A model for intervention practices and services for refugees from Latin America to ameliorate trauma, depression, and somatization, particularly in children and youth is also applicable to Southeast Asians (Table 7.1). Gonsalves (1992) described five stages of acculturation with stage-appropriate refugee tasks, professional roles, and treatment issues.

Immediately after arrival (Stage 1), refugees have to learn a new milieu, meet other refugees, and maintain involvement with their homeland. Culture brokers are tour guides, teachers, and resource specialists who can help alleviate disorientation, sadness, anxiety, and guilt. A destabilization period (Stage 2) may last from 6 months to several years during which survival tools of language, customs, and flexible gender roles are acquired and a support group developed. Teachers and therapists can help with stressors and crises that involve self-doubt, vulnerability to past memories, nostalgia, loneliness, denial, hostility, or resistance. Culture-bound disorders may occur during this stage, as well as physical symptoms, and providers should be alert for PTSD.

Stage 3, exploration and restabilization, generally develops 3 to 5 years after migration. Different cultural learning strategies applied in work and social settings are subsequently integrated into family customs and self-concept. Feelings of isolation can occur as the refugee community is replaced by a more integrated residential neighborhood and conflicts with nonrefugees may surface. In addition, marital conflicts due to role change and child-rearing issues require therapist and culture broker roles as sources of cultural information on values, norms, and behavioral cues.

Stage 4 is a return to normalcy, with retention of some original cultural values and practices in a context of understanding the values of the host society. Family transitions of adolescence or intergenerational conflict can invoke feelings of loss and delayed grief reactions, and depression or anger, violence, and guilt. Family intervention strategies may have to be combined with individual psychotherapy for unresolved earlier issues or personality changes resulting from acculturation.

Stage 5, decompensation, always occurs to some limited extent, but a small number of persons are overwhelmed by reality demands and become unable to cope. Personal adaptation failures, family disintegration, isolation, and identity or existential crises may contribute to major depression, psychotic

Table 7.1 Resettlement: Stages, Provider Roles, Client Tasks, Treatment Foci

Stage	Role	Tasks	Treatment Foci
Arrival	Teacher/broker	Orientation/ involvement	Confusion/anger/guilt/ sadness
Destabilization	Teacher/therapist	Survival tools	Resistance/denial/ hostility
Restabilization	Therapist/broker	Flexibility/ development	Fears
Normalcy	Therapist	Flexibility	Rigidity
Decompensation	Crisis	Connectivity	Pathology

SOURCE: Gonsalves (1992, p. 385, Table 1).

delusions, suicide attempts, or drug/alcohol abuse. Emergency rooms or crisis centers have a major intervention role.

An array of services is desirable and necessary to cope with presenting problems and the cultural and personal constraints to intervention services. Specialized services are required for victims of torture, trauma, multiple losses, and accumulated grief. Mental health education and cultural systems information guides are needed to help make sense of a new environment with a new language and a flexible social etiquette. All conventional therapies including individual, family, group, and cognitive-behavioral require adaptation for each particular group. These adaptations have to acknowledge culture-specific alterations in the service delivery style, contents of communication, and limitations in language skills of both providers and clients. Whenever feasible, a blend of indigenous and Western services is desirable as well as recognition that indigenous services are likely to be used simultaneously, with or without the awareness of professional service providers.

Finally, a community model for primary prevention needs to be developed and used. One model focuses personal, social support, and institutional units on the individual (Owan, 1985b). The personal unit includes the family, extended family, and friendship networks. The social support unit includes fraternal organizations, neighborhoods, and mutual assistance/self-help groups. The institutional unit contains health and mental health settings, voluntary agencies, schools, and churches. A community model recognizes the central importance of the family in all programs and activities but also provides a catalyst for community resources to empower individuals, groups, and institutions to develop their own "culturally syntonic coping skills" (Owan, 1985b, p. 150).

8

Hispanic Americans/Latinos

Hispanic Americans are a diverse and heterogeneous population of over 22 million persons, with 13.5 million Mexican Americans (62%), 2.7 million Puerto Ricans (13%; with an additional 3.3 million in Puerto Rico), and more than 1 million Cubans (5%) (U.S. Bureau of the Census, 1990a). In addition to these three major groups, there are 5 million other Hispanics (12%) from 16 Spanish-speaking countries of Latin America and elsewhere, including Spain (8%). This Spanish-origin population is expected to increase to over 35 million by the year 2000 (Casas & Vasquez, 1996) and comprise 15% of the total population, or 47 million people, by 2020 (Davis, Haub, & Willette, 1988).

Mexican Americans have settled primarily in California, Texas, Arizona, New Mexico, and Colorado. Puerto Ricans are concentrated in New York, New Jersey, Connecticut, Pennsylvania, and Chicago. Nearly half a million Cuban Americans are clustered in Miami, others live predominantly in major cities, and there has been a resettlement network in the New York area since the 1930s (Bach, 1985). Many Central and South American families have settled in Florida, Texas, and New York, although there has been some scattering across the United States. Some of these persons with origins in Spain or Mexico have histories of family residence in California and New Mexico for several hundred years.

Within this population, there are two large groups with special vulnerability to problems of acculturation and/or histories of trauma who may have recourse to interventions that are traditional, culture-specific and/or tailored combinations of culture-general and culture-specific interventions to mitigate acute distress. Refugees seeking political asylum and 6 to 10 million undocumented aliens from Mexico and elsewhere in Central and South America have entered the United States primarily for economic reasons. Nearly 2 million of these immigrants and refugees have come from El Salvador, Nicaragua, Columbia, Guatemala, Ecuador, Honduras, and the Dominican Republic; nearly three quarters of a million are from Cuba and well over 4 million from Mexico (Usdansky, 1993).

The term *Hispanic* has origins as a census descriptor of populations with origins in the Western hemisphere, whereas *Latino* is a self-referent used to express a sense of pan-Hispanic solidarity regardless of ethnicity or national borders (Gutierrez, 1995, p. 217). Latino panethnicity is part of a constellation of multiple identifications that are managed very differently by individuals as primary or secondary self-identifications (Jones-Correa & Leal, 1996). Identification of Hispanics on the basis of surname alone is faulty for over 6% when compared with self-reported Hispanic ethnicity (Winkleby & Rockhill, 1992). This chapter will use the term *Hispanic American* for the most part, although recognizing that *Latino* is often the preferred term and that individuals from particular subgroups may prefer the subgroup label, that is, *Mexican American* or *Chicano.*

A majority of Hispanic Americans from Latin America have Indian genetic origins, African genetic origins, or both, as well as European ancestry (Deloria, 1992). The mixture of racial origins and traditions varies in different geographical locations, but there is always a consistency that includes values, beliefs, perceptions, religion (85% are nominally Roman Catholic), the Spanish language, some presence of folk beliefs, and a Hispanic/Latino group cultural identity (Santiago, 1993). In addition to the Spanish language, common threads of this pan-Hispanic or Latino identity include familism and an accepted social etiquette in human relationships that directly shapes expectations for the behaviors and intervention choices of service providers.

Cultural identity is the predominant identification among Hispanics in contrast to the priority of racial identification in the United States for all persons of color. For example, in racially heterogeneous Puerto Rico, individuals consider themselves Puerto Ricans first, then as part of a continuum of "rainbow people" reflected in Spanish as *blancos* (white), *indios* (dark skin/straight hair Asian), *morenos,* (dark skin with Negroid or Caucasian features), *trigenos* (brunette), and *negros* (black) (Rodriguez, 1989). When they come to the United States, many trigenos and morenos are considered to be black and treated accordingly even though this perception by others is discordant with their own self-perceptions. For example, Rodriquez reports an unpublished study in which college students' self-perceptions of 60% tan, 33% white, and 7% black were in contrast to their reports that others perceived them as 42% black and 58% white. Furthermore, the 1980 census figures found that 48% of New York Puerto Ricans and 40% of Hispanics nationally described themselves as neither black nor white but as "other" with a written Spanish descriptor (U.S. Bureau of the Census, 1984).

Cultural identity is preserved and strengthened by use of the Spanish language, which has continued in the United States in spite of strong opposition to bilingualism (Padilla et al., 1991). Estimates provided at different points in time suggest that 90% speak fluent Spanish (Acosta-Belen, 1988), Spanish is the first language for 70% of all Hispanics, and 50% speak Spanish in the their homes (Bean & Tienda, 1987; Padilla & Ruiz, 1976). Among Puerto Ricans, 91% speak Spanish at home and 70% speak English fluently (Rodriguez, 1989). A recent survey indicated that only a small number of Mexican Americans (8%) were equally comfortable in Spanish or English, with approximately an even split between preferences for an interview in Spanish (45%) or English (48%) (Golding & Aneshensel, 1989; Golding & Burnam, 1990). Many bilingual-bicultural persons have strong preferences regarding which language—Spanish or English—should be used in mental health settings. For quality care, it is imperative to honor these preferences because services in a second language can disguise or exacerbate psychopathology and influence any self-presentation by alterations in motor activity, speech, affect, and general attitude (Marcos, 1994).

This chapter will describe traditional health/illness beliefs and interventions available in countries of origin. Symptoms, psychopathologies, problem-in-living, and culture-bound disorders occurring with high frequencies will be described as a basis for inclusion of relevant interventions. Selected culture-general, combined, and culture-specific interventions for Hispanics in the United States will be presented with criteria for their use. Interventions for the three major Hispanic American subgroups will not be described in separate sections, but all content will clearly indicate the applicable subgroup(s). Furthermore, unless specified, an intervention that is appropriate for Mexican Americans, for example, should not be generalized to apply to Cuban Americans without documentation of effectiveness.

Health/Illness Beliefs

In essence, good mental health for Hispanics is believed to rest on a balance with God and harmony with the family, other persons, and church customs (Weclew, 1975). This assertion is complicated, however, by the presence of folk beliefs in the illness conceptualizations of many persons. For example, Mexican Americans distinguish between serious mental health conditions and minor emotional problems (Newton, 1978). A serious condition results in inability to cope with everyday life situations, loss of self-control (in the absence of talking about problems) or reality contact, and requires help, initially from a relative or friend. Serious conditions are considered to be mental disorders *(enfermidad mentale)* and require help from a mental health specialist or folk healer *(curandero),* especially for a nervous crisis *(crisis nervosa, ataque de nervios).* The most serious condition, being insane *(loco),* is believed to be only partially curable by hospitalization, other interventions, or both. A minor problem is evidenced by disturbed feelings in one area, although self-control and family responsibilities are retained. Inner strength (i.e., toughness, determination, will power) permits problem confrontation and resistance to stress—*(aguantarse)* accepting fate with resignation *(resignarse),* and overcoming adverse circumstances *(sobreponerse).* By contrast, weakness of character limits favorable prognosis by interfering with self-control, responsibility, and reliance on pride *(orgullo)* or shame *(verguenza)* in solving personal problems.

Puerto Ricans share a similar belief that mental illness is caused by individual vulnerability to negative, external influences. Illnesses are also considered to be serious or minor. Sickness from nerves is not necessarily equated with mental disorder and together with sleep disturbances is the most frequent form of distress in Puerto Rico, often adding a dimension of anxiety *(ansiedad),* agitation *(agitamiento),* and restlessness *(desasociego)* to many psychiatric disorders, especially anxiety reactions (Koss-Chioino, 1989). Feelings and emotions are considered to be embedded in personal experience and "nervousness" or "nerves" have become a general label for disordered emotions and emotional disorders.

There is general belief that the physical-physiological body constitutes an envelope for the spirit being cycled through reincarnations. A spiritual body *(perispiritu)* forms an invisible link between the corporeal and incorporeal bodies. External sources, including invasive spirits and discomfort from others' enmity, are often credited with causing distress and bizarre behaviors. Under these circumstances, restoration to good mental health or tranquillity is frequently accomplished using folk-healing practices by spiritists. Spiritists seek to help restore harmony with the spirit world by imaging the spiritual body during sleep and attempting to remove spirit influences affecting the physical body. These practices are often mandatory with traditional persons for culture-specific disorders. Mental health workers, including psychiatrists and psychotherapists within a parallel system, deal with *DSM* psychopathology, particularly as expressed by somatization, bizarre behaviors, and anxiety symptoms using a variety of family, group, behavioral-cognitive, and medication interventions.

Cuban Americans experienced a politically linked immigration of the aristocracy and nouveau riche in the first two waves (1959–1965 and 1965–1973) and these persons received massive assistance in relocation (Bernal & Gutierrez, 1988). The entire Cuban population was not represented in race, occupation, or education until after the early 1980s and these more representative persons made up only about 15% of the Cuban population in the United States. As a consequence of this history, a survey in New York reported by Bernal and Gutierrez indicated some willingness to consult professionals in private practice (with preference for psychiatrists or medical referral) for mental health problems, although there was doubt expressed concerning the likelihood that crazy people could recover. In Miami, which has a developed system of clinics, more acculturated young persons, especially women, were willing to seek psychotherapy.

Santeria, an Afro-Cuban worldview and set of rituals, provides a belief system in which disease is caused by object intrusion as a result of magic, loss of one's soul, spirit intrusion, and the anger of gods who rule over specific parts of the body (Sandoval, 1977). Plants, herbs, and weeds are used by folk healers *(santeros)* because of their curative properties. Santeria has been used to cope with acculturation stressors by the formerly lower-middle- and lower-class Cubans who had become socially mobile and middle-class oriented in the United States. Santeria has retained popularity in the United States because it represents a flexible, adaptive religion with a *santero* providing emotional support, an acceptable cult socialization experience, and care for the soul by brokerage with supernatural powers.

Interventions in
Selected Countries of Origin

Major political, economic, and social changes in Spain occurred as a result of the post-Franco socialist government. These changes included developing ties with the European community (Dowell, Poveda-de-Augustin, & Lowenthal, 1987; Poveda, Garcia, Palomo, & Octavio, 1987), recognizing 17 self-governing regions containing historic nationalities, and the General Health Act of 1986, which inaugurated the Spanish National Health System (Duran & Blanes, 1991). A shift occurred in mental health practices from biomedical approaches and custodial care in hospitals toward a comprehensive network of mental health centers, including psychiatric units in general hospitals in addition to prevention and outpatient care by teams in mental health centers. The role of the family physician in providing care to patients in their homes remained central because a new pattern of medical specialization resulted in family and community medicine practitioners becoming the most frequent specialization. Almost all psychiatrically ill persons now receive antipsychotic medications and live in the community with their families who participate in psychoeducational programs (Canive et al., 1993).

A national population of approximately 40 million supports a Spanish equivalent of the American Psychological Association with over 55,000 members. Their psychologist practitioners are relatively young and two thirds are women. Educational and clinical psychology specializations account for two thirds of all psychologists with fewer in industrial/organizational (15%) and community/social services (9%) (Prieto, 1994). Self-employed professionals are most frequent (37%), followed by agency personnel (33%) and employees of private firms (21%). An academic cadre of nearly 1,000 psychologists provides training.

In Mexico, by contrast, there has been a blend of specialized modern psychiatry and innovative community self-management programs with folk medicine provided by *chamancas,* community leaders who serve as advisers, defenders, and guardians of tradition and ritual (Lartigue & Vivas, 1991) in addition to "herbalists, homeopaths, *curanderos, cuajos* (women specializing in children's diseases), bone setters, shamans, spiritists,and spiritualists" (Spires-Robin & McGarrahan, 1995, p. 121). Folk healers and physicians, however, represent different systems of medicine and have little cooperative contact. Both systems perdure because there are still approximately 10 million indigenous persons (or one ninth of the population) in 56 ethnic and linguistic groups. Some of these groups still live in isolation and have retained their religious worldviews relatively intact (Resnikoff, Pustilaik, & Resnikoff, 1991). These groups endured conquest, slavery, forced conversion to Christianity, and the ravages of new diseases to become the major combatants in the 1910 revolution.

Mental hospitals have existed since 1566, but these facilities were meager and provided only custodial care until the 1984 Health Protection Law funded pharmacological interventions supplemented by behavioral, occupational, and recreational therapies (Lartigue & Vivas, 1991). This law led to development of a national health care system and opportunities for inpatient and outpatient mental health services, particularly in Mexico City, the largest city in the world, with over 21 million inhabitants. In addition, the Mexican Institute of Social Security provided preventive services, primary psychiatric treatment by physicians, and a referral network. Some aftercare services are now available, especially for children, in about one third of the 351 community mental health centers and these facilities usually have clinical psychology departments. Most services, however, are still provided by physicians and the numbers of psychiatrists, psychoanalysts, and other mental health professionals remains insufficient to meet patient needs. To meet mental health personnel needs, a new specialty of mental health rehabilitation clinician has been developed to provide "socialization and therapeutic occupation" for chronic patients (Resnikoff et al., 1991, p. 198). It should also be noted that these authors report prevalence rates for neurosis were more than 13 times higher than psychosis or alcoholism in 1971, although these statistics do not take into account the population diversity.

Puerto Rico's legacy of colonialism fostered two parallel systems of mental health resources—major programs developed in the United States and the practice of *mesa blanca* by spiritists *(espiritistas)* (Koss-Chioino, 1989). Puerto Rico was divided into catchment areas following the Community Mental Health Act in 1963 and service centers began outreach programs in local communities. Folk healing by spiritists was imported from France before 1850. The Puerto Rican ethos of sociality, hospitality, and receptivity to expressed feelings persuaded existing folk healers *(curanderos)* to become spiritists. In spite of denigration by the Church, folk healers are typically consulted first, especially in crisis, and there is often simultaneous use of both systems. Estimates that 36% to 60% of all Puerto Ricans have consulted spiritists are contrasted with only 18% in one representative sample, although respondents could choose not to answer the item, and other persons had seen *santeros* (Hohmann et al., 1990). Koss-Chioino pioneered a therapist/spiritist project that began in the late 1970s to develop an infrastructure between these two systems, provide training to both cadres of healers, and create a new psychotherapeutic approach based on synthesis, and contribute data on how psychopathology is expressed in Puerto Rico.

Mental health services in Cuba prior to 1959 were equated with treatment of crazy persons and there was strong stigma preventing people from seeking psychological interventions (Bernal & Gutierrez, 1988). Only a few clinical psychologists, primarily trained in the United States, were available. Hospital care for chronic mental patients was custodial under psychiatric aegis. Santeria provided a religious folk/mental health care system for the majority of the population (Sandoval, 1979). Among the immigrants to the United States were many Cuban health professionals who revalidated their licenses and their services became available to subsequent immigrants, particularly third-wave Marial Cubans (Portes, Kyle, & Eaton, 1992). Although Cuban mental health services have altered to encompass health psychology and preventive services since the early waves of immigration, these changes are not relevant for Cuban Americans whose beliefs and expectations came with them to the United States.

Services in Latin American countries have generally been premised on long familiarity with mental health resources in Europe and more recently in the United States and available primarily for middle-class, educated persons during periods of economic stability. In countries such as Argentina and Chile, prior to their military dictatorships, there was a strong psychoanalytic and psychiatric presence. In addition, indigenous healers have been active in many countries where there are large populations with local Indian or African origins.

In Nicaragua, Guatemala, and El Salvador, the aftermath of war and political terrorism has stimulated a variety of therapeutic approaches including art, massage, play, and movement within community-organized networks. In Nicaragua, there has been international cooperation on mental health problems since the 1979 revolution with an infusion of international cooperation and personnel to develop a psychoanalytic intervention model and community resources (Maldonado-Martinez, 1990; Saraceno, Briceno, Asioli, & Liberati, 1990). Predominant diagnoses were depressive and anxiety neuroses followed by schizophrenia, with nearly one half of outpatients reporting family problems (Penayo, 1989). Fifteen community-based mental health centers have replaced mental hospitals (Kraudy, Liberati, Asioli, & Saraceno, 1987). There are distinct differences among six major ethnic groups in their presenting problems. Modern interventions are preferred by upper-class urban residents whereas poor, less educated, and rural residents in three ethnic groups prefer traditional healing (Barrett, 1993).

In El Salvador, the prolonged war normalized dehumanized social relationships resulting in widespread somatization and changes in mental functioning and personality (Martin-Baro, 1989). PTSD is common and a community treatment program has been designed to reassure victims that they remain the same person in spite of trauma. Anxiety, survivor guilt, feelings of helplessness, and losses of control are reduced by relating symptoms to traumatic events (Bowen, Carscadden, Beighle, & Fleming, 1992).

Symptoms, Psychopathologies, Problems-in-Living, and Culture-Bound Disorders

Hispanic subgroup histories in the United States, their mental health problems, problems-in-living, and culture-specific disorders are diverse. Three major studies of psychopathology during the late 1970s and 1980s, the National Institute of Mental Health Epidemiologic Catchment Area Program

(NIMH-ECA), the Hispanic Health and Nutrition Examination H-HANES), and a Puerto Rican survey conducted by Canino et al. in 1987 have been reviewed (Escobar, 1993). The NIMH-ECA study used two sets of interview data from the same informants. Prevalence rates of existing symptoms were followed one year later by incidence data for new symptoms collected at five sites nationally, including Los Angeles, where 43% of all respondents were Hispanics, predominantly Mexican Americans. Their rates for schizophrenia were generally low, with males reporting more alcohol abuse, less drug abuse, and depression whereas women reported more phobias and dysthymia and less drug and alcohol abuse than non-Hispanics. Mexican Americans born in Mexico had consistently lower prevalence rates for symptoms than those born in the United States. The H-HANES national survey included multistage, stratified samples of Puerto Ricans and Cuban Americans as well as Mexican Americans for several geographic areas. The Puerto Rican samples included more poor, unemployed, and unmarried persons, and also reported prevalence rates for major depressive disorders and depressive symptoms that were twice the magnitude of the other Hispanic groups. In the survey conducted in Puerto Rico, there were no differences from mainland Puerto Ricans, although rates were higher among uneducated persons and women presented more affective and anxiety disorders.

In an earlier review of Mexican American schizophrenia incidence and prevalence studies, Cuéllar (1982) suggested that behavioral deterioration and regression were often characteristic of schizophrenia in this population. He documented the influence of sociocultural factors during seven stages of the diagnostic process as contributing to pervasive and cumulative unreliability in diagnosing schizophrenia and other disorders among Mexican Americans. As a consequence, frequent misdiagnosis of schizophrenia was found to occur as well as confounding schizophrenia with culture-bound disorders. Depression also had a prevalence rate among Hispanics comparable to that of other groups when socioeconomic factors in earlier studies were taken into account (Cuéllar & Roberts, 1984; Roberts, 1980). Many Hispanics also sought medical assistance for psychological problems presenting with physical symptoms and somatic complaints. A review of *DSM* and somatization among Hispanic psychiatric patients found much higher rates using diagnostic rating scales, which could not be verified by the criteria for somatoform disorders (Escobar, 1987). Escobar suggested that the *DSM* systems "tend to minimize cross-cultural differences in symptomatology and yield rather concordant syndromes sharing essential core symptoms stripped of their cultural character" (p. 178). Reported prevalence rates can be misleading because of dependence on the screening measure used, although the three major studies all used the same interview schedule. Nonetheless, in a review of these methods of epidemiological data collection, López and Núñez (1987) concluded that all of these instruments minimized recognition and inclusion of cultural factors.

Problems-in-Living

Hispanics share all problems-in-living with other groups, but problems of families and youth are often experienced more intensely as a result of acculturation stress, discrimination, alcohol/drug addiction, poverty, inadequate housing, and a high proportion of single-parent families. Palacios and Franco (1986) have described the unique problems of Mexican American women who must reconcile preservation of traditional values/customs with adoption of new values and behaviors from the dominant society. These women are treated not only as subordinate to men but are also victimized by discrimination because of race or ethnicity. Their major problems stem from feelings of failure to meet their gender roles, involving culture-specific standards as wives and mothers with subsequent anger and depression. Moreover, as psychiatric hospital patients, women expose not only family conflict, impaired interpersonal relations, and low stress tolerance, but also an absence of work and problem-solving skills.

In comparison with Anglos, alcohol consumption is heavier among Hispanic men who drink, with 43% reporting alcohol problems nationally whereas women have higher abstinence rates (Lex, 1987). Among Hispanics, depression accompanying alcohol abuse is twice as frequent among women, single men, and those with low incomes, although drinking occurs with much greater frequency in younger males and those with higher incomes (Caetano, 1987). Alcohol-related problems include higher rates of driving infractions and public drunkenness than the general population. There are also differences in drinking patterns by country of origin. For example, Puerto Rico has a lifetime prevalence rate of 12.6% for alcohol abuse-dependence determined from a structured diagnostic interview with a 12:1 preponderance of abuse for males when compared with women (Canino et al., 1987). For marginal men especially, machismo has been distorted to "symbolize masculine entitlement, sexual potency, and toughness, which includes the right to drink, especially as a reward for earning a living in a milieu that offers only limited economic opportunities" (Lex, 1987, p. 297).

Acculturative Stress

Acculturative stressors for first-generation immigrants and refugees vary somewhat by country of origin but stem from adaptation to new rules and expected behaviors. Poverty, discrimination, and learning English as a second language are accompanied by having to cope with losing a familiar way of life. Hispanic immigrants share language difficulties, acceptance of skin color differences, and strong social and family ties, and they may be illegal immigrants or victims of war and oppression (Smart & Smart, 1995). These authors describe acculturative stress effects on physical health, decision making, and occupational functioning in a context of role entrapment and status leveling. *Role entrapment* results from stereotypes that stigmatize their language ability, skin color, speech, and educational level in a way that damages expectations for a good life in the United States. *Status leveling* reduces all newcomers to the lowest common denominator regardless of individual differences. An absence of role models and minimal rewards for English proficiency contribute to strained or ineffective relationships with potential providers.

Discrimination is often encountered by Hispanics because their unique ethnicity is often ignored and they are perceived in racial terms as black, white, or Indian. Intergenerational problems are especially severe among immigrant families in which the children acculturate more rapidly than their parents and conflict with parental authority results. Traditional families of low acculturation to mainstream society in Miami experience stress as a result of prejudice and their minority status in a closed society. Among families with children born in the United States, this stress leads to behavior problems reported by teachers and children (Vega, Khoury, Zimmerman, Gil, & Warheit, 1995). Among immigrant families, however, it is the children with language problems who have more difficulty socializing and report more behavior problems. This study suggested that acculturative family stress is first apparent in child behavior problems due to learning a second language, but subsequent intergenerational family conflicts produce child behavior problems resulting from discrimination and perception of diminished opportunity coupled with expectations for success.

Women present with acculturation issues related to gender roles, language, loss, and grief (Espin, 1987). Sex role problems occur because traditional roles conflict with the greater role flexibility in mainstream society. Social and emotional problems among Head Start children were evidenced in school by playing alone, quarreling, teasing, and attacking peers, whereas mothers reported displays of temperament (Grossman & Shigaki, 1994). For boys, solitary play was the major risk factor; for girls, temper outbursts was the major risk factor. Hispanic youths are frequently gang members who adopt divergent versions of traditional values from both cultures and experience marginal cultural orientation. These youths are from families unable to inculcate the values of familism and isolated from the culturally nourishing contexts of school, church, and community. Often abused and witness to the battering of mothers and sisters by aggressive, intimidating males, they model alcohol/drug use and a tough, violent street persona (Belitz & Valdez, 1984). The gang becomes a surrogate family, with older gang members as the models for a socialization process that has now existed for three to four generations.

Culture-Bound Disorders

The cultural character of symptoms has been examined using idiomatic expressions of anger among Puerto Ricans (Malgady, Rogler, & Cortes, 1996; Rogler, Cortes, & Malgady, 1994). This research began by having neighborhood residents identify idioms of distress that were subsequently incorporated into an Anger Idioms Scale. Comparisons were then made between community mental health center clients diagnosed primarily as having affective disorders and a comparable nonclinical sample. The interviews with both groups of paid participants were conducted in Spanish by trained bilingual professionals using the Anger Idiom Scale and standard measures of depression and trait anxiety translated and adapted for Puerto Ricans. The results transformed *DSM* symptoms into anger idioms and factors for aggressive, assertive, and vindictive anger idioms were identified. This emic research permits symptoms to be classified into syndromes on the basis of their cultural origins and provides one alternative to *DSM* diagnostic categories that can be directly related to subsequent culture-specific interventions.

A second approach used historically identified culture-bound disorders, some of which are now contained in the *DSM-IV* glossary (American Psychiatric Association, 1994). Because many Hispanics in the United States have roots among various Indian tribes in the Americas, African slaves, and Spanish soldiers or clergy, they share a wide range of symptomatology with other groups. They experience "fright disorders" with soul loss such as *susto* (also known as *espanto, tripe ida, perdida la alma*), which may result in death when untreated. *Susto* usually stems from a specific fear or event. Feelings of sadness, depression, and low self-worth occur with effects on sleep, appetite, and family relations, in a context of a variety of somatic symptoms (Hughes & Wintrob, 1995). In the 1970s, there was an abiding belief in the services of *curandismo* for these conditions by almost all families that has diminished over time. A more recent study found 43.4% of families among carefully sampled Colorado women had undergone treatment by a *curandero* for a variety of conditions including 8.7% *susto* and 23.2% *empacho* (i.e., food sticking to the stomach lining) (Rivera, 1988).

Nervios refers to a vulnerability to stress in everyday life from family disruptions or economic difficulties as well as a syndrome resulting from chronic distress. *Nervios* is a socially acceptable response to high levels of stress; it includes a wide range of somatic symptoms and varies in degree of disability from mild to extreme. Comparisons of symptoms, cause, and meaning have been made between urban and rural Costa Rica, Guatemala, and Eastern Kentucky Appalachia coal miners, Newfoundland women, and for Puerto Ricans in New York City (Low, 1985). *Ataques de nervios,* a panic attack version of *nervios,* usually occurs in women with a sudden onset, often in reaction to family stress, illness, accident, or death (Oquendo, Horwath, & Martinez, 1992). There is an experienced loss of emotional and physical control with intense bodily sensations and alterations in consciousness that may include dizziness, fainting, hallucinations, and amnesia, although rapid restoration of functioning is typical (Guarnaccia, Rivera, Franco, & Neighbors, 1996).

Acculturation and Psychopathology

Over 50% of the Hispanic population in the United States is composed of immigrants (Suazo, 1990). For Mexican Americans, a large research literature was reviewed for a multivariate stress model of interactive components that functioned over time (Cervantes & Castro, 1985). This model permitted following a stressful event through mediation and coping. Acculturative stress for Hispanics is lifelong, pervasive, and intense, involving loss of social support, self-esteem, and identity, all of which are unique components of Hispanic acculturation (Smart & Smart, 1995).

In examining psychopathology prevalence and incidence rates for Hispanic Americans, it is necessary to control for acculturation. For example, with increasing acculturation, Mexican American women present more depression and anxiety (Burham, Hough, Karno, Escobar, & Telles, 1987). Moreover, although Colombian patients presented core depression symptoms similar to those presented in the United States on two depression measures, somatization symptoms were more prevalent among these patients (Escobar, Gomez, & Tuason, 1983). In research studies, it has not proven feasible to control for errors in psychiatric diagnoses due to marginal *DSM* reliabilities for many conditions and the lack of culturally competent diagnostic skills among many clinicians. The process of acculturation for immigrants is accompanied by stressors in the form of life events and ongoing strains that may differ in kind and intensity from those encountered by subsequent generations in the United States (Cervantes & Castro, 1985;

Golding, Potts, & Aneshensel, 1991). As suggested earlier, a major source of stress results from being perceived and identified by others in racial terms, as either white or black, rather than having cultural identity acknowledged and being accepted as Hispanic or Latino.

For Mexicans and Mexican Americans in Los Angeles, a traditional cultural orientation, or low acculturation, has been related to lower prevalence rates for eight surveyed disorders (Burham et al., 1987). Explanations for this finding include a possible selective migration of more robust persons who experience a lower sense of deprivation because of comparison with life in Mexico. Mexicans of low and high acculturation did not differ appreciably in prevalence rates except for more frequent problems with alcohol and drug abuse among more highly acculturated persons. Mexican Americans born in the United States had higher rates of alcohol and drug abuse, depression, phobias, and antisocial personality with increasing acculturation. Puerto Ricans and Mexicans of all socioeconomic levels living in Puerto Rico or Mexico City have reported higher symptom scores on a screening scale (Langer, 1962) than those living in New York City (Haberman, 1976). These differences may represent culturally acceptable but different modes of symptom expression and less inhibition in reporting symptomatology because the symptoms are not perceived as necessarily socially undesirable.

Although some authors find acculturation and distress or disorder to be positively related, the relationship of acculturative stress to adjustment is both complex and controversial (Betancourt & López, 1993; Rogler, Cortes, & Malgady, 1991). A meta-analytic study of 49 reports, 111 samples, and 11 adjustment contexts suggested that intelligence, field independence, and anxiety were related to acculturation (Moyerman & Forman, 1992). Lower socioeconomic status (SES) persons in all 11 contexts had the greatest increases in symptomatology and conflict (i.e., addictions, career conflict, anxiety). This finding is supported by data for acculturated, higher-income Mexican Americans (i.e., bicultural and assimilated cultural orientations) indicating more efficient coping styles for dealing with stressors as a result of their more effective use of support networks (Griffith & Villavicencio, 1985).

Culture-General Interventions

The available public mental health resources are neither readily accessible nor credible for many Hispanics. As a result, Hispanics as a group have underused services because the mental health system in the United States was not designed to care for many of these persons because of different health/illness beliefs, previous inexperience with sophisticated mental health services, or special problems among refugees and immigrants resulting from trauma and acculturation stressors (DeAngelis, 1995). In spite of detailed agendas for mental health research and services primarily by Hispanic social scientists (e.g., Marín & Marín, 1991; Ponterotto & Casas, 1991; Rogler et al., 1983; Rogler, Malgady, & Rodriguez, 1989), underuse still exists except in mental health settings where clients and providers can be matched for ethnicity, first language, or both (Takeuchi, Sue, & Yeh, 1995).

Psychoanalysis, components of psychoanalytic method, and derivative insight-oriented therapies have been used with Hispanics (e.g., Bluestone & Vela, 1982; Maduro, 1982; Maduro & Martinez, 1974; Rendon, 1993). Bluestone and Vela used insight-oriented therapy with selected lower-class, well-motivated Puerto Ricans in New York City whose lives were free from external chaos and who were capable of insight. These patients were informed that psychological problems required more time to treat than medical problems and urged to be on time for appointments. Modifications included a more authoritative stance, discouragement of passive dependency, attention to aggressive feelings coupled with fear of consequence for their overt expression, and the use of humor, proverbs, and metaphors. These modifications, however, are sufficient to consider this study an example of a combined intervention and it is important to consider the guidelines (see Table 8.1) in differentiating between culture-general and combined-intervention approaches. Although dynamic interventions may have a limited clientele among lower-class persons, they should be effective with middle-class bicultural clients as culture-general interventions with less modification.

Behavioral approaches have enjoyed popularity in Spain and Latin America. These approaches share a problem orientation; specific tasks; and active, directive therapists; and have been adapted and delivered using an acceptable behavioral-emotional style (Juarez, 1985). These techniques can be used to train parents, teachers, and community persons. Behavioral models have been recommended for more widespread application in the United States because they include contractual agreements specifying objectives and methods, permitting client choices consistent with their cultural values (e.g., Boulette, 1976; Casas, 1976; Ruiz & Casas, 1981). Behavioral-cognitive therapy has a history of use for depression in Puerto Rican women (Cómas-Dias, 1981) and children with interpersonal difficulties, and children who believe that they are "bad" because of their behavior problems (Juarez, 1985). Cognitive restructuring and modeling also represent structured problem-focused techniques that may be used with Hispanics.

Cultural considerations, however, should never be ignored in the implementation of any assessment or intervention process. To what extent a cultural context is necessary and how the clinician can provide an acceptable

Table 8.1 Culture-General Intervention Guidelines

Acculturation status
   Acculturated and bicultural clients may benefit, but marginal clients may respond to combined interventions, and traditional clients often require culture-specific interventions.

Service delivery style/social etiquette
   All clients appreciate/respond to high frequencies of affiliative/affectional behaviors *(simpatico)* or respect *(respecto);* personal, informal, individualized attention *(personalismo);* chatting to create warm atmosphere *(platicando).*

Language
   Services should be provided in first language. Bicultural/bilingual clients may or may not prefer services in Spanish; choice should be respected if feasible.

Social class
   All clients show respect for persons in authority/higher socioeconomic positions.

Client-therapist match
   Ethnic match whenever feasible or first language match.

Age/gender
   Respect for older therapists by younger clients. Respect by women for male therapists, although presenting problems of abuse may dictate women therapist.

---

context for intervention are questions to be answered prior to treatment with all multicultural clients. Following a frank discussion of whether cultural issues need to be considered figure or ground during the treatment process, bicultural, bilingual clients, or both may prefer to choose among feasible interventions. Even when the client decision is for a culture-general intervention with English as the designated language, cultural information can often provide a context permitting clients access to procedures. For example, the service delivery style should be perceived by the client as credible, and part of credibility is therapist role flexibility to recognize the client as a person in a life context that many contain many diverse problems requiring attention. The therapist should be able to modify roles of counselor or psychtherapist and become adviser, advocate, or facilitator, as needed. Although many Anglo therapists believe their exclusive role is psychotherapy, an inability to be flexible can conflict with cultural values and minimize their effectiveness. Culture-general interventions are predicated on reasonable clinician certainty that the client's cultural orientation is bicultural or acculturated, but it may not be necessary to administer an acculturation scale routinely for this information before applying culture-general interventions if the necessary information is obtained during an interview.

   As suggested here, guidelines for modifications of mainstream interventions provide some plausible signposts to indicate for whom culture-general interventions may be appropriate (Table 8.1). The therapist should fit the client's expectations whenever feasible, that is, preferably an older Hispanic male of the same subgroup or national origin, with behavioral characteristics associated with expertise including an affiliative (simpatico) service delivery style and Spanish language competence. These expectations, however, will vary somewhat with client acculturation status, social class, first language, expectations for language to be used in therapy, ethnicity of therapist, and flexibility.

Clients are often articulate on what they need from an intervention. Providers who are aware that the broad range of multiple presenting needs for their services is an index of diversity within a cultural group will be able to be more effective. Clients who are refugees or immigrants often require roles of advocacy and knowledge of referral sources in the Hispanic community for support or healing, in addition to roles of counselor or psychotherapist. Cultural competence requires flexibility in selection of potentially helpful roles requiring knowledge of the client's culture, life history, and current life situation, as well as the resources available in the client's cultural community and potential sources of stress in the larger society.

Combined Approaches

Table 3.3 (Chapter 3, this volume) suggests relevant questions that can be helpful in the mutual decision to use a combinatory intervention. In applying combined approaches, Hispanic client preferences are even more critical regarding choice of language because English may be the client's second language and the clinician may or may not be fluent in Spanish. Whenever the clinician is not fluent, the client's facility with English must be sufficient to understand and participate in the selected intervention procedures or referral should be made to a Spanish-speaking clinician for implementation. Unless a language test is used (Yansen & Shulman, 1996), however, it may be difficult to evaluate a client's mastery of English solely on the basis of an interview. Nonetheless, there should be agreement between client and clinician before any treatment is initiated.

Cultural identity information for Mexican American clients that goes well beyond categorization of cultural identity status may be obtained with the Acculturation Rating Scale for Mexican Americans (ARSMA–ARSMA-II) (Cuéllar, Arnold, & Maldonado, 1995), the Cultural Lifestyle Inventory (Mendoza, 1989), or the Multicultural Experience Inventory (Ramirez, 1984). A detailed discussion of acculturation measures for Hispanics is available elsewhere (Dana, 1996b). Acculturation information can provide a basis for examining personal conflicts and reactions to stressors in daily experiences. The information provided by a cultural formulation also contributes to awareness of cultural factors in psychosocial functioning, the client-clinician relationship, and an overall assessment for *DSM-IV* diagnosis and subsequent interventions. A complete *DSM-IV* cultural formulation for *nervios* and *ataques* in a Puerto Rican migrant woman is also available as a guide (Lewis-Fernandez, 1996b).

Family Therapy

Family therapy and group therapy will be used to illustrate how cultural considerations can alter standard treatments. Family therapy models developed in the professional mainstream have been adapted for Puerto Ricans (Canino & Canino, 1982), Mexican Americans (Soto-Fulp & DelCampo, 1994), and Cuban Americans (Szapocznik & Kurtines, 1993) in the United States. These three forms of combined interventions for families represent different degrees of incorporating cultural variables into family therapy. The adaptations provide alterations in service delivery style and technique to accommodate intracultural distinctiveness, differences in presenting problems, and the context of family functioning. In Puerto Rico, Canino and Canino dramatically altered and personalized the service delivery process using bilingual therapists acting as temporary *copadres* (godparents) and surrogates for the extended family. Their goal was to mobilize extended family supports for individuals who experienced poverty, discrimination, and stressful migration effects. There was no designated "patient" and the process was typically brief and focused on problem solving.

For Mexican American families, there has been focus on problems provided by intercultural marriages, intracultural family acculturation differences, and the impact of extended family cohesiveness on severe life crises (Soto-Fulp & DelCampo, 1994). First, as in Puerto Rico, the service delivery style embodied *personalismo* to create bonds of trust, respect, and acceptance of therapists who were self-disclosing, and active with all family members. Second, the process remained similarly directive, structured, and explicit. Third, the goals included fostering clear boundaries among individuals; family groups; and spousal, parental, or sibling dyads. When the marital dyad, for example, is separated from the family system, conflicts could be addressed and reduced without pressure from other family members. This is necessary because familism demands traditional family values and perpetuates a child focus, an intensity of relationship that can conflict with the acculturation process of adolescents toward responsibility, independence, and autonomy. Fourth, the therapists did not have to be of the same ethnicity as their clients, but had to recognize, explore, appreciate, and come to terms with their own ethnicity to be emotionally available to respond to client cultural issues. Cultural differences between therapists and clients can become positive attributes leading to beneficial outcomes for both parties in a therapy transaction.

Szapocmik and Kurtines (1993) examined individual dynamics within the Cuban American family context and family dynamics within a culturally pluralistic environment. Acculturation occurred less rapidly for parents than for their children and adolescents, exacerbating intergenerational discord and leading to conduct problems. The family struggle for family unity and connectedness was countered by adolescent demands for autonomy. As a consequence, the children were deprived of needed emotional support and parents were denied their leadership expectations. Structural family therapy, a mainstream intervention in which families were seen conjointly, was selected as applicable to the value orientations and interpersonal style preferences of these children and adolescents (Szapocznik, Scopetta, Aranalde, & Kurtines, 1978). Before this combined intervention was applied, a values orientation test was developed from the Kluckhohn-Strodtbeck model of value orientations described in Chapter 3 of this volume, that differentiated Cuban American adolescents from their Anglo peers on style of social relations and time. The value characteristics of Cuban adolescents included a relative position within a hierarchy and orientation to the present.

This information modified structural family therapy in several ways. First, this treatment was called "one-person family therapy" because of focus on an adolescent family member, the identified patient (Szapocznik, Kurtines, Foote, Perez-Vidal, & Hervis, 1983). The psychopathology presented by this family member was symptomatic of family dysfunction and the purpose of intervention was not only to reduce this pathology in the designated family member but also to demonstrate change in the entire family. Second, the therapist role was as a responsible authority who employed the existing hierarchical systems within home, school, and probation settings in the therapeutic process. Third, the adolescent's focus on the present was used to create crises and capitalize on them during the treatment process. Fourth, the parents were subsequently taught the skills required to facilitate an adolescent transition to independence, that is, the Anglo style of social relations. When this combined intervention was compared with psychodynamic child therapy (Szapocznik et al., 1989) and conjoint family therapy (Szapocznik, Kurtines, Foote, Perez-Vidal, & Hervis, 1986), the one-person family therapy was comparable in efficacy in reducing symptomatology in the identified patient, but also protected family integrity for at least a year.

Group Therapy

Group therapy has been recommended for Hispanics, but alterations are required for various Hispanic populations because these patients are significantly less productive verbally than Anglos in group sessions (Shen,

Sanchez, & Huang, 1984). McKinley (1987) worked with lower-class Puerto Rican women in New York City and altered both the structure and contents of group therapy to fit her clients' problems-in-living. Carefully selected and prepared groups of 9 or 10 women who entered treatment with pessimism and isolated suffering were gradually enabled to share their problems and recognize individual unmet needs in their submerged selves and, finally, were able to make decisions for changes in their lives.

A brief summary of issues and contents of this group therapy follows. McKinley (1987) extrapolated from Bernstein's (1964) work with the language system of lower socioeconomic groups indicating "their language is characterized by a restricted vocabulary, with relatively few qualifiers, adjectives, and adverbs, particularly those that describe feelings, and a preference for concrete or functional as opposed to abstract thinking" (McKinley, p. 287). Early power and status experiences have limited the opportunities for children to express personal feelings and thoughts, particularly negative emotions, because parents should be honored and physical punishment is invoked for verbal or behavioral infractions. Hispanic patients may enjoy the group process without participation, except in crisis, because therapist power is diluted and the patients stimulate each other by sharing common experiences. Group therapy can also accommodate traditional persons whose time frame is flexible leading to irregular attendance and a gradual process in which other members encourage sustained presence and increasing participation. Erratic attendance is also related to fears that others will flout the rule of confidentiality and gossip *(bochinche).* Because gossip can serve as an expression of culturally repressed aggression and sexuality that patients may be deprived of in daily life, group therapy can address these fears and encourage more self-assertiveness within a context of mutual aid and cooperation. Somatization provides another safe content for shared discussions, but may also evidence emotional distress and social control turning anger and aggression against the self. Group experience can forge links for understanding how emotional and relationship stressors produce symptoms not only of somatization, but of depression, *ataques,* and *nervios* as well. Similarly, concerns about sexuality, particularly in first-generation women, are addressed by permission for discussion to reduce fear and guilt over expression of hidden issues.

A. S. Ruiz (1975), in California, has developed Chicano group catalysts, or techniques to facilitate interaction among groups equal in numbers of men and women high school, college, and Neighborhood Youth Corps students. A bilingual/bicultural counselor conducts groups in which Spanish and English are used interchangeably to deal with "unfinished business," reintegrate denied parts of the self, validate group identity, clarify values, and facilitate self-actualization by providing alternatives to coerced assimilation. *Una palabra* (a word) focuses on students with difficulties speaking Spanish who share negative feelings about themselves as a consequence. Spanish words and phrases are used to stimulate associated feelings, feedback, emotional reactions, and action alternatives. Reclaim your *nombre* (name) and color of skin revive positive and negative experience to increase self-acceptance. Other techniques including "Chicano Handclap," *sonidos* (sounds), and *el grito* (yell) use specific stimuli to focus attention on feelings and nonverbal communication.

Alcohol Treatment

In Mexico, historically, there was limited alcohol use among the Aztecs in religious ceremonies, but their social norms restricted consumption by young males otherwise. The introduction of more relaxed Spanish norms resulted in increased consumption and abuse. In Mexican American culture, alcohol was used to celebrate life and served a ubiquitous social function. The machismo attitude obligated young males to consume and tolerate large quantities of alcohol (Panitz & McConche, 1983). Although acculturated and bicultural Mexican Americans now accept alcoholism as a disease, traditional and marginal individuals believe in external causes, such as a hex or punishment by God. Intervention preferences thus stem from health/illness beliefs, although families may delay interventions for both their male and female members to protect their name, a source of pride and respect (Maril & Zavaleta, 1979). Mainstream interventions often use confrontation that belies respect and challenges machismo. As a consequence, these treatments may be refused with frequent outcomes of family violence. In the United States, alcoholism is often treated by a *curandero* either before or instead of hospitalization and natural healers have used induced aversion (Trotter, 1979). In Mexico, cures for Aztec Indians are often affected by conversion to Protestantism and subsequent abstinence.

The Texas Tech program in Lubbock, Texas, provides 4 to 6 weeks of inpatient care in a combined multimodal and multidisciplinary intervention for alcoholism (Arredondo, Weddige, Justice, & Fitz, 1987). Admission to the Texas Tech program follows acculturation assessment using the ARSMA and establishment of the patient's literacy level in English for subsequent bibliotherapy and writing assignments. A machismo concept is incorporated "that includes being brave, honest, hardworking, patriotic, and the family provider" (Arredondo et al., 1987, p. 183). The family support system of *copadres* (coparent sponsors of a child), grandparents, aunts, uncles, and cousins participate in Alanon family education and psychotherapy. Attendance at Alcoholics Anonymous (AA) meetings is required during hospitalization to emphasize shared life experiences, helping others, and spirituality. Patients and their families are subsequently introduced to Mexican American community AA and Alanon groups.

Family intervention in the community for alcohol and drug abuse incorporating cultural elements into a psychoeducational program has been provided by the Austin Women's Addiction Referral and Education Center (Aguilar, DiNitto, Franklin, & López-Pilkington, 1991). This intervention uses four sessions held 2 weeks apart to allow for counselor assistance with homework. It includes didactic materials, group discussions, participation in a variety of community groups, role plays, structured experiential exercises, visual aids, and analogies, as part of a 9- to 12-month program in which continued attendance in a self-help meeting is essential. Cultural elements are introduced throughout this process by reframing, language switching, reliance on Catholic religious percepts, and an indigenous helping network in the community. Reframing occurs initially by not using a disease model, because a moral weakness causal explanation is culturally accepted by many Mexican Americans. Similarly, the incentive for involvement and recovery is reframed as a gift to others in the family, for example, to children by becoming a better mother and to the husband by being a better wife. This is important because women alcohol/drug abusers are stigmatized for being in conflict with their idealized roles of wife and mother and are often reluctant to enter treatment or remain in treatment over a period of time. Taking care of oneself is linked to sustaining the physical and emotional resources necessary to care for other family members more adequately. The cultural rule of secrecy, or "don't talk" about personal problems outside the family is reframed as being detrimental to children whereas openness about problems becomes a source of pride rather than shame. Because women-only groups are not accepted, men are encouraged to attend. This invitation respects their role in the family and reduces concerns that the meetings may be used to encourage behaviors that are unacceptable in their wives. Language switching is often used to present concepts more clearly, particularly when meanings of words such as anger and rage differ in Spanish and English (e.g., *coraje* refers to both anger and rage). Catholicism is discussed to reinforce family values and gender roles and turning to the church is recommended for help with family problems. An indigenous helping network includes a youth advocacy agency for at-risk 9- to 17-year-old children and adolescents that provides outreach for the families and sustained participation in groups such as AA, Narcotics Anonymous, Adult Children of Alcoholics, or Alanon.

Culture-Specific Interventions and Healing Practices

Table 3.3 (Chapter 3, this volume) suggests questions that should be explored before recommending or implementing culture-specific interventions. These services should be conducted in Spanish for traditional clients. Although an exact ethnicity match (e.g., Mexican American with Mexican American) is desirable, the clinician should be Hispanic whenever feasible. Bicultural and even marginal clients may present identity issues that can be explored with bicultural/bilingual Anglo therapists. A detailed cultural identity description using acculturation measures should be prepared prior to examining identity issues. Cultural elements are conspicuous in these interventions and new interventions should rely on introduced cultural elements to match the client's value structure by similar therapeutic assumptions and to use the client's culture to address conflicting cultural norms, as recommended by Costantino, Malgady, and Rogler (1985).

Interventions for Symptoms and Psychopathology

Howard (1991) suggested that life-story construction and identity development are outcomes of storytelling. When stories go awry, psychotherapy can serve to repair life stories. *Cuento* therapy (storytelling) makes use of folktales as educational and therapeutic tools. Folktales tap the repository of cultural heritage by delineating societal rules, customs, and morality, often through the actions of heroes and heroines. *Cuento* therapy employs both original, unaltered folktales and altered versions to instill knowledge, values, and skills useful for coping with stress. Because their role in child development has been considered elemental and sacred in Puerto Rico, mothers are used as cotherapists who read either original or altered tales to small groups of their children from grades K through 3 (Costantino, Malgady, & Rogler, 1986). Two bilingual/bicultural therapists, a man and a woman, balanced sex-role modeling, in 20 weekly sessions of 90 minutes each. Control groups, also with therapists, use art-play materials or nonintervention video sessions. Pre- , post- , and follow-up testing indicated that first grade children in the adapted folktale group showed significantly less trait anxiety, followed by the original and art-play groups, whereas the nonintervention group was less affected. The Comprehension subtest of the WISC-R improved for both original and adapted folktale groups.

There are increases in complexity with age from fictional folktales to historical biographies and from preferences for either pictures or words. Subsequent research included new hero/heroine modeling for Puerto Rican eighth and ninth grade adolescents (Malgady, Rogler, & Costantino, 1990) and storytelling using pictorial stimuli for more diverse Hispanic populations (Costantino, Malgady, & Rogler, 1994). The modeling study used biographies of male and female models who had achieved in spite of poverty, prejudice, and illness. Small groups of paid students read passages aloud for analysis by a teacher and a therapist to identify the source of stress and adaptive coping strengths reflecting ethnic pride and positive self-concepts. Questions were asked by participants as bridges to their own lives and led to role playing an open-ended skit based on the story. After an introductory session, there were 18 weekly 90-minute modeling sessions. Control groups met with similar personnel for discussions of current events. Prepost measures of ethnic identity, using an ARSMA adaptation, self-concept, trait anxiety, and symptoms of distress were used. Ethnic identity was strengthened and anxiety was reduced, but self-concept improved only for adolescents in father-absent households, which accounted for 40% of Puerto Rican families by 1970 (Gurak, 1981).

Pictorial stimuli were used in a second study to initiate storytelling with older Puerto Rican, Dominican, San Salvadoran, Nicaraguan, Peruvian, and Colombian children selected for comorbid symptoms of anxiety, conduct, and phobic disorders (Costantino et al., 1994). Small groups participated in eight weekly 90-minute sessions conducted by Hispanic therapists in experimental and attention-control conditions. The pictorial stimuli were eight Tell-Me-A-Story (TEMAS) pictures of multiracial Hispanic adolescents in a variety of life settings (Costantino, Malgady, & Rogler, 1988). Group-developed composite stories were used to synthesize adaptive solutions, and personal experiences were subsequently related to these stories by group members. Maladaptive themes were discussed to provide more adaptive solutions and the groups subsequently dramatized the composite stories using role playing. The attention-control groups discussed children's videos with their teachers and therapists. Prepost measures suggested experimental group improvement in conduct problems, hyperactivity, and anxiety for both sexes. Sex differences occurred in reduction of phobic symptoms for sixth grade boys and for girls in the fifth and sixth grades. Failure to find prepost differences in depression may have been due to low pretest depression scores.

Interventions for Identity Issues

When the presenting problems indicate that cultural issues are critical for treatment, culture-specific interventions are necessary. Identity issues require exploration, supportive understanding, and use of a structured process that recognizes a sequence of stages for resolution of conflict and distress (Ruiz, 1990). These problems will frequently involve the client's ethnic identity, discrepancies between specific cultural values/behaviors and family or general community expectations/norms, and experiences with prejudice and discrimination that can result in life crises or make coping in daily life more difficult. In Table 8.2, Ruiz suggests intervention procedures for each of the four stages in Mexican American identity formation described in Chapter 4, this volume, Table 4.5. Causal stage interventions seek to decrease negative thinking about the self and simultaneously strengthen ethnic identity. Cognitive stage interventions continue to process the erroneous beliefs that contribute to negative thinking. At this point, there is more awareness of the consequences of identity fragmentation and defenses against awareness. Problem-specific distress is now evidenced and a working-through stage provides a counseling process using cultural identity assessment and culture-specific interventions, or "ethnocultural assessment" and "ethnotherapy," in Ruiz's (1990) terms. Finally, a successful resolution provides increased acceptance of self that includes culture and ethnicity.

Interventions for *Nervios-Ataque de Nervios*

Culture-specific interventions are also required whenever presenting symptoms and idioms of distress signal the presence of culture-specific disorders consistent with traditional health/illness beliefs. These health/illness beliefs should be explored as part of the development of a cultural formulation. Effective intervention must support the cultural belief in the temporary, situational, nature of *nervios-ataques* and the expectation of immediate relief from distress by not labeling the person as mentally ill or removing him or her from the family for hospitalization. Oquendo (1994) suggests that help can be provided by the client's support network, beginning with a family meeting in which temporary relinquishment of ordinary responsibilities is provided by others and, whenever possible, the source of immediate stress can be addressed or relieved. The local market *(bodega/ botanica)* can provide herbs, plants, and nonprescription drugs. If a clinician is present during one of these self-limiting *ataques,* patience and a comforting presence will help to reduce anxiety. Oquendo also suggests application of ammonium smelling salts or an alcohol swab for seizure-like behavior, mutism, or depressed consciousness, and intramuscular benzodiazines whenever there is risk of self-injury, although the clinical effectiveness of this intervention has not been demonstrated. Among Puerto Ricans in New York City, a majority of patients participating in one treatment program had also been treated by spiritists, informal home remedies, and community-based religious approaches including prayer for Catholics and group ceremonies for Pentecostals (Swerdlow, 1992).

Table 8.2 Stages of Mexican American Ethnic Identity Formation and Associated Interventions

Stage	Intervention
1. Causal	a. Stop negative ethnic thinking
	b. Teach ethnic affirmation
	c. Encourage participation in activities leading to ethnic pride
2. Cognitive	Identify erroneous beliefs
	• Group membership, poverty, prejudice
	• Escape from poverty-prejudice only via assimilation
	• Success possible only by assimilation
3. Consequence	Awareness of fragmented ethnic identity Shame/embarrassment: Accent, name, language, custom, appearance (skin color), neighborhood. Estrangement and defenses (denial, identification with aggressor, splitting, and so on)
4. Working through	Experienced distress due to inability to cope (beginning of willingness of enter counseling), use of ethnocultural assessment. Then eclectic application of ethnography, pluralistic counseling, ethnocultural identification, natural support system
5. Resolution	Greater acceptance of self, culture, ethnicity.

Culture-Specific Service-Delivery Settings

Culture-specific community mental health settings can provide acceptable services that incorporate cultural components for problems articulated by their community residents. A nationwide study identified culturally competent program sites and examined the characteristics that resulted in increased use and effectiveness of services (Issacs & Benjamin, 1991). Two of these programs, one in Los Angeles and another in New York City, are used as examples of within-culture differences in specific services.

In 1987, the Roybal Family Mental Health Services Utah Street School Colocation Project began in a health services agency located within a predominantly Mexican American neighborhood experiencing a high crime rate, drug use, gang activity, and violence (Issacs & Benjamin, 1991). The school had no Hispanic teachers and one Anglo counselor for 900 children. The project was designed to meet mental health needs of the school children as a means of improving academic performances by stimulating attendance, minimizing suspicions, and reducing behavior problems. Bilingual/bicultural professional staff and paraprofessional community workers with flexible roles were located in the school, and workshops were used initially for parent orientation and requests for services. Cultural identity assessments with the family were used to gain understanding of the acculturation process and outcome. Linguistic assessments with children were also completed prior to designing and implementing services using the family as the primary support and intervention context. A network of informal community support was developed and services were integrated between the school and a large public housing project. Group and individual psychotherapy with the children incorporated cultural elements to reinforce traditions and values. Outreach to families in their homes and by telephone or notes was used to increase their involvement in determining educational and treatment goals for their children. An advisory body from the agencies and community examines the program status on a regular basis and informal evidence suggests that the school objectives for treated children have been largely met.

The Roberto Clemente Family Guidance Center also has community access; a family focus; does cultural assessments; provides responsive services; uses natural, informal support systems; and has an integrated network of services with bicultural/bilingual staff (Issacs & Benjamin, 1991). This Center serves Puerto Rican first- or second-generation migrant families on the lower East side of Manhattan who live in low-income public housing in neighborhoods where over half of the buildings are abandoned or burned. Unemployment is 60%, and 43% of adults speak no English. Within the Center, the physical decor is faithful to the community culture. An ecological systems model is used for a full range of services focusing on specific problems-in-living, particularly those of loss or confusion of cultural identity and the major cultural conflict areas of adolescents (Inclan & Herron, 1989). These areas include clashes of culture (from political relationships between the United States and Puerto Rico), generational conflicts (parent-child differences in moral standards and cultural practices), socioeconomics (contiguous living with wealthy Anglo American communities), and individual identity/role conflicts (contrast between an agricultural economy with a function/adaptive transition to adulthood and mainstream conceptualizations of adolescent role responsibilities). These cultural issues create family problems of adaptation, marriage, school, and adolescence. These problems are addressed first by required, formal cultural competence inservice training of all staff in seminars that include, for example, ecological/family/cultural perspectives, differences among Hispanic ethnic groups, the migration process, historical context of Puerto Rican families, values orientation and family therapy, and the influence of religion. This training uses videotaped sessions that all therapists are required to make with consenting clients and occurs with weekly individual and group supervision. Client representatives are responsible for evaluation of services using interviews and observations concerning client satisfaction with arrival and waiting time, patient status, instructions for care and comprehension of these instructions, and staff attitudes. Not only are satisfaction levels high but new clients are referred primarily by former clients.

Agency cultural competence characteristics derived from intensive study of existing settings has been supplemented by development of a reliable checklist based on the entire literature of 700 relevant items (Dana, Behn, & Gonwa, 1992). This checklist has been applied in agencies to foster their self-evaluations. For example, this checklist was used in a mental health service located within a health-care delivery setting in rural Washington state serving a 90% Hispanic population (Dana, 1991), and this study is cited here to represent services in a more typical but less financially favored culture-specific agency setting. The results indicated that policy was congruent with the population served and both clients and community representatives were represented on the agency board of directors. Most staff members were bicultural/bilingual and problems were examined within a cultural context using a culture-specific treatment model, although no formal assessments were used. In-office counseling was provided for individual and family crises and there was brief problem-specific counseling. There were, however, no staff members responsible for interface between clients and community resources, as occurred in New York and Los Angeles, to facilitate networking within the Hispanic community and to augment involvement with agencies in the mainstream community. Prevention, outreach, and education resources had not been developed, although there was an active inservice training program. The dilemma of underfunding and the relative newness of this program precluded a wider array of available services within the minority community in spite of clear understanding by the administrators of what is entailed in providing culturally competent services.

9

———

——

——

Epilogue

As stated in the Preface, I have sought to maximize between- and within-group differences as a deliberate antidote for a history of minimizing all group differences. I do want to reverse the direction of the traditional Null Hypothesis, as Robert Malgady (1996) has done, to focus on differences rather than similarities, but I have chosen to do it with words rather than a meta-analysis of existing research literature, which also needs to occur. A premise of difference conveys respect as a beginning for understanding and provides a new perception of flaws in the extant literature.

I believe that cultural or racial identity should become the focus of attention if professional providers are to be honest about the major source of inner turmoil and external stressors leading to problems, symptomatology, and psychopathology. Simultaneously, this focus also permits caution to be exercised in applying the *DSM* to persons from multicultural groups by requiring a step-by-step exploration of cultural/racial issues in the diagnostic process by using a cultural formulation. If this is done conscientiously, there can be a dramatic reduction in pathologization in addition to increased accuracy of resulting diagnoses. These benefits should be reflected by increased use of services, improved client satisfaction with these services, and in the development of a legitimate new area for research attention.

To provide substance for the credibility of these assumptions, this book articulates an assessment-intervention model for cultural competence in providing mental health services to multicultural populations in the United States. Use of this model can sensitize providers to a sequence of opportunities for cultural information to inform the multiple decisions required to ensure and implement services likely to have beneficial outcomes. In this book, the model has been outlined and only imperfectly articulated in the conclusion to Chapter 4 as a basis for continued development.

The assessment portion of this model has been described in Chapters 2 and 3, with examples contained in Chapters 5, 6, 7, and 8. African American professionals have insisted that assessment be directed at both a developmental continuum for black persons of Anglocentricity/Afrocentricity and a delineation of Afrocentric behaviors and values. This stance exists because race matters and is always at issue in receiving services from Anglo Americans. Hispanic American professionals are no less adamant about ethnicity because they want to be perceived as Hispanics first and members of a particular racial group second. Considerations of cultural integrity and continued use of the Spanish language are paramount in this decision. As a consequence, psychometrically responsible and sustained research efforts have been made to examine identity from the perspective of Mexican Americans, Cuban Americans, and Puerto Ricans. By contrast, Asian American professionals have not attended to differences in Asian groups per se, but have opted primarily for measures of pan-Asian cultural identity. Their focus in assessment is on an evaluation of deficiencies in research on existing standard assessment instruments and, very recently, on a preference for delineating general response set/response style differences from Anglo Americans. American Indian professionals, probably due to their smaller numbers, have not emphasized assessment as a priority, although they have contributed substantive critical reviews.

The intervention portion of this model, presented in Chapter 3, has been applied in Chapters 5-8 by selection of intervention examples for illustration. Although these chapters were all designed to serve this function, each one does this differently because various steps in the model have been selectively attended to by researchers and practitioners within each group.

African American professionals desire their interventions to nurture pride in racial identity as a source of strength and psychological health for coping with racism, economic discrimination, and self-destructive activities within ghetto communities. Rationales for these interventions are now available, but their research documentation has not occurred because it has required over 20 years to develop the intervention models and describe them in the literature. Hispanics have taken the step of adapting mainstream Anglo emic interventions by incorporation of culture-specific elements before applications, particularly with families, and have provided research demonstrating efficacy. These combinations always include a simpatico style of service delivery in addition to cultural elements typically derived from research findings. Again, this has occurred because of an earlier research tradition with a great many competent researchers in funded research settings. This research should be carefully considered with an eye toward extrapolation to develop interventions for other groups that also combine culture-specific elements in the procedures with an acceptable social etiquette and the client's first language in providing services.

Asian American professionals have also focused on providing services to families using first languages and proper social etiquette, but have chosen to do this using a systems approach within culture-specific communities. Another precursor to developing interventions has been unequivocal documentation of the importance of matching providers and clients on ethnicity and language to reduce drop-out rates and improve benefits from subsequent interventions.

American Indian professionals have reached consensus concerning the necessity of defining their own problems, in particular, within tribal reservation settings, prioritizing these problems, and developing community-originated, setting-specific interventions. These interventions require community participation and support for their success, which may be only local in nature and not generalizable to other tribes. A focus for these interventions is the strengthening of identity as a source of inner harmony for individuals, as well as self-sufficiency and greater internal cohesion for communities. In these endeavors, American Indians have the unique advantage of having retained a cadre of traditional healers and have acquired the bicultural coping ability to use mainstream Anglo American services as well whenever available. Moreover, there is a groundswell in Indian communities toward development of local and pan-Indian idioms of distress and problems-in-living. This is absolutely necessary because the *DSM* has pathologized them to a greater extent than other cultural/racial groups due to irreconcilable differences from an Anglo American worldview as well as the continued presence of an Indian self with permeable boundaries, internal organization, and other constituents that seldom occur in an Anglo American self. Interventions, including healing rituals/ ceremonies or combined interventions for identity recognition, clarification, and enhancement, can also examine identity conflicts to restore an expanded cultural self-awareness containing the essentials of cultural belief, or what it entails in being an Indian person.

This book is a primer, a sketch of what I believe can become a legitimate assessment/intervention model whose general outlines and steps will have very different content for each cultural/racial group. The details of this model for each group cannot, however, be supplied by Anglo American professionals, and fleshing out the model may alter the model's components due to culture-specific applications and examples. As a result, the emphasis on differences among groups can be continued and, hopefully, become acceptable as the demonstration of the Null Hypothesis reversal in intervention practices.

References

Abkar, N. (1991). Mental disorders among African Americans. In R. G. Jones (Ed.), *Black psychology* (3rd ed., pp. 339-352). Berkeley, CA: Cobb & Henry.

Abott, K. A. (1970). *Cultural change, psychosocial functioning, and the family: A case study in the Chinese American community in San Francisco.* Unpublished doctoral dissertation, University of California, Berkeley.

Abramowitz, S. I., & Murray, J. (1983). Race effects in psychotherapy. In J. Murray & P. R. Abramson (Eds.), *Bias in psychotherapy* (pp. 215-255). New York: Praeger.

Acosta, F. X., Yamamoto, J., Evans, L. A., & Skilbeck, W. M. (1983). Preparing low-income Hispanic, black, and white patients for psychotherapy: Evaluation of a new orientation program. *Journal of Clinical Psychology, 39,* 872-877.

Acosta-Belen, E. (1988). From settlers to newcomers: The Hispanic legacy in the United States. In E. Acosta-Belen & B. R. Sjostrom (Eds.), *The Hispanic experience in the United States: Contemporary issues and perspectives* (pp. 81-106). New York: Praeger.

Adibimpe, V. R. (1981). Hallucinations and delusions among black psychiatric patients. *Journal of the National Medical Association, 73,* 517-520.

Adibimpe, V. R. (1994). Race, racism, and epidemiological surveys. *Hospital and Community Psychiatry, 45,* 27-31.

Adibimpe, V. R., Chung-Chou, C., Klein, H. E., & Lange, M. H. (1982). Racial and geographic differences in the psychopathology of schizophrenia. *American Journal of Psychiatry, 139,* 888-891.

Aguilar, M. A., DiNitto, D. M., Franklin, C., & López-Pilkinton, B. (1991). Mexican Amerian families: A psychoeducational approach for addressing chemical dependency and codependency. *Child and Adolescent Social Work, 8,* 309-326.

Akutsu, P. D., Snowden, L. R., & Organista, K. C. (1996). Referral patterns in ethnic-specific and mainstream programs for ethnic minorities and whites. *Journal of Counseling Psychology, 43,* 56-64.

Alarcon, R. D., & Foulks, E. F. (1993, January). Cultural factors and personality disorders: A review of the literature. In NIMH-sponsored Group on Culture and Diagnosis, *Cultural proposals and supporting papers for DSM-IV* (3rd rev., pp. 250-254). Pittsburgh, PA: University of Pittsburgh.

Albaugh, B. J., & Anderson, P. O. (1974). Peyote in the treatment of alcoholism among American Indians. *American Journal of Psychiatry, 131,* 1247-1250.

Albee, G. W. (1970). The uncertain future of clinical psychology. *American Psychologist, 25,* 1071-1080.

Albee, G. W. (1982). The uncertain direction of clinical psychology. In J. R. McNamara & A. G. Barclay (Eds.), *Critical issues, developments, and trends in professional psychology* (pp. 295-312). New York: Praeger.

Allen, I. M. (1996). PTSD among African Americans. In A. J. Marsella, M. J. Friedman, E. T. Gerrity, & R. M. Scurfield (Eds.), *Ethnocultural aspects of Posttraumatic Stress Disorder: Issues, research, and clinical applications* (pp. 209-238). Washington, DC: American Psychological Association.

Allen, J., & French, C. (1994). *Northern Plains Bicultural Immersion Scale—Preliminary manual and scoring instructions.* Vermillion: University of South Dakota.

Allen, J., & French, C. (1996). *Northern Plains Bicultural Immersion Scale-Preliminary manual and scoring directions* (Version 5). Vermillion: University of South Dakota.

Allen, J., & French, C. (Eds.). (in press). *Psychological assessment of Northern Plains Indians.* Vermillion: University of South Dakota Press.

Allen, R. L., Dawson, M. C., & Brown, R. E. (1989). A schema-based approach to modeling an African American racial belief system. *American Political Science Review, 83,* 421-442.

Allison, K. W., Crawford, I., Echemendia, R., Robinson, L., & Kemp, D. (1994). Human diversity and professional competence: Trainiong in clinical and counseling psychology revisited. *American Psychologist, 49,* 792-796.

Allison, K. W., Echemendia, R. J., Crawford, I., & Robinson, W. L. (1996). Predicting cultural competence: Implications for practice and training. *Professional Psychology: Research and Practice, 27,* 386-393.

Altschuler, L. L., Xida, W., Haiging, Q., & Qiang, H. (1988). Who seeks mental health care in China? Diagnoses of Chinese outpatients according to *DSM-III* and the Chinese classification system. *American Journal of Psychiatry, 145,* 872-875.

American Psychiatric Association. (1994). *Diagnostic and statistical manual of mental disorders* (4th ed.). Washington, DC: Author.

American Psychological Association. (1981). Ethical principles of psychologists (rev. ed.). *American Psychologist, 36,* 633-638.

American Psychological Association. (1989). *Draft of guidelines for psychological practice with ethnic and culturally diverse populations.* Washington, DC: Task Force on Delivery of Services to Minority Populations.

American Psychological Association. (1992). Ethical principles of psychologists and code of conduct. *American Psychologist, 47,* 1597-1611.

American Psychological Association. (1993). Guidelines for providers of psychological services to ethnic, linguistic, and culturally diverse populations. *American Psychologist, 48,* 45-48.

Anderson, L. P. (1991). Acculturative stress: A theory of relevance to black Americans. *Clinical Psychology Review, 11,* 685-702.

Andrews, F. M., & Withey, S. B. (1976). *Social indicators of wellbeing: America's perceptions of life quality.* New York: Plenum.

Aponte, J. F., & Barnes, J. M. (1995). Impact of acculturation and moderator variables on the intervention and treatment of ethnic groups. In J. F. Aponte, R. Y. Rivers, & J. Wohl (Eds.), *Psychological interventions and cultural diversity* (pp. 19-39). Boston: Allyn & Bacon.

Aponte, J. F., & Crouch, R. T. (1995). The changing ethnic profile of the United States. In J. F. Aponte, R. Y. Rivers, & J. Wohl (Eds.), *Psychological interventions and cultural diversity* (pp. 1-18). Boston: Allyn & Bacon.

Arredondo, R., Weddige, R. L., Justice, C. L., & Fitz, J. (1987). Alcoholism in Mexican Americans: Intervention and treatment. *Hospital and Community Psychiatry, 38,* 180-183.

Asamen, J. K., & Berry, G. L. (1987). Self-concept, alienation, and perceived prejudice: Implications for counseling Asian Americans. *Journal of Multicultural Counseling and Development, 15,* 146-160.

Asante, M. (1990). *Kemet, Afrocentricity, and knowledge.* Trenton, NJ: Africa-World Press.

Asante, M. K. (1987). *The Afrocentric idea.* Philadelphia, PA: Temple University Press.

Atkinson, D. R. (1983). Ethnic similarity in counseling psychology: A review of research. *Counseling Psychologist, 11*(3), 79-92.

Atkinson, D. R., Furlong, M. J., & Poston, W. C. (1986). Afro-American preferences for counselor characteristics. *Journal of Counseling Psychology, 33,* 326-330.

Atkinson, D. R., & Gim, R. H. (1989). Asian American cultural identity and attitude toward mental health services. *Journal of Counseling Psychology, 36,* 209-212.

Atkinson, D. R., Morten, G., & Sue, D. W. (1989). *Counseling American minorities: A cross-cultural perspective* (3rd ed.). Dubuque, IA: William C. Brown.

Atkinson, D. R., Poston, W. C., Furlong, M. J., & Mercado, P. (1989). Ethnic group preferences for counselor characteristics. *Journal of Counseling Psychology, 36,* 68-72.

Atkinson, D. R., Thompson, C. E., & Grant, S. K. (1993). A three-dimensional model for counseling racial-ethnic minorities. *Counseling Psychologist, 21,* 257-277.

Atkinson, D. R., Whiteley, S., & Gim, R. H. (1990). Asian American acculturation and preferences for help providers. *Journal of College Student Development, 31,* 155-161.

Attneave, C. L. (1974). Medicine men and psychiatrists in the Indian Health Service. *Psychiatric Annals, 4,* 49, 53-55.

Awanbor, D. (1982). The healing process in African psychotherapy. *American Journal of Psychotherapy, 36,* 206-213.

Axelson, J. A. (1992). *Counseling and development in a multicultural society* (2nd ed.). Pacific Grove, CA: Brooks/Cole.

Azibo, D. A. Y. (1988). Understanding the proper and improper usage of the comparative research framework. *Journal of Black Psychology, 15,* 81-91.

Bach, R. L. (1985). Cubans. In D. W. Haines (Ed.), *Refugees in the United States: A handbook* (pp. 77-180). Westport, CT: Greenwood.

Baldwin, A. J., & Bell, Y. R. (1984). The African Self-Consciousness Scale: An Africentric personality questionnaire. *Western Journal of Black Studies, 9*(2), 65-68.

Bandura, A. (1986). *Social foundations of thought and action: A social cognitive theory.* Englewood Cliffs, NJ: Prentice Hall.

Barrett, B. (1993). Health care behavior on Nicaragua's west coast. *Social Science and Medicine, 37,* 355-368.

Basoglu, M. (Ed.). (1992). *Torture and its consequences: Current treatment approaches.* New York: Cambridge University Press.

Bass, B. A. (1982). The validity of socioeconomic factors in assessment and treatment of Afro-Americans. In B. A. Bass, G. E. Wyatt, & G. J. Powell (Eds.), *The Afro-American family: Assessment, treatment, and research issues* (pp. 69-83). New York: Grune & Stratton.

Bean, F. D., & Tienda, M. (1987). *The Hispanic population in the United States.* New York: Russell Sage.

Bekhuis, T., Cook, H., Holt, K., & Scott-Lennox, J. (1995). Ethnicity, church affiliation, and beliefs about the causal agents of health: A comparative study employing a multivariate analysis of covariance. *Health Education Research, 10,* 73-82.

Belitz, J., & Valdez, D. (1994). Clinical issues in the treatment of Chicano male gang youth. *Hispanic Journal of Behavioral Sciences, 16,* 57-74.

Bell, C., & Mehta, H. (1979). The misdiagnosis of black patients with manic-depressive illness. *Journal of the National Medical Association, 72,* 141-145.

Bell, C. C., Shakoor, B., Thompson, B., Dew, D., Hughley, E., Mays, R., & Shorter-Gooden, K. (1984). Prevalence of isolated sleep paralysis in black subjects. *Journal of the National Medical Association, 76,* 501-508.

Benjamin, M. P., & Morgan, P. C. (1989). *Refugee children traumatized by war and violence: The challenge offered to the service delivery system.* Washington, DC: CASSP Technical Assistance Center, Georgetown University Child Development Center.

Bennett, M. J. (1986). Toward ethnorelativism: A developmental model of intercultural sensitivity. In R. M. Paige (Ed.), *Cross-cultural orientation: New conceptualizations and applications* (pp. 27-69). Lanham, MD: University Press of America.

Bennett, S. K., Atkinson, D. R., & Rowe, W. (1993, August). *White racial identity: An alternative perspective.* Paper presented at the annual meeting of the American Psychological Association, Toronto, Canada.

Bennett, S. K., & BigFoot-Sipes, D. S. (1991). American Indian and white college student preferences for counselor characteristics. *Journal of Counseling Psychology, 38,* 440-445.

Bergman, R. L. (1971). Navajo peyote use: Its apparent safety. *American Journal of Psychiatry, 128*(6), 51-55.

Bergman, R. L. (1973). A school for medicine men. *American Journal of Psychiatry, 130,* 663-666.

Bernal, G., & Gutierrez, M. (1988). Cubans. In L. Cómas-Dias & E. E. H. Griffith (Eds.), *Clinical guidelines in cross-cultural mental health* (pp. 233-261). New York: John Wiley.

Bernstein, B. (1964). Social class, speech systems, and psychotherapy. *British Journal of Sociology, 55,* 54-64.

Berry, J. W. (1989). Psychology of acculturation. *Nebraska Symposium on Motivation, 39,* 201-234.

Berry, J. W., & Blondel, T. (1982). Psychological adaptation of Vietnamese refugees in Canada. *Canadian Journal of Community Mental Health, 1*(1), 81-88.

Berry, J. W., & Kim, U. (1988). Acculturation and mental health. In P. R. Dasen, J. N. Berry, & N. Sartorius (Eds.), *Health and cross-cultural psychology: Toward applications* (pp. 207-236). Newbury Park, CA: Sage.

Bersoff, D. N. (1994). Explicit amibguity: The 1992 Ethics Code as an oxymoron. *Professional Psychology: Research and Practice, 25,* 182-187.

Betancourt, H., & López, S. R. (1993). The study of culture, ethnicity, and race in American psychology. *American Psychologist, 48,* 629-637.

Beverly, C. C. (1975). Toward a model for counseling black alcoholics. *Journal of Non-White Concerns, 3,* 169-176.

Biegel, D. E., & Naparstek, A. J. (Eds.). (1982). *Community support systems and mental health.* New York: Springer.

Billson, J. M. (1995). *Keepers of the culture: The power of tradition in women's lives.* New York: Lexington.

Bloom, B. L. (1984). *Community mental health: A general introduction.* Pacific Grove, CA: Brooks/Cole.

Bluestone, H., & Vela, R. M. (1982). Transcultural aspects in the psychotherapy of the Puerto Rican poor in New York City. *Journal of the American Academy of Psychoanalysis, 10,* 269-293.

Boehnlein, J. K. (1987). Clinical relevance of grief and mourning among Cambodian refugees. *Social Sciences in Medicine, 25,* 765-772.

Boehnlein, J. K., Kinzie, J. D., Leung, P. K., Matsunaga, D., Johnson, R., & Shore, J. D. (1992/1993). The natural history of medical and psychiatric disorders in an American Indian community. *Culture, Medicine, and Psychiatry, 16,* 543-554.

Bojholm, S., & Vesti, P. (1992). Multidisciplinary approach in the treatment of torture survivors. In M. Basoglu (Ed.), *Torture and its consequences: Current treatment approaches* (pp. 299-309). New York: Cambridge University Press.

Boulette, R. R. (1976). Assertive training with low-income Mexican American women. In M. R. Miranda (Ed.), *Psychotherapy with the Spanish speaking: Issues in research and service delivery* (pp. 66-171). Los Angeles: University of California, Spanish-Speaking Mental Health Center.

Bowen, D. J., Carscadden, L., Beighle, K., & Fleming, I. (1992). Posttraumatic stress disorder among Salvadoran women: Empirical evidence and descriptions of treatment. *Women and Therapy, 13,* 267-280.

Bowman, B., & Edwards, M. (1984). The Indochinese refugee: An overview. *Australian and New Zealand Journal of Psychiatry, 18,* 40-52.

Boyd-Franklin, N. (1989). *Black families in therapy.* New York: Guilford.

Boyd-Franklin, N., & Shenouda, N. T. (1990). A multisystems approach to the treatment of a black, inner-city family with a schizophrenic mother. *American Journal of Orthopsychiatry, 60,* 186-195.

Boyer, L., Klopfer, B., Brawer, F. B., & Kawai, H. (1964). Comparisons of the shamans and pseudoshamans of the Apaches of the Mescalero Indian reservation. *Journal of Personality Assessment, 28,* 173-180.

Bradshaw, C. A. (1990). A Japanese view of dependency: What can amae psychology contribute to feminist theory and therapy? *Women and Therapy, 9*(1-2), 67-86.

Brantley, T. (1983). Racism and its impact on psychotherapy. *American Journal of Psychiatry, 140,* 1605-1608.

Brown v. Board of Education. (1954). 347 U.S. 483.

Brown, D. R. (1990). Depression among Blacks: An epidemiological perspective. In D. S. Ruiz & J. P. Comer (Eds.), *Handbook of mental health and mental disorder among black Americans* (pp. 71-93). New York: Greenwood.

Brown, D. R., Gary, L. E., Greene, A. D., & Milburn, N. C. (1992). Patterns of social affiliation as predictors of depressive symptoms among urban Blacks. *Journal of Health and Social Behavior, 33*(September), 242-253.

Bui, K. V. T., & Takeuchi, D. T. (1992). Ethnic minority adolescents and the use of community mental health care services. *American Journal of Community Psychology, 20,* 403-417.

Bulhan, H. A. (1985). *Franz Fanon and the psychology of oppression.* New York: Plenum.

Burham, M. A., Hough, R. L., Karno, M., Escobar, J. I., & Telles, C. A. (1987). Acculturation and lifetime prevalence of psychiatric disorders among Mexican Americans in the Los Angeles. *Journal of Health and Social Behavior, 28,* 89-102.

Burlew, A. K., & Smith, L. R. (1991). Measures of racial identity: An overview and a proposed framework. *Journal of Black Psychology, 17*(2), 53-71.

Byron, D, M. (1995). *The relationship of cultural identification to depression and alcohol use among urban American Indians.* Unpublished doctoral dissertation, California School of Professional Psychology, San Deigo.

Caetano, R. (1987). Alcohol use and depression among U.S. Hispanics. *British Journal of Addiction, 82,* 1245-1251.

Caldwell, C. H. (1996). Predisposing, enabling, and need factors related to patterns of help seeking among African American women. In H. W. Neighbors & J. S. Jackson (Eds.), *Mental health in black America* (pp. 146-160). Thousand Oaks, CA: Sage.

Campbell, A. (1981). *The sense of well-being in America: Recent patterns and trends.* New York: McGraw-Hill.

Canino, G., & Canino, I. A. (1982). Culturally syntonic family therapy for migrant Puerto Ricans. *Hospital and Community Psychiatry, 33,* 299-303.

Canino, G. J., Bird, H., Shrout, P. E. , Rubio, M., Geil, K. P., & Bravo, M. (1987). The prevalence of alcohol abuse and/or dependence in Puerto Rico. In M. Gaviria & J. D. Arana (Eds.), *Health and behavior: Research agenda for Hispanics* (Simon Bolivar Research Monograph Series No. 1, pp. 127-143). Chicago, IL: Simon Bolivar Hispanic American Research and Training Program.

Canino, G. J., Bird, H. R., Shrout, P. E., Rubio-Stipe, M., Bravo, M., Martinez, R., Sesman, M., & Grievara, L. M. (1987). The prevalence of specific psychiatric disorders in Puerto Rico. *Archives of General Psychiatry, 44,* 727-735.

Canive, J. M., Sanz-Fuentenebro, J., Tuason, V. B., Vasquez, C., Schrader, R. M., Alberdi, J., & Fuentenebro, F. (1993). Psychoeducation in Spain. *Hospital and Community Psychiatry, 44,* 679-681.

Carlson, E. B., & Rosser-Hogan, R. (1993). Mental health status of Cambodian refugees 10 years after leaving their homes. *American Journal of Orthopsychiatry, 63,* 223-231.

Carter, R. T. (1990). *The influence of race and racial identity in psychotherapy.* New York: John Wiley.

Carter, R. T. (1991). Cultural values: A review of empirical research and implications for counseling. *Journal of Counseling and Development, 70,* 164-173.

Carter, R. T. (1995). *The influence of race and racial identity in psychotherapy: Toward a racially inclusive model.* New York: John Wiley.

Carter, R. T., & Helms, J. E. (1987). The relationship between black value-orientations and racial identity attitudes. *Measurement and Evaluation in Counseling and Development, 19*(4), 185-195.

Carter, R. T., & Helms, J. E. (1988). The relationship between racial identity attitudes and social class. *Journal of Negro Education, 57*(1), 22-30.

Carter, M. M., Sbrocco, T., & Carter, C. (1996). African Americans and anxiety disorders research: Development of a testable theoretical framework. *Psychotherapy, 33,* 449-463.

Casas, J. M. (1976). Applicability of a behavioral model in serving the mental health needs of the Mexican American. In M. R. Miranda (Ed.), *Psychotherapy with the Spanish speaking: Issues in research and service delivery* (pp. 61-65). Los Angeles: University of California, Spanish-Speaking Mental Health Center.

Casas, J. M. (1988). Cognitive-behavioral approaches: A minority perspective. *Counseling Psychologist, 16,* 106-110.

Casas, J. M., & Vasquez, M. J. T. (1996). Counseling the Hispanic: A guiding framework for a diverse population. In P. B. Pedersen, J. G. Draguns, W. J. Lonner, & J. E. Trimble (Eds.), *Counseling across cultures* (4th ed., pp. 146-176). Thousand Oaks, CA: Sage.

Castillo, R. J. (1996). *Culture and mental illness: A client-centered approach.* Pacific Grove, CA: Brooks/Cole.

Cervantes, R. C., & Arroyo, W. (1994). *DSM-IV:* Implications for Hispanic children and adolescents. *Hispanic Journal of Behavioral Sciences, 16,* 8-27.

Cervantes, R. C., & Castro, F. G. (1985). Stress, coping, and Mexican American mental health: A systematic review. *Hispanic Journal of Behavioral Sciences, 7,* 1-73.

Chan, F., Lam, C. S., Wong, D., Leung, P., & Fang, X. S. (1988). Counseling Chinese Americans with disabilities. *Journal of Applied Rehabilitation Counseling, 19*(4), 21-25.

Chang, S. C. (1989). Psychiatric diagnosis in China. *American Journal of Psychiatry, 146,* 1079-1080.

Chapa, J., & Valencia, R. R. (1993). Latino population growth, demographic characteristics, and educational stagnation: An examination of recent trends. *Hispanic Journal of Behavioral Sciences, 15*(2), 165-187.

Charles, C. (1979). Brief comments on the occurrence, etiology, and treatment of indisposition. *Social Science and Medicine, 13B,* 135-136.

Cheatham, H. E., Tomlinson, S. M., & Ward, T. J. (1990). The African self-consciousness construct and African American students. *Journal of College Student Development, 31,* 492-499.

Cheung, G. K., & Snowden, L. R. (1990). Community mental health and ethnic minority populations. *Community Mental Health Journal, 26,* 277-291.

Chiles, L. M. (1982). The federal budget and the new federalism: Trends affecting mental health. *American Psychologist, 37,* 835-842.

Chin, J. L. (1991). The South Cover Community Health Center program: An approach to community-based training. In H. F. Myers, P. Wohlford, L. P. Guzman, & R. J. Echemendia (Eds.), *Ethnic minority perspectives on clinical training and services in psychology* (pp. 149-153). Washington, DC: American Psychological Association.

Chin, R. (1984). Conceptual paradigm for a racial-ethnic community: The case of the Chinese American community. In S. Sue & T. Moore (Eds.), *The pluralistic society: A community mental health perspective* (pp. 222-236). New York: Human Sciences Press.

Chu, J., & Sue, S. (1984). Asian-Pacific Americans and group practice. *Social Work With Groups, 7,* 23-36.

Chu, J. A. (1988). Ten traps for therapists in the treatment of trauma survivors. *Dissociation, 1,* 24-32.

Chung, R. C. Y., & Kagawa-Singer, M. (1993). Predictors of psychological distress among Southeast Asian refugees. *Social Science and Medicine, 36,* 631-639.

Chung, R. C. Y., & Lin, K. M. (1994). Help-seeking behavior among Southeast Asian refugees. *Journal of Community Psychology, 22,* 109-120.

Clark, K. (1971). The pathos of power: A psychological perspective. *American Psychologist, 26,* 1047-1057.

Clark, K. B. (1965). *Dark ghetto: Dilemmas of social power.* New York: Harper & Row.

Clinton, J. J., McCormick, K., & Besteman, J. (1994). Enhancing clinical practice: The role of practice guidelines. *American Psychologist, 49,* 30-33.

Cobbs, P. M. (1972). Ethnotherapy in groups. In L. N. Solomon & B. Berzon (Eds.), *New perspectives on encounter groups* (pp. 383-403). San Francisco: Jossey-Bass.

Cohen, R. L. (1989). Fabrication of justice. *Social Justice Research, 3,* 31-46.

Cole, J. D., Watt, N. F., West, S. G., Hawkins, J. D., Asarnow, J. R., Markman, H. J., Ramey, S. L., Shure, M. B., & Long, B. (1993). The science of prevention: A conceptual framework and some directions for a national research program. *American Psychologist, 48,* 1013-1022.

Cómas-Diaz, L. (1981). Effects of cognitive and behavioral group treatment in the depressive symptomatology of Puerto Rican women. *Journal of Consulting and Clinical Psychology, 49,* 627-632.

Cómas-Diaz, L., & Jacobsen, F. M. (1987). Ethnocultural identification in psychotherapy. *Psychiatry, 50,* 232-241.

Committee of the Family, Group for Advancement of Psychiatry. (1995). A model for the classification and diagnosis of relational disorders. *Psychiatric Services, 46,* 926-931.

Conway, J. (1982, June). *Some characteristics of exemplary young clinical psychologists: The scientists, the professionals, and the scientist professional.* Paper presented at the annual meeting of the Canadian Psychological Association, Montreal, Quebec.

Cooper, R. (1983). The Hmong of Laos: Economic factors in refugee exocus and return. In G. L. Hendricks, B. T. Downing, & A. S. Deinard (Eds.), *The Hmong in transition* (pp. 23-40). Staten Island, NY: Center for Migration Studies of New York; Southeast Asian Refugee Studies, University of Minnesota.

Costa, P. T., Jr., & McRae, R. R. (1992). *Revised NEO Personality Inventory (NEO-PI-R) and NEO Five-Factor Inventory (NEO-FFI) professional manual.* Odessa, FL: Psychological Assessment Resources.

Costantino, G., Malgady, R. G., & Rogler, L. H. (1985). Cuento therapy: Folktales as a culturally sensitive psychotherapy for Puerto Rican children. Maplewood, NJ: Waterfront.

Costantino, G., Malgady, R. G., & Rogler, L. H. (1986). Cuento therapy: A culturally sensitive modality for Puerto Rican children. *Journal of Consulting and Clinical Psychology, 54,* 739-746.

Costantino, G., Malgady, R. G., & Rogler, L. H. (1988). *TEMAS (Tell-Me-A-Story) manual.* Los Angeles, CA: Western Psychological Services.

Costantino, G., Malgady, R. G., & Rogler, L. H. (1994). Storytelling through pictures: Culturally sensitive psychotherapy for Hispanic children and adolescents. *Journal of Clinical Child Psychology, 23,* 13-20.

Coulehan, J. L. (1980). Navajo Indian medicine: Implications for healing. *Journal of Family Practice, 10*(l), 55-61.

Crissman, L. W. (1991). Chinese immigrant families in Australia: A variety of experiences. *Journal of Comparative Family Studies, 22,* 25-37.

Cross, W. E., Jr. (1978). The Thomas and Cross models of psychological Nigrescence: A review. *Journal of Black Psychology, 5*(1), 13-31.

Cuéllar, I. (1982). The diagnosis and evaluation of Mexican American schizophrenics. In R. M. Becerra, M. Karno, & J. I. Escobar (Eds.), *Mental health and Hispanic Americans: A clinical perspective* (pp. 61-81). New York: Grune & Stratton.

Cuéllar, I. (1993, November). Clinical assessment of Hispanic patients: Cross-cultural considerations. In F. Paredes (Chair), *Neuropsychological tests and procedures.* Symposium conducted at the meeting of the Texas Psychological Association, Austin, TX.

Cuéllar, I., Arnold, B., & Maldonado, R. (1995). Acculturation Rating Scale for Mexican Americans-II: A revision of the original ARSMA scale. *Hispanic Journal of Behavioral Sciences, 17,* 275-304.

Cuéllar, I., Dana, R. H., & Gonzalez, G. (1995). *Competent psychological assessment with Hispanics: A cultural formulation using DSM-IV.* Unpublished manuscript.

Cuéllar, I., & Gonzalez, R. (1983). Clinical psychiatric case presentation: Culturally responsive diagnostic formulation in an Hispanic female. *Hispanic Journal of Behavioral Sciences, 5,* 93-103.

Cuéllar, I., Harris, L. C., & Jasso, R. (1980). An acculturation scale for Mexican American normal and clinical populations. *Hispanic Journal of Behavioral Sciences, 2,* 199-217.

Cuéllar, I., & Roberts, R. E. (1984). Psychological disorders among Chicanos. In J. L. Martinez & R. H. Mendoza (Eds.), *Chicano psychology* (2nd ed., pp. 133-161). New York: Academic Press.

Culturally Relevant Ethnic Minority Services Coalition. (1989a). Seattle Indian Health Board's culturally oriented mental health program. In Culturally Relevant Ethnic Minority Services Coalition, *Multiethnic mental health services: Six demonstration programs in Washington state* (pp. 163-190). Mount Vernon, WA: Northwest Graphics.

Culturally Relevant Ethnic Minority Services Coalition. (1989b). Tribal mental health program of Skagit Community Mental Health Center. In Culturally Relevant Ethnic Minority Services Coalition, *Multiethnic mental health services: Six demonstration programs in Washington state* (pp. 191-234). Mount Vernon, WA: Northwest Graphics.

D'Souza, D. (1991). *Illiberal educations: The politics of race and sex on campus.* New York: Vintage.

Dahlstrom, W. G., Lachar, D., & Dahlstrom, L. E. (1986). *MMPI patterns of American minorities.* Minneapolis: University of Minnesota Press.

Daly, A., Jennings, J., Beckett, J. O., & Leashore, B. R. (1995). Effective coping strategies of African Americans. *Social Work, 40,* 240-248.

Dana, R. H. (1964). The impact of fantasy on a residential treatment program. *Corrective Psychiatry and Journal of Social Therapy, 10,* 202-212.

Dana, R. H. (1965). The Seven Squares Test: Phenomenon naming versus causal naming. *Perceptual and Motor Skills, 20,* 69-70.

Dana, R. H. (1978). Comparisons of competence training in two successful clinical training programs. *Psychological Reports, 42,* 919-926.

Dana, R. H. (1982). *A human science model for personality assessment with projective techniques.* Springfield, IL: Charles C Thomas.

Dana, R. H. (1987). Training for professional psychology: Science, practice, and identity. *Professional Psychology: Research and Practice, 18,* 9-16.

Dana, R. H. (1991). *Cultural competence in three human service agencies.* Unpublished manuscript, Portland State University, Regional Research Institute.

Dana, R. H. (1992a). A commentary on assessment training in Boulder and Vail model programs: In praise of differences! *Journal of Training and Practice in Professional Psychology, 6*(2), 19-26.

Dana, R. H. (1992b). Assessment of cultural orientation. *SPA Exchange, 2*(2), 14-15.

Dana, R. H. (1993a). *Multicultural assessment perspectives for professional psychology.* Boston: Allyn & Bacon.

Dana, R. H. (1993b, March). How can we invest assessment procedures with knowledge of Mexican Americans as cultural beings? In R. Dana (Chair), *Assessment of clients as cultural entities.* Symposium conducted at the meeting of the Society for Personality Assessment, Chicago, IL.

Dana, R. H. (1994). Testing and assessment ethics for all persons: A beginning and an agenda. *Professional Psychology: Research and Practice, 25,* 349-354.

Dana, R. H. (1996a). *Response to Velasquez et al.: Silk purse or sow's ear—An MMPI commonground.* Unpublished manuscript.

Dana, R. H. (1996b). Assessment of acculturation in Hispanic populations. *Hispanic Journal of Behavioral Sciences, 18,* 317-338.

Dana, R. H. (1997a). *Managed mental health care for multicultural populations: Occam's Razor and quality of care.* Paper presented at the National Research Center on Asian American Mental Health, University of California, Davis.

Dana, R. H. (1997b). Personality assessment and the cultural self: Emic and etic contexts as learning resources. In L. Handler, & M. Hilsenroth (Eds.), *Teaching and learning personality assessment.* Hillsdale, NJ: Lawrence Erlbaum.

Dana, R. H., Behn, J. D., & Gonwa, T. (1992). A checklist for the examination of cultural competence in social service agencies. *Research on Social Work Practice, 2,* 220-233.

Dana, R. H., Conner, M. G., & Allen, J. (1996). Quality of care and cost containment in managed mental health policy, education, research, advocacy. *Psychological Reports, 79,* 1395-1422.

Dana, R. H., & Matheson, L. (1992). An application of the Agency Cultural Competence Checklist to a program serving small and diverse ethnic communities. *Psychosocial Rehabilitation Journal, 15*(4), 101-105.

Dana, R. H., & May, W. T. (1986). Health care megatrends and health psychology. *Professional Psychology: Research and Practice, 17,* 251-255.

Dana, R. H., & May, W. T. (Eds.). (1987). *Internship training in professional psychology.* New York: Hemisphere.

Dana, R. H., & Voigt, W. (1962). The Seven Squares Test. *Perceptual and Motor Skills, 15,* 751-753.

Davidson, A. R. (1977). The etic-emic dilemma: Can methodology provide a solution in the absence of theory? In Y. H. Poortinga (Ed.), *Basic problems in cross-cultural psychology* (pp. 49-55). The Netherlands: Swets & Zeitlinger.

Davidson, J. P. (1975). Empirical development of a measure of Black student identity (Doctoral Dissertation, University of Maryland, 1974). *Dissertation Abstracts International,* DA8617150.

Davis, C., Haub, C., & Willette, J. L. (1988). U.S. Hispanics: Changing the face of America. In E. Acosta-Belen & B. R. Sjostrom (Eds.), *The Hispanic experience in the United States: Contemporary iiisues and perspectives* (pp. 3-55). New York: Praeger.

De la Cancela, V., & Sotomayer, G. M. (1993). Rainbow warriers: Reducing institutional racism in mental health. *Journal of Mental Health Counseling, 15,* 55-71.

DeAngelis, T. (1994). Ethnic-minority issues recognized in *DSM-IV. APA Monitor, 25*(11), 36.

DeAngellis, A. (1995, July). Mental health care is elusive for Hispanics. *APA Monitor,* p. 49.

DeLeon, P. H., VandenBos, G. R., & Bulatao, E. Q. (1991). Managed mental health care: A history of federal policy initiative. *Professional Psychology: Research and Practice, 22,* 15-25.

Deloria, V., Jr. (1992). American Indians. In J. D. Buenker & L. A. Ratner (Eds.), *Multiculturalism in the United States* (pp. 31-52). New York: Greenwood.

DeVos, G. (1975). Ethnic pluralism: Conflict and accomodation. In G. DeVos & L. Romanucci-Ross (Eds.), *Ethnic identity: Cultural continuities and change* (pp. 5-41). Palo Alto, CA: Mayfield.

Dick, L. (1995). "Pibloktoq" (Arctic hysteria): A construction of European-Inuit relations? *Arctic Anthropology, 32,* 1-42.

Dien, S. D. (1983). Big me and little me: A Chinese perspective on self. *Psychiatry, 46,* 281-286.

Dillard, J. L. (1973). *Black English: Its history and use in the United States.* New York: Vintage.

Dinges, N. G., Trimble, J. E., Manson, S. M., & Pasquale, F. L. (1981). Counseling and psychotherapy with American Indians and Alaska Natives. In A. J. Marsella & P. B. Pedersen (Eds.), *Cross-cultural counseling and psychotherapy* (pp. 243-276). New York: Pergamon.

Dodson, J. E. (1983). Black families: The clue to cultural appropriateness as an evaluative concept for health and human services. In A. E. Johnson (Ed.), *The Black experience: Considerations for health and human services* (pp. 43-52). Davis, CA: International Dialogue Press.

Doi, T. (1962). Amae: A key concept for understanding Japanese personality structure. In R. Smith & R. Beardsley (Eds.), *Japanese culture: Its development and characteristics* (pp. 122-129). Chicago, IL: Aldine.

Doi, T. (1971). *The anatomy of dependence.* Tokyo: Kodansha International.

Doi, T. (1973). *The anatomy of dependence.* Tokyo: Kodansha International.

Doi, T. (1984). Psychotherapy: A cross-cultural perspective from Japan. In P. B. Pedersen, N. Sartorius, & A. J. Marsella (Eds.), *Mental health services: The cross-cultural context* (pp. 267-279). Beverly Hills, CA: Sage.

Doi, T. (1990). The cultural assumptions of psychoanalysis. In J. W. Stigler, R. A. Shweder, & G. Herdt (Eds.), *Cultural psychology: Essays on comparative human development* (pp. 446-453). New York: Cambridge University Press.

Domino, G., Affonso, D., & Slobin, M. (1987). Community psychology in the People's Republic of China. *Psychologia, 30,* 1-11.

Dowell, D. A., Poveda-de-Augustin, J. M., & Lowenthal, A. (1987). Changing mental health services in Madrid: International issues. *Hospital and Community Psychiatry, 38,* 68-72.

Dufrene, P. M., & Coleman, V. D. (1992). Counseling Native Americans: Guidelines for group process. *Journal of Specialists in Group Work, 17,* 229-234.

Dunnigan, T. (1983). Processes of identity maintenance on Hmong society. In G. L. Hendricks, B. T. Downing, & A. S. Deinard (Eds.), *The Hmong in transition* (pp. 41-53). Staten Island, NY: Center for Migration Studies of New York; Southeast Asian Refugee Studies, University of Minnesota.

Duran, E., & Blanes, T. (1991). Spain: Democracy followed by devolution. In L. Appleby & R. Araya (Eds.), *Mental health services in the global village* (pp. 54-68). London: Gaskell.

Eaton, W. W., & Kessler, L. G. (Eds.). (1985). *Epidemiologic field methods in psychiatry.* New York: Academic Press.

Ebihara, M. (1985). Khmer. In D. W. Haines (Ed.), *Refugees in the United States: A reference handbook* (pp. 127-147). Westport, CT: Greenwood.

Edwards, E. D., & Edwards, M. E. (1984). Group work practice with American Indians. *Social Work With Groups, 7*(3), 7-21.

Ellison, R. (1952). *Invisible man.* New York: Random House.

Epstein, N. B., Baldwin, L. M., & Bishop, D. S. (1983). The McMaster Family Assessment Device. *Journal of Marital and Family Therapy, 9,* 171-180.

Epstein, N. B., & Bishop, D. (1981). Problem-centered systems therapy of the family. In A. S. Gurman & D. R. Kniskern (Eds.), *Handbook of family therapy* (pp. 444-490). New York: Brunner Mazel.

Escobar, J. I. (1987). Cross-cultural aspects of the somatization trait. *Hospital and Community Psychiatry, 38,* 174-180.

Escobar, J. I. (1993). Psychiatric epidemiology. In A. C. Gaw (Ed.), *Culture, ethnicity, and mental illness* (pp. 43-73). Washington, DC: American Psychiatric Press.

Escobar, J. I., Gomez, J., & Tuason, V. B. (1983). Depressive symtomatology in North and South American patients. *American Journal of Psychiatry, 140,* 47-51.

Espin, O. M. (1987). Psychological impact of migration on Latinas: Implications for psychotherapeutic practice. *Psychology of Women Quarterly, 11,* 489-503.

Etzioni, A. (1968). *The active society.* New York: Free Press.

Evans, L. A., Acosta, F. X., Yamamoto, J., & Hurwicz, M. L. (1986). Patient requests: Correlates and their therapeutic implications for Hispanic, black, and caucasian patients. *Journal of Clinical Psychology, 42,* 213-221.

Eyton, J., & Neuwirth, G. (1984). Cross-cultural validity: Ethnocentrism in health ctudies with special reference to the Vietnamese. *Social Science in Medicine, 18,* 447-453.

Fabrega, H., Jr. (1991). Somatization in cultural and historical perspective. In L. J. Kirmayer & J. M. Robbins (Eds.), *Current concepts of somatization: Research and clinical perspectives* (pp. 181-199). Washington, DC: American Psychiatric Press.

Fairchild, H. H. (1985). Black, Negro, or Afro-American? The differences are crucial! *Journal of Black Studies, 16,* 47-55.

Fairweather, G. W. (Ed.). (1980). *The Fairweather lodge: A twenty-five year retrospective.* San Francisco: Jossey-Bass.

Fanon, F. (1967). *Black skin, white masks* (C. L. Markmann, Trans.). New York: Grove.

Fischer, E. H., & Turner, J. L. (1970). Orientations to seeking help: Development and research utility of an attitude scale. *Journal of Consulting and Clinical Psychology, 35,* 79-90.

Flaskerud, J. H. (1990). Matching client and therapist ethnicity, langauge, and gender: A review of research. *Issues in Mental Health Nursing, 11,* 321-336.

Frank, R. G., Sullivan, M. J., & DeLeon, P. H. (1994). Health care reform in the states. *American Psychologist, 49,* 855-867.

Freeman, J. (1989). *Hearts of sorrow: Vietnamese American lives.* Stanford, CA: Stanford University Press.

French, L. (1989). Native American alcoholism: A transcultural counseling perspective. *Counselling Psychology Quarterly, 2*(2), 153-166.

Friedman, S., Paradis, C. M., & Hatch, M. (1994). Characteristics of African American and white patients with panic disorder and agoraphobia. *Hospital and Community Psychiatry, 45,* 798-803.

Fuchs, M., & Bashshur, R. (1975). Use of traditional Indian medicine among urban Native Americans. *Medical Care, 13*(11), 915-927.

Fujii, J. S., Fukushima, S. N., & Yamamoto, J. (1993). Psychiatric care of Japanese Americans. In A. C. Gaw (Ed.), *Culture, ethnicity, and mental illness* (pp. 305-345). Washington, DC: American Psychiatric Press.

Gall, S. B., & Gall, T. L. (Eds.). (1993). *Statistical record of Asian Americans.* Detroit. MI: Gale Research.

Gary, L. E. (1987). Attitudes of black adults toward community mental health services. *Hospital and Community Psychiatry, 38,* 1100-1105.

Gaw, A. (1975). An integrated approach in a delivery of health care to a Chinese community in America: The Boston experience. In A. Kleinman (Ed.), *Medicine in Chinese cultures* (pp. 327-350). Washington, DC: Government Printing Office.

Geller, J. D. (1988). Racial bias in the evaluation of patients for psychotherapy. In L. D. Cómas-Diaz & E. E. H. Griffith (Eds.), *Clinical guidelines in cross-cultural mental health* (pp. 112-134). New York: John Wiley.

Ghee, K. L. (1990). The psychological importance of self definition and labeling: Black versus African American. *Journal of Black Psychology, 17,* 75-93.

Gilbert, D., & Kahl, J. A. (1987). *The American class structure: A new synthesis.* Chicago: Dorsey.

Gilchrist, L., Schinke, S., Trimble, J., & Cvetkovich, G. (1987). Skills enhancement to prevent substance abuse among American Indian adolescents. *International Journal of the Addictions, 22*(9), 869-879.

Glazer, N., & Moynihan, D. P. (1976). Introduction. In D. Glazer & D. P. Moynihan (Eds.), *Ethnicity: Theory and experience* (pp. 1-26). Cambridge, MA: Harvard University Press.

Glazer, W. M. (1992). Psychiatry and medical necessity. *Psychiatric Annals, 22,* 362-366.

Golding, J. M., & Aneshensel, C. S. (1989). Factor structure of the Center for Epidemiologic Studies Depression Scale among Mexican Americans and non-Hispanic whites. *Psychological Assessment, 3,* 163-178.

Golding, J. M., & Burnam, M. A. (1990). Immigration stress and depressive symptoms in a Mexican American community. *Journal of Nervous and Mental Disease, 178,* 161-171.

Golding, J. M., Potts, M. K., & Aneshensel, C. S. (1991). Stress exposure among Mexican Americans and non-Hispanic whites. *Journal of Community Psychology, 19,* 37-59.

Gong-Guy, E., Cravens, R. B., & Patterson, T. E. (1991). Clinical issues in mental health service delivery to refugees. *American Psychologist, 46,* 642-648.

Gonsalves, C. J. (1992). Psychological stages of the refugee process: A model for therapeutic interventions. *Professional Psychology: Research and Practice, 23,* 382-389.

Gould, K. H. (1995). The misconstruing of multiculturalism: The Stanford debate and social work. *Social Work, 40,* 198-205.

Graham, S. (1992). "Most of the subjects were white and middle-class": Trends in published research on African Americans in selected APA journals, 1970-1989. *American Psychologist, 47,* 629-639.

Granger, J. M., & Portner, D. L. (1985). Ethnic- and gender-sensitive social work practice. *Journal of Social Work Education, 21,* 38-47.

Graziano, A. M. (1969). Clinical innovation and the mental health power structure. *American Psychologist, 24,* 8-18.

Greenhill, M. (1978). Toward a theory of clinical science. *Psychosomatics, 19,* 519-520.

Grekin, P. M., Jemelka, R., & Trupin, E. W. (1994). Racial differences in the criminalization of the mentally ill. *Bulletin of the American Academy of Psychiatry and the Law, 22,* 411-420.

Griffith, E. E. H., & Baker, F. M. (1993). Psychiatric care of African Americans. In A. C. Gaw (Ed.), *Culture, ethnicity, and mental illness* (pp. 147-173). Washington, DC: American Psychiatric Press.

Griffith, J., & Villavicencio, S. (1985). Relationships among acculturation, sociodemographic characteristics, and social supports in Mexican American adults. *Hispanic Journal of Behavioral Sciences, 7,* 75-92.

Griffin, J. T. (1991). Racism and humiliation in the African American community. *Journal of Primary Prevention, 12,* 149-167.

Grossman, J., & Shigaki, I. S. (1994). Investigation of familial and school-based risk factors for Hispanic Head Start children. *American Journal of Orthopsychiatry, 64,* 456-467.

Guarnaccia, P. J., Rivera, M., Franco, F., & Neighbors, C. (1996). The experiences of ataques de nervios: Toward an anthropology of emotions in Puerto Rico. *Culture, Medicine, and Psychiatry, 20,* 343-367.

Gurak, D. T. (1981). Family structural diversity of Hispanic ethnic groups. *Research Bulletin, 4,* 6-10.

Gurin, P., & Hatchett, S. (1982). *Group identity and subjective mental health.* Unpublished manuscript, University of Michigan, Institute for Social Research, Ann Arbor.

Gustafson, J. P. (1976). The group matrix of individual therapy. *Contemporary Psychoanalysis, 12*(2), 227-229.

Gutierrez, D. J. (1995). *Walls and mirrors: Mexican Americans, Mexican immigrants, and the politics of ethnicity.* Berkeley: University of California Press.

Gutman, A. (Ed.). (1994). *Multiculturalism: Examining the politics of recognition.* Princeton, NJ: Princeton University Press.

Guzman, L. P. (1993). Guidelines for treating ethnic minority clients. *Independent Practitioner, 13*(1), 22-25.

Haberman, P. W. (1976). Psychiatric symptoms among Puerto Ricans in Puerto Rico and the United States. *Ethnicity, 3,* 133-144.

Hacker, A. (1992). *Two nations: Black and white, separate, hostile, unequal.* New York: Scribner's.

Halberstadt-Freud, H. C. (1991). Mental health care in China. *International Review of Psychoanalysis, 18*(1), 11-18.

Harré, R. (1984). *Personal being.* Cambridge, MA: Harvard University Press.

Harrell, S. (1991). Pluralism, performance, and meaning in Taiwanese healing: A case study. *Culture, Medicine and Psychiatry, 15,* 45-68.

Hayes-Bautista, D. E. (1974). Becoming Chicano: A "dis-assimilation" theory of transformation of ethnic identity. *Dissertation Abstracts International, 34,* 5332A. (University Microfilms No. 74-4708, 283)

Hays, P. A. (1995). Multicultural applications of cognitive-behavior therapy. *Professional Psychology: Research and Practice, 26,* 309-315.

Heller, D. (1985). *Power in psychotherapeutic practice.* New York: Human Sciences Press.

Heller, K., & Monahan, J. (1977). *Psychology and community change.* Homewood, IL: Dorsey.

Helms, J. E. (1984). Toward an explanation of the influence of race in the counseling process: A black-white model. *Counseling Psychologist, 12,* 153-165.

Helms, J. E. (Ed.). (1990a). *Black and white racial identity: Theory, research, and practice.* New York: Greenwood.

Helms, J. E. (1990b). Toward a model of white racial identity development. In J. E. Helms (Ed.), *Black and white racial identity: Theory, research, and practice* (pp. 49-66). Westport, CT: Greenwood.

Helms, J. E. (1992). Why is there no study of cultural equivalence in standardized cognitive ability testing? *American Psychologist, 47,* 1083-1101.

Helms, J. E., & Carter, R. T. (1991). Relationships of white and black racial identity attitudes and demographic similarity to counselor preferences. *Journal of Counseling Psychology, 38,* 446-457.

Henkin, W. A. (1985). Toward counseling the Japanese in America: A cross-cultural primer. *Journal of Counseling and Devlopment, 63,* 500-503.

Hinton, W. L., Chen, Y. C. J., Du, N., Tran, C. G., Lu, F. G., Miranda, J., & Faust, S. (1993). *DSM-III-R* disorders in Vietnamese refugees. *Journal of Nervous and Mental Disease, 181,* 113-122.

Ho, M. K. (1984). Social group work with Asian-Pacific Americans. *Social Work With Groups, 7,* 49-61.

Ho, M. K. (1987). *Family therapy with ethnic minorities.* Newbury Park, CA: Sage.

Hoberman, H. M. (1992). Ethnic minority status and adolescent mental health service utilization. *Journal of Mental Health Administration, 19,* 246-267.

Hobfoll, S. F., Spielberger, C. D., Breznitz, S., Figley, C., Folkman, S., Lepper-Green, B., Milgram, N. A., Sandler, I., Sarason, I., & van der Kolk, B. (1991). War-related stress: Addressing the stress of war and other traumatic events. *American Psychologist, 46,* 848-855.

Hohmann, A. A., Richeport, M., Marriott, B. M., Canino, G. J., Rubio-Stipec, M., & Bird, H. (1990). Spiritism in Puerto Rico: Results of an island-wide community study. *British Journal of Psychiatry, 156,* 328-335.

Homma-True, R., Greene, B., López, S. R., & Trimble, J. E. (1993). Ethnocultural diversity in clinical psychology. *Clinical Psychologist, 46,* 50-63.

Hong, G. K. (1988). A general family practitioner approach for Asian American mental health services. *Professional Psychology: Research and Practice, 19,* 600-605.

Hornby, R. (1992a). *Training culturally appropriate interventions for Native Americans* (Application No. 0536). Washington, DC: Comprehensive Program Fund for the Improvement of Secondary Education.

Hornby, R. (1992b). *Competency training for human service providers.* Unpublished manuscript.

Hoshmand, L. L. S. T. (1989). Alternate research paradigms: A review and teaching proposal. *Counseling Psychologist, 17,* 3-79.

Howard, G. S. (1991). Culture tales: A narrative approach to thinking, cross-cultural psychology, and psychotherapy. *American Psychologist, 46,* 187-197.

Howard-Pitney, B., LaFromboise, T. D., Basil, M., September, B., & Johnson, M. (1992). Psychological and social indicators of suicide ideation and suicide attempts in Zuni adolescents. *Journal of Consulting and Clinical Psychology, 60,* 473-476.

Hsu, F. L. K. (1971). Psychosocial homeostasis and Jen: Conceptual tools for advancing psychological anthropology. *American Anthropologist, 73,* 23-44.

Hsu, F. L. K. (1985). The self in cross-cultural perspective. In A. J. Marsella, G. DeVos, & F. L. K. Hsu (Eds.), *Culture and self: Asian and western perspectives* (pp. 24-55). New York: Tavistock.

Hughes, C. C., & Wintrob, R. M. (1995). Culture-bound syndromes and the cultural context of clinical psychiatry. In J. M. Oldham & M. B. Riba (Eds.), *Review of psychiatry* (Vol. 14, pp. 565-597). Washington, DC: American Psychiatric Press.

Hui, T., Snowden, L. R., Jerrell, J. M., & Nguyen, T. D. (1991). Ethnic populations in public mental health: Services choice and level of use. *American Journal of Public Health, 81,* 1429-1434.

Hung, N. M. (1985). Vietnamese. In D. W. Haines (Ed.), *Refugees in the United States: A reference handbook* (pp. 195-208). Westport, CT: Greenwood.

Huntington, S. P. (1993). The clash of civilizations. *Foreign Affairs, 72*(3), 22-49.

Ibrahim, F. A. (1985). Effective cross-cultural counseling and psychotherapy. *Counseling Psychologist, 13,* 625-638.

Inclan, J. E., & Herron, D. G. (1989). Puerto Rican adolescents. In J. T. Gibbs & L. N. Huang (Eds.), *Children of color: Psychological interventions with minority youth* (pp. 251-275). San Francisco, CA: Jossey-Bass.

Irigon, F., Claravall, V., & Christian, A. (1990, June). *Cultural issues related to effective mental health treatment for Asian-Pacific Islander population.* Paper presented at the Washington Second Annual Statewide Mental Health Conference, Yakima, WA.

Irwin, L. (1992). Cherokee healing: Myth, dreams, and medicine. *American Indian Quarterly, 16*(2), 237-257.

Ishiyama, F. I. (1986). Positive reinterpretation of fear of death: A Japanese (Morita) psychotherapy approach to anxiety treatment. *Psychotherapy, 23,* 556-562.

Ishiyama, F. I. (1990). A Japanese perspective on client inaction: Removing attitudinal blocks through Morita therapy. *Journal of Counseling and Development, 68,* 566-570.

Issacs, M. R., & Benjamin, M. P. (1991). *Toward a culturally competent system of care* (Vol. 2). Washington, DC: CAASP Technical Assistance Center, Georgetown University Child Development Center.

Jackson, D. N. (1989). *Basic Personality Inventory manual.* Port Huron, MI: Sigma Assessment Associates.

Jackson, G. G. (1976). The African genesis of the black perspective. *Professional Psychology, 7,* 292-308.

Jackson, J. S. (Ed.). (1991). *Life in black America.* Newbury Park, CA: Sage.

Jackson, J. S., Chatters, L. M., & Taylor, R. J. (Eds.). (1993). *Aging in black America.* Newbury Park, CA: Sage.

Jackson, J. S., McCullough, W. R., Gurin, G., & Broman, C. L. (1991). Race identity. In J. S. Jackson (Ed.), *Life in black America* (pp. 238-253). Newbury Park, CA: Sage.

Jacobsen, F. M. (1988). Ethnocultural assessment. In L. Cómas-Diaz & E. E. H. Griffith (Eds.), *Clinical guidelines in cross-cultural mental health* (pp. 135-147). New York: John Wiley.

Jahoda, G. (1977). In pursuit of the emic-etic distinction: Can we ever capture it? In Y. P. Poortinga (Ed.), *Basic problems in cross-cultural psychology* (pp. 55-63). The Netherlands: Swets & Zeitlinger.

Jenkins, F. H. (1996). Culture, emotion, and PTSD. In A. J. Marsella, M. J. Friedman, E. T. Gerrity, & R. M. Scurfield (Eds.), *Ethnocultural aspects of posttraumatic stress disorder: Issues, research, and clinical applications* (pp. 165-182). Washington, DC: American Psychological Association.

Jensen, L. C., McGhie, A. P., & Jensen, J. R. (1991). Do men and women's worldviews differ? *Psychological Reports, 68,* 312-314.

Jilek, W. (1975). Native renaissance: The survival and revival of indigenous therapeutic ceremonials among North American Indians. *Transcultural Psychiatric Research Review, 15,* 117-147.

Johnson, D. L., & Johnson, C. A. (1965). Totally discouraged: A depression syndrome of the Dakota Sioux. *Transcultural Psychiatric Research, 1,* 141-143.

Johnson, F. A. (1994). African perspectives on mental disorder. In J. E. Mezzich, Y. Honda, & M. C. Kastrop (Eds.), *Psychiatric diagnosis in a world perspective* (pp. 57-66). New York: Springer-Verlag.

Johnson, M. E., & Lashley, K. H. (1989). Influence of Native Americans' cultural commitment on preferences for counselor ethnicity and expectations about counseling. *Journal of Multicultural Counseling and Development, 17*(July), 115-122.

Johnson, R. (1993). Clinical issues in the use of the *DSM-III-R* with African American children. *Journal of Black Psychology, 19,* 447-460.

Jones, A. C. (1985). Psychological functioning in black Americans: A conceptual guide for use in psychotherapy. *Psychotherapy, 22,* 363-369.

Jones, A. C. (1989). Psychological functioning in African American adults: Some elaborations on a model with clinical applications. In R. L. Jones (Ed.), *Black adult development and aging* (pp. 297-307). Berkeley, CA: Cobb & Henry.

Jones, J. M. (1991). A call to advance psychology's role in minority issues. *APA Monitor, 21*(6), 23.

Jones-Correa, M., & Leal, D. L. (1996). Becoming "Hispanic": Secondary panethnic identification among Latino-origin populations in the United States. *Hispanic Journal of Behavioral Sciences, 18,* 214-254.

Jordaan, J. P., Myers, R. A., Layton, W. L., & Morgan, H. H. (Eds.). (1968). *The counseling psychologist.* New York: Teachers College Press.

Jordan, J. B. (1988). Interventions with Native Americans. In D. Cappezzi & L. Golden (Eds.), *Preventing adolescent suicide* (pp. 299-322). Muncie, IN: Accelerated Development.

Juarez, R. (1985). Core issues in psychotherapy with the Hispanic child. *Psychotherapy, 22,* 441-448.

Jung, M. (1984). Structural family therapy: Its application to Chinese families. *Family Process, 23,* 365-374.

Kahn, M. W., & Delk, J. L. (1973). Developing a community mental health clinic on the Papago Indian Reservation. *International Journal of Social Psychiatry, 19,* 299-306.

Kahn, M. W., Lejero, L., Antone, M., Francisco, D., & Manual, J. (1988). An indigenous community mental health service on the Tohono O'odham (Papago) Indian reservation: Seventeen years later. *American Journal of Community Psychology, 16,* 369-378.

Kahn, M. W., Lewis, J., & Galvez, E. (1974). An evaluation of a group therapy procedure with reservation adolescent Indians. *Psychotherapy: Theory, Research and Practice, 11,* 241-244.

Kahn, M. W., Williams, C., Galvez, E., Lejero, L., Conrad, R., & Goldstein, G. (1975). The Papago Psychology Service: A community mental health program on an American Indian reservation. *American Journal of Community Psychology, 3,* 81-97.

Karenga, M. (1997). *Kwanzaa: Origin, concepts, practice.* Los Angeles, CA: Kawaida.

Katz, J. H. (1985). The sociopolitical nature of counseling. *Counseling Psychologist, 13,* 615-624.

Katz, R., & Rohde, E. (1981). Community alternatives to psychotherapy. *Psychotherapy: Theory, Research and Practice, 18,* 365-374.

Kearney, M. (1975). Worldview theory and study. In B. J. Siegel (Ed.), *Annual review of psychology* (Vol. 4, pp. 247-270). Palo Alto, CA: Annual Reviews.

Kendrick, E. A., MacMillan, M. F., & Pinderhughes, C. A. (1983). A racial minority: Black Americans and mental health care. *American Journal of Social Psychiatry, 3*(2), 11-18.

Kerckhoff, A. C., & McCormick, T. C. (1955). Marginal status and marginal personality. *Social Forces, 34*(1), 48-55.

Kessler, R. C., McGonagle, K. A., Zhao, S., Nelson, C. B., Hughes, M., Eshleman, S., Wittchen, H. U., & Kendler, K. S. (1994). Lifetime and 12-month prevalence of DSM-III-R psychiatric disorders in the United States. *Archives of General Psychiatry, 51,* 8-19.

Kiesler, C. A., & Simpkins, S. (1992). *The unnoticed majority: Psychiatric outpatient care in general hospitals.* New York: Plenum.

Kim, S. C. (1985). Family therapy for Asian Americans: A strategic-cultural framework. *Psychotherapy, 22,* 342-348.

Kimble, G. A. (1984). Psychology's two cultures. *American Psychologist, 39,* 833-839.

Kinzie, J. D., Boehnlein, J. K., Leung, P. K., Moore, L. J., Riley, C., & Smith, D. (1990). The prevalence of posttraumatic stress disorder and its clinical significance among Southeast Asian refugees. *American Journal of Psychiatry, 147,* 913-917.

Kinzie, J. D., Leung, P., & Boehlnein, J. K. (1987). Antidepressent blood levels in South Asians. *Journal of Nervous and Mental Disease, 175,* 480-485.

Kinzie, J. D., Leung, P. K., Boehnlein, J., Matsunaga, D., Johnson, R., Manson, S., Shore, J. H., Heinz, J., & Williams, M. (1992). Psychiatric epidemiology of an Indian village: A 19-year replication study. *Journal of Nervous and Mental Disease, 180,* 33-39.

Kirk, S. A., & Kutchens, H. (1992). The setting of *DSM:* The rhetoric of science in psychiatry. Hawthorne, NJ: Aldine de Gruyter.

Kitano, H. H. L., Fujino, D., & Takahashi, J. (in press). Interracial marriage: Where are the Asian Americans and where are they going? In L. Lee & N. Zane (Eds.), *Handbook of Asian American psychology*. Thousand Oaks, CA: Sage.

Kitano, H. H. L., & Maki, M. T. (1996). Continuity, change, and diversity. In P. Pedersen, J. G. Draguns, W. J. Lonner, & J. E. Trimble (Eds.), *Counseling across cultures* (4th ed., pp. 124-145). Thousand Oaks, CA: Sage.

Kleinman, A. (1988). *Rethinking psychiatry: From clinical category to personal experience*. New York: Free Press.

Kluckhohn, F. R., & Strodtbeck, F. L. (1961). *Variations in value orientations*. Evanston, IL: Row Paterson.

Koizumi, K., & Harris, P. (1992). Mental health care in Japan. *Hospital and Community Psychiatry, 43*, 1100-1103.

Kondo, A. (1953). Morita therapy. *American Journal of Psychoanalysis, 13*, 31-37.

Korman, M. (1974). National conference on levels and patterns of professional training in psychology: Major themes. *American Psychologist, 29*, 301-313.

Korte, T. (1993, June 3). Navajos seek help of traditional healers. *The Oregonian*, p. 24.

Koss-Chioino, J. (1989). *Women as healers, women as patients: Mental health care and traditional healing in Puerto Rico*. Boulder, CO: Westview.

Kramer, M. (1995). Projected changes in the population of the United States-1990, 2000 and 2010: Implication for mental health and primary health care. *International Journal of Methods in Psychiatric Research, 5*, 123-137.

Kraudy, E., Liberati, A., Asioli, F., & Saraceno, B. (1987). Organization of services and patterns of psychiatric care in Nicaragua: Result of a survey in 1986. *Acta Psychiatrica Scandinavica, 76*, 545-551.

Kreitman, N., Sainsbury, P., Morrissey, J., Towers, J., & Scrivener, J. (1961). The reliability of psychiatric assessment: An analysis. *Journal of Mental Science, 107*, 887-908.

Kutchens, H., & Kirk, S. A. (1995, May). *DSM-IV:* Does bigger and newer mean better? *Harvard Mental Health Letter*, pp. 4-6.

LaBarre, W. (1941). A cultist drug-addiction in an Indian alcoholic. *Bulletin of the Menninger Clinic, 5*, 40-46.

Ladinsky, J. L., Volk, N. D., & Robinson, M. (1987). The influence of traditional medicine in shaping medical care practices in Vietnam today. *Social Science and Medicine, 25*, 1105-1110.

LaFromboise, T. D. (1988). American Indian mental health policy. *American Psychologist, 43*, 388-397.

LaFromboise, T. D. (1991). *Zuni life skills development curriculum*. Madison, WI: University of Wisconsin Press.

LaFromboise, T. D., Foster, S., & James, A. (1996). Ethics in multicultural counseling. In P. B. Pedersen, J. G. Draguns, W. J. Lonner, & J. E. Trimble (Eds.), *Counseling across cultures* (4th ed., pp. 47-72). Thousand Oaks, CA: Sage.

LaFromboise, T. D., & Howard-Pitney, B. (1995). The Zuni life skills development curriculum: Description and evaluation of a suicide prevention program. *Journal of Counseling Psychology, 42*, 479-486.

LaFromboise, T. D., Trimble, J. E., & Mohatt, G. V. (1990). Counseling intervention and American Indian tradition: An integrative approach. *Counseling Psychologist, 18*, 628-654.

Land, H., & Levy, A. (1992). A school-based prevention moel for depressed Asian adolescents. *Social Work in Education, 14*, 165-175.

Landrine, H., & Klonoff, E. A. (1994). The African American Acculturation Scale: Development, reliability, and validity. *Journal of Black Psychology, 20,* 104-127.

Landrine, H., & Klonoff, E. A. (1996). *African American acculturation: Deconstructing race and reviving culture.* Thousand Oaks, CA: Sage.

Langer, T. S. (1962). A 22-item screening score of psychiatric symptoms indicating impairment. *Journal of Health and Human Behavior, 3,* 269-276.

Laosebikan, S. (1973). Mental health in Nigeria. *Journal of Black Studies, 4,* 221-228.

Lartigue, T., & Vivas, J. (1991). Mental health services in Mexico. *Journal of Sociology and Social Welfare, 18*(2), 57-83.

Lawson, W. B., Hepler, N., Holladay, J., & Cuffel, B. (1994). Race as a factor in inpatient and outpatient admissions and diagnosis. *Hospital and Community Psychiatry, 45,* 72-74.

Lazarus, R. S. (1984). Puzzles in the study of daily hassles. *Journal of Behavioral Medicine, 7,* 375-384.

Lazarus, R. S., & Folkman, S. (1984). *Stress, appraisal, and coping.* New York: Springer.

Leary, K. (1995). "Interpreting in the dark": Race and ethnicity in psychoanalytic psychotherapy. *Psychoanalytic Psychotherapy, 12,* 127-140.

Leary, T. (1957). *Interpersonal diagnosis of personality.* New York: Ronald.

Lebra, T. S. (1986). Self-reconstruction in Japanese religious psychotherapy. In T. S. Lebra & W. P. Lebra (Eds.), *Japanese culture and behavior: Selected readings* (Rev. ed., pp. 354-368). Honolulu: University of Hawaii Press.

Lebra, W. P. (1969). Shaman and client in Okinawa. In W. Caudill & T. Y. Lin (Eds.), *Mental health research in Asia and the Pacific* (pp. 216-222). Honolulu, HI: East-West Center.

Lee, C. P., Juan, G., & Hom, A. B. (1984). Group work practice with Asian clients: A sociocultural approach. *Social Work With Groups, 7,* 37-48.

Lee, E. (1982). A social systems approach to assessment and treatment for Chinese American families. In M. McGoldrick, J. K. Pearce, & J. Giordano (Eds.), *Ethnicity and family therapy* (pp. 527-551). New York: Guilford.

Lefley, H. P. (1979a). Female case of falling-out: A psychological evaluation of a small sample. *Social Science and Medicine, 13B,* 115-116.

Lefley, H. P. (1979b). Prevalence of potential falling-out cases among the black, Latin, and non-Latin white population of the city of Miami. *Social Science and Medicine, 138,* 113-114.

Leong, F. T. L. (1986). Counseling and psychotherapy with Asian Americans: Review of the literature. *Journal of Coounseling Psychology, 33,* 196-206.

Leong, F. T. L. (1992). Guidelines for minimizing premature termination among Asian American clients in group counseling. *Journal for Specialists in Group Work, 17,* 218-228.

Leong, F. T. L., Wagner, N. S., & Tata, S. P. (1995). Racial and ethnic variations in help-seeking attitudes. In J. G. Ponterotto, J. M. Casas, L. A. Suzuki, & C. M. Alexander (Eds.), *Handbook of multicultural counseling* (pp. 415-438). Thousand Oaks, CA: Sage.

Leung, A. C. N. (1993). Psychotherapy a la Chinese: Forms of folk psychotherapy practiced by the Chinese. *Independent Practitioner, 13*(1), 25-28.

LeVine, E. S., & Padilla, A. M. (1980). *Crossing cultures in therapy: Pluralistic counseling for the Hispanic.* Pacific Grove, CA: Brooks/Cole.

Lewis, T. H. (1975). A syndrome of depression and mutism in the Ogalala Sioux. *American Journal of Psychiatry, 132,* 753-755.

Lewis-Fernandez, R. (1996a). Cultural formulation of psychiatric diagnosis. Case No. 02. Diagnosis and treatment of nervios and ataques in a female Puerto Rican migrant. *Culture, Medicine, and Psychiatry, 20,* 155-163.

Lewis-Fernandez, R. (1996b). Cultural formulation of psychiatric diagnosis. *Culture, Medicine, and Psychiatry, 20,* 133-144.

Lex, B. W. (1987). Review of alcohol problems in ethnic minority groups. *Journal of Consulting and Clinical Psychology, 55,* 293-300.

Li, S., & Phillips, M. R. (1990). With doctors and mental illness in mainland China: A preliminary study. *American Journal of Psychiatry, 147,* 221-224.

Li-Repac, D. (1980). Cultural influences on perception: A comparison between Caucasian and Chinese American therapists. *Journal of Cross-Cultural Psychology, 11,* 327-342.

Lieberman, R. P. (1994). Treatment and rehabilitation of the seriously mentally ill in China: Impressions of a society in transition. *American Journal of Orthopsychiatry, 64,* 68-77.

Lin, T. Y. (1982). Culture and psychiatry: A Chinese perspective. *Australian and New Zealand Journal of Psychiatry, 16,* 235-245.

Lin, T. Y., & Lin, M. C. (1978). Service delivery issues in Asian North American communities. *American Journal of Psychiatry, 135,* 454-456.

Lipsey, M. (1974). Research and relevance: A survey of graduate students and faculty in psychology. *American Psychologist, 29,* 541-555.

Lockart, B. (1981). Historic distrust and the counseling of American Indians and Alaska Natives. *White Cloud Journal, 2*(3), 31-34.

Locke, M. (1983). Japanese responses to social change—Making the strange familiar. *Western Journal of Medicine, 139,* 829-834.

Loescher, G., & Scanlan, J. A. (1986). *Calculated kindness: Refugees and America's half-open door, 1945 to the present.* New York: Free Press.

Loevinger, J. (1976). *Ego development.* San Francisco: Jossey-Bass.

Long, K. A. (1983). The experience of repeated and traumatic loss among Crow Indian children. *American Journal of Orthopsychiatry, 53,* 116-126.

Lonner, W. J. (1980). The search for psychological universals. In H. C. Triandis & W. W. Lambert (Eds.), *Handbook of cross-cultural psychology: Perspectives* (Vol. 1, pp. 143-204). Boston: Allyn & Bacon.

Loo, C., Fong, K. T., & Iwamas, G. (1988). Ethnicity and cultural diversity: An analysis of work published in community psychology journals, 1965-1985. *Journal of Community Psychology, 16,* 332-349.

López, S. R. (1996). Multicultural assessment: Widening our cultural lenses. *Contemporary Psychology, 41,* 455-456.

López, S. R., Grover, K. P., Holland, D., Johnson, M. J., Kain, C. D., Kanel, K., Mellins, C. A., & Rhyne, M. C. (1989). Development of culturally sensitive therapists. *Professional Psychology: Research and Practice, 20,* 369-376.

López, S. R., & Hernandez, P. (1986). How culture is considered in evaluations of psychopathology. *Journal of Nervous and Mental Disease, 176,* 598-606.

López, S. R., & Hernandez, P. (1987). When culture is considered in the evaluation and treatment of Hispanic patients. *Psychotherapy, 24,* 120-126.

López, S. R., López, A. A., & Fong, K. T. (1991). Mexican Americans' initial preferences for counselors: The role of ethnic factors. *Journal of Counseling Psychology, 38,* 487-496.

López, S., & Núñez, J. A. (1987). Cultural factors considered in selected diagnostic criteria and interview schedules. *Journal of Abnormal Psychology, 96,* 270-272.

Lorenzo, M. K., & Adler, D. A. (1984). Mental health services for Chinese in a community mental health center. *Social Casework, 65,* 600-609.

Loring, M., & Powell, B. (1984). Gender, race, and *DSM-III:* A study of the objectivity of psychiatric diagnostic behavior. *Journal of Health and Social Behavior, 29*(March), 1-22.

Low, S. (1985). Culturally interpreted symptoms or culture-bound syndromes: A cross-cultural review of nerves. *Social Science and Medicine, 21,* 187-196.

Lu, F. G., Lin, R. F., & Mezzich, J. E. (1995). Issues in the assessment and diagnosis of culturally diverse individuals. In J. M. Oldham & M. B. Riba (Eds.), *Review of psychiatry* (Vol. 14, pp. 477-510). Washington, DC: American Psychiatric Press.

Luckert, K. W. (1972). Traditional Navaho theories of disease and healing. *Arizona Medicine, 29,* 570-573.

Lykes, M. B. (1985). Gender and individualistic versus collectivist bases for notions about the self. *Journal of Personality, 53,* 356-383.

MacMillan, A. M. (1957). The Health Opinion Survey: Technique for estimating prevalence of psychoneurotic and related types of disorders in communities. *Psychological Reports, 3,* 325-339.

Maduro, R. J. (1982). Working with Latinos and the use of dream analysis. *Journal of the American Academy of Psychoanalysis, 10,* 609-628.

Maduro, R. J., & Martinez, C. F. (1974). Latino dream analysis: Opportunity for confrontation. *Social Casework, 55,* 461-469.

Mail, P. D., McKay, R. B., & Katz, M. (1989). Expanding practice horizons: Learning from American Indian patients. *Patient Education and Counseling, 13,* 91-102.

Majors, R., & Nikelly, A. (1983). Serving the black minority: A new direction for psychotherapy. *Journal of Non-White Concerns, 11*(4), 142-151.

Maldonado-Martinez, I. (1990). Mental health: The history of an internationalist cooperation with Nicaragua. *Family Systems Medicine, 8,* 327-337.

Malgady, R. G. (1996). The question of cultural bias in assessment and diagnosis of ethnic minority clients: Let's reject the Null Hypothesis. *Professional Psychology: Research and Practice, 27,* 73-77.

Malgady, R. G., Rogler, L. H., & Cortes, D. E. (1996). Cultural expression of psychiatric symptoms: Idioms of anger among Puerto Ricans. *Psychological Assessment, 8,* 265-268.

Malgady, R. G., Rogler, L. H., & Costantino, G. (1990). Hero-heroine modeling for Puerto Rican adolescebnts: A preventive mental health intervention. *Journal of Consulting and Clinical Psychology, 58,* 702-712.

Mandiberg, J. M. (1993). Between a rock and a hard place: The mental health system in Japan. In J. M. Mandiberg (Ed.), *Innovations in Japanese mental health services* (pp. 3-12). San Francisco, CA: Jossey-Bass.

Manicas, P. T., & Secord, P. F. (1983). Implications for psychology of the new philosophy of science. *American Psychologist, 38,* 399-413.

Mann, J. W. (1958). Group relations and the marginal personality. *Human Relations, 11,* 77-92.

Manson, S., Beals, J., O'Nell, T., Piasecki, J., Bechtold, D., Keane, E., & Jones, M. (1996). Wounded spirits, ailing hearts: PTSD and related disorders among American Indians. In A. J. Marsella, M. J. Friedman, E. T. Gerrity, & R. M. Scurfield (Eds.), *Ethnocultural aspects of posttraumatic stress disorder: Issues, research, and clinical applications* (pp. 255-283). Washington, DC: American Psychological Association.

Manson, S. M., & Shore, J. H. (1981). Psychiatric epidemiological research among American Indians and Alaska Natives: Methodological issues. *White Cloud Journal, 2*(2), 48-56.

Marano, L. (1982). Windigo psychosis: The anatomy of an emic-etic confusion. *Current Anthropology, 23,* 385-412.

Marcos, L. R. (1994). The psychiatric examination of Hispanics: Across the language barrier. In R. G. Malgady & O. Rodriquez (Eds.), *Theoretical and conceptual issues in Hispanic mental health* (pp. 144-153). Malabar, FL: Krieger.

Maril, R. L., & Zavaleta, A. N. (1979). Drinking patterns of low-income Mexican American women. *Journal of Studies on Alcohol, 40,* 480-484.

Marín, G., & Marín, B. V. (1991). *Research with Hispanic populations.* Newbury Park, CA: Sage.

Marsella, A. J., Friedman, M. J., Gerrity, E. T., & Scurfield, R. M. (Eds.). (1996). *Ethnocultural aspects of posttraumatic stress disorder: Issues, research, and clinical applications.* Washington, DC: American Psychological Association.

Martin-Baro, I. (1989). Political violence and war as causes of psychosocial trauma in El Salvador. *International Journal of Mental Health, 18,* 3-30.

Massey, D. S., Gross, A. B., & Shibuya, K. (1994). Migration, segregation, and the geographic concentration of poverty. *American Sociological Review, 59,* 425-445.

Massey, D. S., & Hajnal, Z. L. (1995). The changing geographic structure of black-white segregation in the United States. *Social Science Quarterly, 76,* 527-542.

Matheson, L. (1986). If you are not an Indian, how do you treat an Indian? In H. P. Lefley & P. B. Pedersen (Eds.), *Cross-cultural training for mental health professionals* (pp. 115-130). Springfield, IL: Charles C Thomas.

Mathews, L. (1996, July 6). Census bureau considers adding "multiracial" to its categories. *The Oregonian,* p. A19.

Matsuoka, J. (1993). Demographic characteristics as determinants in qualitative differences in the adjustment of Vietnamese refugees. *Journal of Social Service Research, 17*(3/4), 1-21.

May, R. (1967). *Psychology and human dilemma.* Princeton, NJ: Van Nostrand.

May, R. (1972). *Power and innocence: A search for the sources of violence.* New York: Norton.

May, P. A., & Moran, J. R. (1995). Prevention of alcohol misuse: A review of health promotion efforts among American Indians. *American Journal of Health Promotion, 9,* 288-299.

Mays, V. M., Caldwell, C. H., & Jackson, J. S. (1996). Mental health symptoms and service utilization patterns of help seeking among African American women. In H. W. Neighbors & J. S. Jackson (Eds.), *Mental health in black America* (pp. 161-176). Thousand Oaks, CA: Sage.

McClure, G. M. (1988). Adolescent mental health care in China. *Journal of Adolescence, 11*(1), 1-10.

McKinley, V. (1987). Group therapy as a treatment modality of special value for Hispanic patients. *International Journal of Group Psychotherapy, 37,* 255-268.

McNally, R. J. (1992). Psychopathology of posttraumatic stress disorder (PTSD): Boundaries of the syndrome. In M. Basoglu (Ed.), *Torture and its consequences: Current treatment approaches* (pp. 229-252). New York: Cambridge University Press.

McNeilly, M. D., Anderson, N. B., Armstead, C. A., Clark, R., Corbett, M., Robinson, E. L., Pieper, C. F., & Lepisto, E. M. (1996). The Perceived Racism Scale: A multidimensional assessment of the experience of white racism among African Americans. *Ethnicity & Disease, 6,* 154-166.

Meinhardt, K., Tom, S., Tse, P., & Yu, C. Y. (1985/1986). Southeast Asian refugees in the "Silicon Valley": The Asian Health Assessment Project. *Amerasia, 12*(2), 43-65.

Mendoza, R. H. (1989). An empirical scale to measure type and degree of acculturation in Mexican American adolescents and adults. *Journal of Cross-Cultural Psychology, 20,* 372-385.

Meredith, G. M. (1966). Amae and acculturation among Japanese-American college students in Hawaii. *Journal of Social Psychology, 68,* 175-182.

Meyer, G. G. (1974). On helping the casualties of rapid change. *Psychiatric Annals, 4,* 44-48.

Mezzich, J. E. (1995). Cultural formulation and comprehensive diagnosis: Clinical and research perspectives. *Psychiatric Clinics of North America, 18,* 649-657.

Millet, P. E., Sullivan, B. F., Schwebel, A. I., & Myers, L. J. (1996). Black Americans' and white Americans' views of etiology and treatment of mental health problems. *Community Mental Health Journal, 32,* 235-242.

Milliones, J. (1980). Construction of a black consciousness measure. *Psychotherapy: Theory, Research and Practice, 17,* 175-182.

Miura, M., & Usa, S. I. (1974). A psychotherapy of neurosis: Morita therapy. In T. S. Lebra & W. P. Lebra (Eds.), *Japanese culture and behavior: Selected readings* (pp. 407-430). Honolulu: University of Hawaii Press.

Mohatt, G. (1985). *Cross-cultural perspectives on prevention and training: The healer and prevention.* Unpublished paper, University of Alaska-Fairbanks, College of Human and Rural Development.

Mohatt, G. (1988). Psychological method and spiritual power in cross-cultural psychotherapy. *Journal of Contemplative Psychotherapy, 5,* 85-115.

Mollica, R. F., Wyshak, G., & Lavelle, J. (1987). The psychosocial impact of war trauma and torture on Southeast Asian refugees. *American Journal of Psychiatry, 144,* 1567-1572.

Montero, D. (1979). *Vietnamese Americans: Patterns of resettlement and socioeconomic adaptation in the United States.* Boulder, CO: Westview.

Montes, J. H., Eng, E., & Braithwaite, R. L. (1995). A commentary on minority health as a paradigm shift in the United States. *American Journal of Health Promotion, 9,* 247-250.

Montgomery, D. E., Fine, M. A., & James-Myers, L. (1990). The development and validation of an instrument to assess an optimal Afrocentric worldview. *Journal of Black Psychology, 17,* 37-54.

Moore, L. J., & Boehnlein, J. K. (1991). Posttraumatic stress disorder, depression, and somatic symptoms in the U.S. Mien patients. *Journal of Nervous and Mental Disease, 179,* 728-733.

Morey, L. C. (1991). *Personality Assessment Inventory manual.* Odessa, FL: Personality Assessment Resources.

Moyerman, D. R., & Forman, B. D. (1992). Acculturation and adjustment: A meta-analytic study. *Hispanic Journal of Behavioral Sciences, 14,* 163-200.

Muensterberger, W. (1984). Transcultural psychoanalysis: The case of a Chinese army officer. *Journal of Psychoanalytic Anthropology, 7,* 3-21.

Munakata, T. (1986). Japanese attitudes toward mental illness and mental health care. In T. S. Lebra & W. P. Lebra (Eds.), *Japanese culture and behavior: Selected readings* (Rev. ed., pp. 369-378). Honolulu: University of Hawaii Press.

Murase, K. (1992). Models of service delivery in Asian American communities. In S. M. Furuto, R. Biswas, D. K. Chung, K. Murase, & F. Ross-Sherif (Eds.), *Social work practice with Asian Americans* (pp. 101-120). Newbury Park, CA: Sage.

Murase, T. (1974). Naikan therapy. In T. S. Lebra & W. P. Lebra (Eds.), *Japanese culture and behavior: Selected readings* (pp. 431-442). Honolulu: University of Hawaii Press.

Murase, T., & Johnson, F. (1974). Naikan, Morita, and Western psychotherapy. *Archives of General Psychiatry, 31,* 121-128.

Murphy, J. M., & Hughes, C. C. (1965). The use of psychophysiological symptoms as indicators of disorder among the Eskimos. In J. M. Murphy & A. Leighton (Eds.), *Approaches to cross-cultural psychiatry* (pp. 64-107). Ithaca, NY: Cornell University Press.

Murray, H. A. (1938). *Explorations in personality.* New York: Oxford University Press.

Myers, H. F. (1982). Research on the Afro-American family: A critical review. In B. A. Bass, G. E. Wyatt, & G. J. Powell (Eds.), *The Afro-American family: Assessment, treatment, and research issues* (pp. 35-68). New York: Grune & Stratton.

Myers, H. F., Alvy, K. T., Arrington, A., Richardson, M. A., Marigna, M., Huff, R., Main, M., & Newcomb, M. D. (1992). The impact of a parent training program on inner-city African American families. *Journal of Community Psychology, 20,* 132-147.

Myrdal, G. (1944). *An American dilemma: The Negro problem and modern democracy.* New York: Harper and Row.

Nagata, D. K. (1990). The Japanese American internment: Exploring the transgenerational consequences of traumatic stress. *Journal of Traumatic Stress, 3,* 47-69.

Nagata, D. K. (1991). Transgenerational impact of the Japanese American internment: Clinical issues in working with children of former internees. *Psychotherapy, 28,* 121-128.

Naierman, N., Haskins, B., & Robinson, G. (1978). *Community mental health centers—A decade later.* Cambridge, MA: Abt Associates.

Narayanan, L., Menon, S., & Levine, E. L. (1995). Personality structure: A culture-specific examination of the five-factor model. *Journal of Personality Assessment, 64,* 51-62.

Narikiyo, T. A., & Kameoka, V. A. (1992). Attributions of mental illness and judgments about help seeking among Japanese American and white American students. *Journal of Counseling Psychology, 39,* 363-369.

Nathan, P. E. (1994). *DSM:IV:* Empirical, accessible, not yet ideal. *Journal of Clinical Psychology, 50,* 103-110.

Neal, A. M., Rich, L. N., & Smucker, W. D. (1994). The presence of panic disorder among African American hypertensives: A pilot study. *Journal of Black Psychology, 20,* 29-35.

Neal, A. M., & Turner, S. M. (1991). Anxiety disorder research with African Americans: Current status. *Psychological Bulletin, 109,* 400-410.

Neff, J. A. (1984). Race differences in psychological distress: The effects of SES, urbanicity, and measurement strategies. *American Journal of Community Psychology, 12,* 337-351.

Neff, J. A., & Husaini, B. A. (1987). Urbanicity, race, and psychological distress. *Journal of Community Psychology, 15,* 520-536.

Neighbors, H. W., & Jackson, J. S. (Eds.). (1996). *Mental health in black America.* Thousand Oaks, CA: Sage.

Neighbors, H. W., Jackson, J. S., Broman, C., & Thompson, E. (1996). Racism and the mental health of African Americans: The role of self and system blame. *Ethnicity & Disease, 6,* 167-175.

Neighbors, H. W., & Lumpkin, S. (1990). The epidemiology of mental disorder in the Black population. In D. S. Ruiz & J. P. Comer (Eds.), *Handbook of mental health and mental disorders among Black Americans* (pp. 55-71). New York: Greenwood.

Neligh, G. (1988). Major mental disorders and behavior among American Indians and Alaska Natives. In S. M. Manson & N. G. Dinges (Eds.), *Behavioral health issues among American Indians and Alaska Natives: Explorations on the frontiers of the biobehavioral sciences* (Vol. 1, Monograph No. 1, pp. 116-159). Denver, CO: National Center for American Indian and Alaska Native Mental Health Research.

Newhill, C. E. (1990). The role of culture in the development of paranoid psychopathology. *American Journal of Orthopsychiatry, 60,* 176-185.

Newton, F. (1978). The Mexican American emic system of mental illness: An exploratory study. In J. M. Casas & S. E. Keefe (Eds.), *Family and mental health in the Mexican American community* (Monograph No. 7, pp. 69-90). Los Angeles: University of California, Spanish-Speaking Mental Health Center.

Ng, F. (1993). Toward a second generation Hmong history. *Amerasia Journal, 19*(3), 51-69.

Ng, M. L. (1985). Psychoanalysis for the Chinese applicable or not applicable? *International Review of Psychoanalysis, 12,* 449-460.

NIMH-Sponsored Group on Culture and Diagnosis. (1993). *Cultural proposals and supporting papers for* DSM-IV (3rd rev.). Pittsburgh, PA: University of Pittsburgh, Department of Psychiatry and Epidemiology.

Nishimura, K. (1987). Shamanism and medical cures. *Current Anthropology, 28*(4), 59-64.

Nishio, K., & Bilmes, M. (1987). Psychotherapy with Southeast Asian American clients. *Professional Psychology: Research and Practice, 18,* 342-346.

Nofz, M. P. (1988). Alcohol abuse and culturally marginal American Indians. *Social Casework, 69*(2), 67-73.

Norton, D. G. (1978). *The dual perspective.* New York: Council on Social Work Education.

O'Connell, J. C. (1985). A family systems approach for serving rural, reservation Native American communities. *Journal of American Indian Education, 24*(2), 1-6.

O'Nell, T. D. (1989). Psychiatric investigations among American Indians and Alaska Natives: A critical review. *Culture, Medicine, and Psychiatry, 13,* 51-87.

O'Nell, T. D. (1992/1993). "Feeling worthless": An ethnographic investigation of depression and problem drinking at the Flathead reservation. *Culture, Medicine, and Psychiatry, 16,* 447-469.

O'Sullivan, M. J., Peterson, P. D., Cox, G. B., & Kirkeby, J. (1989). Ethnic populations: Community mental health services 10 years later. *American Journal of Community Psychology, 17,* 17-30.

Obot, I. S. (1996). Problem drinking, chronic disease, and recent life events. In H. W. Neighbors & J. S. Jackson (Eds.), *Mental health in black America* (pp. 45-61). Thousand Oaks, CA: Sage.

Okazaki, S., & Sue, S. (1995). Methodological issues in assessment research with ethnic minorities. *Psychological Assessment, 7,* 367-375.

Olmedo, E. L. (1979). Acculturation: A psychometric perspective. *American Psychologist, 34,* 1061-1070.

Olney, D. (1993). Population trends. In G. L. Hendricks, B. T. Downing, & A. S. Deinard (Eds.), *The Hmong in transition* (pp. 179-184). New York: Center for Migration Studies of New York and Southeast Asian Refugee Studies, University of Minnesota.

Oquendo, M., Horwath, E., & Martinez, A. (1992). Ataques de nervios: Proposes diagnostic criteria for a culture specific syndrome. *Culture, Medicine, & Psychiatry, 16,* 367-376.

Oquendo, M. A. (1994). Differential diagnosis of ataque de nervios. *American Journal of Orthopsychiatry, 65,* 60-65.

Orbe, M. P. (1995). African American communication research: Toward a deeper understanding of interethnic communication. *Western Journal of Communication, 59,* 61-78.

Owan, T. C. (Ed.). (1985a). Southeast Asian Mental Health: *Treatment, prevention, services, training, and research* (DHHS Publication No. [ADM] 85-1399). Rockville, MD: National Institute of Mental Health.

Owan, T. C. (1985b). Southeast Asian Mentl Health: Transition from treatment services to prevention—A new direction. In T. C. Owan (Ed.), *Southeast Asian Mental Health: Treatment, prevention, services, training, and research* (DHHS Publication No. [ADM] 85-1399, pp. 141-167). Rockville, MD: National Institute of Mental Health.

Padgett, D. K., Patrick, C., Burns, B. J., & Schlesinger, H. J. (1994). Women and outpatient mental health services: Use by black, Hispanic, and white women in a national insured population. *Journal of Mental Health Administration, 21,* 347-360.

Padilla, A. M., Lindholm, K. J., Chen, A., Duran, R., Hakuta, K., Lambert, W., & Tucker, G. R. (1991). The English-only movement: Myths, reality, and implications for psychology. *American Psychologist, 46,* 120-130.

Padilla, A. M., & Ruiz, R. A. (1976). *Latino mental health: A review of literature.* Rockville, MD: U.S. Department of Health, Education, and Welfare.

Palacios, M., & Franco, J. N. (1986). Counseling Mexican American women. *Journal of Multicultural Counseling and Development, 14*(3), 124-131.

Paniagua, F. A. (1994). *Assessing and treating culturally diverse clients: A practical guide.* Thousand Oaks, CA: Sage.

Panitz, D. R., & McConche, R. D. (1983). The role of machismo and the Hispanic family in the etiology and treatment of alcoholism in Hispanic American males. *American Journal of Family Therapy, 11,* 31-44.

Parham, T. A. (1989). Cyles of psychological Nigrescence. *Counseling Psychologist, 17,* 187-226.

Parham, T. A., & Helms, J. E. (1981). The influence of black students' racial identity attitudes on preference for counselor's race. *Journal of Counseling Psychology, 28,* 250-257.

Parson, E. R. (1985). The intercultural setting: Encountering black Vietnam veterans. In S. Sonnenberg, A. Blank, & J. Talbott (Eds.), *The trauma of war: Stress and recovery in Vietnam veterans* (pp. 361-387). Washington, DC: American Psychiatric Press.

Pascarosa, P., Futterman, S., & Halsweig, M. (1976). Observations of alcoholics in the peyote ritual: A pilot study. *Annals of the New York Academy of Sciences, 273,* 518-524.

Patterson, D. G., & Lofquist, L. (1960). A note on the training of clinical and counseling psychologists. *American Psychologist, 15,* 365-366.

Paul, G. L., & Lentz, R. J. (1977). *Psychological treatment of chronic mental patients: Milieu versus social-learning programs.* Cambridge, MA: Harvard University Press.

Payton, C. R. (1994). Implications of the 1992 Ethics Code for diverse groups. *Professional Psychology: Research and Practice, 25,* 317-320.

Pearson, R. E. (1985). The recognition and use of natural support systems in cross-cultural counseling. In P. Pedersen (Ed.), *Handbook of cross-cultural counseling and psychotherapy* (pp. 299-306). Westport, CT: Greenwood.

Pearson, V. (1992). Community and culture: A Chinese model of community care for the mentally ill. *International Journal of Social Psychiatry, 38*(3), 163-178.

Pedersen, P. B. (1995). Culture-centered ethical guidelines for counselors. In J. G. Ponterotto, J. M. Casas, L. A. Suzuki, & C. M. Alexander (Eds.), *Handbook of multicultural counseling* (pp. 34-49). Thousand Oaks, CA: Sage.

Pedersen, P. B., & Marsella, A. J. (1982). The ethical crisis for cross-cultural counseling and therapy. *Professional Psychology, 13,* 492-500.

Penayo, U. (1989). Experiences of a psychiatric outpatient in Nicaragua. *Social Psychiatry and Psychiatric Epidemiology, 24*(3), 151-155.

Persons, J. B. (1986). The advantages of studying psychological phenomena rather than psychiatric diagnosis. *American Psychologist, 41,* 1252-1260.

Pettigrew, T. F. (1964). *A profile of the Negro American.* Princton, NJ: Van Nostrand.

Phenice, L. A., & Griffore, R. J. (1994). College students' stereotypes. *College Student Journal, 28,* 373-375.

Philippe, J., & Romain, J. B. (1979). Indisposition in Haiti. *Social Science and Medicine, 13B,* 1252-1260.

Phillips, F. B. (1990). NTU psychotherapy. *Journal of Black Psychology, 17,* 55-74.

Pike, K. L. (1966). *Language in relation to a unified theory of the structure of human behavior.* The Hague: Mouton.

Pinderhughes, E. (1982). Afro-American families and the victim system. In M. McGoldrick, J. K. Pierce, & J. Giordiano (Eds.), *Ethnicity and family therapy* (pp. 108-122). New York: Guilford.

Pinderhughes, E. (1989). *Understanding race, ethnicity, and power: The key to efficacy in clinical practice.* New York: Free Press.

Plasky, P., & Lorion, R. P. (1984). Demographic parameters of self-disclosure to psychotherapists and others. *Psychotherapy, 21,* 483-490.

Plous, S., & Williams, T. (1995). Racial stereotpyes from the days of American slavery: A continuing legacy. *Journal of Applied Social Psychology, 25,* 795-817.

Polkinghorne, D. E. (1988). *Narrative knowing and the human sciences.* Albany: State University of New York Press.

Pomales, J., & Williams, V. (1989). Effects of level of acculturation and counseling style on Hispanic students' perceptions of counselor. *Journal of Counseling Psychology, 36,* 79-83.

Ponce, F. Q., & Atkinson, D. R. (1989). Mexican American acculturation, counselor ethnicity, counseling style, and perceived counselor credibility. *Journal of Counseling Psychology, 36,* 203-208.

Ponterotto, J. G. (1988). Racial consciousness development among white counselor trainees: A stage model. *Journal of Multicultural Counseling and Development, 16*(4), 146-156.

Ponterotto, J. G. (1997). Multicultural counseling training: A competence model and national survey. In D. B. Pope-Davis & H. L. K. Coleman (Eds.), *Multicultural counseling competencies: Assessment, education and training, and supervision* (pp. 111-130). Thousand Oaks, CA: Sage.

Ponterotto, J. G., & Alexander, C. M. (1996). Assessing the multicultural competence of counselors and clinicians. In L. A. Suzuki, P. Meller, & C. M. Alexander (Eds.), *Handbook of multicultural counseling* (pp. 34-50). Thousand Oaks, CA: Sage.

Ponterotto, J. G., Alexander, C. M., & Grieger, I. (1995). A multicultural competency checklist for counseling training programs. *Journal of Multicultural Counseling and Development, 23,* 11-20.

Ponterotto, J. G., Alexander, C. M., & Hinkston, J. A. (1988). Afro-American preferences for counselor characteristics: A replication and extension. *Journal of Counseling Psychology, 35,* 175-182.

Ponterotto, J. G., & Casas, J. M. (Eds.). (1991). *Handbook of racial-ethnic minority counseling research.* Springfield, IL: Charles C Thomas.

Pope, K. S., & Garcia-Peltoniemi, R. E. (1991). Responding to victims of turture: Clinical issues, professional responsibilities, and useful resources. *Professional Psychology: Research and Practice, 22,* 269-276.

Pope-Davis, D. B., Breaux, C., & Liu, W. M. (1997). A multicultural immersion experience: Filling a void in multicultural training. In D. B. Pope-Davis & H. L. K. Coleman (Eds.), *Multicultural counseling competencies: Assessment, education and training, and supervision* (pp. 227-241). Thousand Oaks, CA: Sage.

Pope-Davis, D. B., & Coleman, H. L. K. (Eds.). (1997). *Multicultural counseling competencies: Assessment, education and training, and supervision.* Thousand Oaks, CA: Sage.

Popp, C., & Takemoto, Y. (1993). The application of the core conflictual relationship theme method to Japanese psychoanalytic psychotherapy. *Journal of the American Academy of Psychoanalysis, 21,* 229-252.

Portes, A., Kyle, D., & Eaton, W. W. (1992). Mental illness and help-seeking behavior among Mariel Cuban and Haitian refugees in South Florida. *Journal of Health and Social Behavior, 33,* 283-298.

Portes, A., & Rumbaut, R. G. (1990). *Immigrant America: A portrait.* Berkeley: University of California Press.

Poveda, J. M., Garcia, S., Palomo, E., & Octavio, O. (1987). Mental health in Spain, 1960-1985. *International Journal of Mental Health, 16*(1-2), 182-197.

Powers, W. K. (1982). *Yuwipi: Vision and experience in Ogalala ritual.* Lincoln: University of Nebraska Press.

Price, R. H., Cowen, E. L., Lorion, R. P., & Ramos-McKay, J. (Eds.). (1988). *14 ounces of prevention: A casebook for practitioners.* Washington, DC: American Psychological Association.

Price, R. H., Van Ryn, M., & Vinokur, A. D. (1992). Impact of preventive job search interventions on the liklihood of depression among the enemployed. *Journal of Health and Social Behavior, 33*(June), 158-167.

Prieto, J. M. (1994). Contemporary psychology in Spain. *Annual Review of Psychology, 45,* 51-78.

Raimy, V. (Ed.). (1950). *Training in clinical psychology.* New York: Prentice Hall.

Ramirez, M., III. (1984). Assessing and understanding biculturalism-multiculturalism in Mexican American adults. In J. L. Martinez, Jr. & R. H. Mendoza (Eds.), *Chicano psychology* (pp. 77-94). Orlando, FL: Academic Press.

Ramirez, S. Z., Wassef, A., Paniagua, F. A., Linskey, A., & O'Boyle, M. (1994). Perceptions of mental health providers concerning cultural factors in the evaluation of Hispanic children and adolescents. *Hispanic Journal of Behavioral Sciences, 16,* 28-42.

Randall, E. J. (1994). Cultural relativism in cognitive therapy with disadvantaged African American women. *Journal of Cognitive Psychotherapy, 8,* 195-207.

Rappaport, H., & Rappaport, M. (1981). The integration of scientific and traditional healing. *American Psychologist, 36,* 774-781.

Rendon, M. (1993). The psychoanalysis of ethnicity and the ethnicity of psychoanalysis. *American Journal of Psychoanalysis, 53,* 109-122.

Resnikoff, R., Pustilnik, S., & Resnikoff, D. (1991). Mexico: Struggling for a better future. In L. Appleby & R. Araya (Eds.), *Mental health services in the global village* (pp. 184-202). London: Gaskell.

Ridley, C. R., Mendoza, D. W., & Kanitz, B. E. (1994). Multicultural training: Reexamination, operationalization, and integration. *Counseling Psychologist, 22,* 27-289.

Ridley, C. R., Mendoza, D. W., Kanitz, B. F., Angermeier, L., & Zenk, R. (1994). Cultural sensitivity in multicultural counseling: A perceptual schema model. *Journal of Counseling Psychology, 41,* 125-136.

Rin, H. (1975). The synthesizing mind in Chinese ethno-cultural adjustment. In G. De Vos & L. Romanucci-Rpss (Eds.), *Ethnic identity: Cultural communities and change* (pp. 137-155). Palo Alto, CA: Mayfield.

Rivera, G., Jr. (1988). Hispanic folk medicine utilization in urban Colorado. *Sociology and Social Research, 72,* 237-241.

Roberts, R. E. (1980). Prevalence of psychological distress among Mexican American. *Journal of Health and Social Behavior, 21,* 134-145.

Robin, R. W., Chester, B., & Goldman, D. (1996). Cumulative trauma and PTSD in American Indian communities. In A. J. Marsella, M. J. Friedman, E. T. Gerrity, & R. M. Scurfield (Eds.), *Ethnocultural aspects of posttraumatic stress disorder: Issues, research, and clinical applications* (pp. 239-253). Washington, DC: American Psychological Association.

Robinson, J. L. (1995). *Racism or attitude: The ongoing struggle of black liberation and self-esteem.* New York: Plenum.

Robinson, T. L., & Howard-Hamilton, M. (1994). An Afrocentric paradigm: Foundation for a healthy self-image and healthy interpersonal relationships. *Journal of Mental Health Counseling, 16,* 327-339.

Rodriguez, C. E. (1989). *Puerto Ricans: Born in the U.S.A.* Boston, MA: Unwin Hyman.

Rogler, L. H., Cooney, R. S., Costantino, G., Earley, B. F., Grossman, B., Gurak, D. T., & Rodriguez, O. (1983). *A conceptual framework for mental health research on Hispanic populations.* New York: Fordham University, Hispanic Research Center.

Rogler, L. H., Cortes, D. E., & Malgady, R. G. (1991). Acculturation and mental health status among Hispanics. *American Psychologist, 46,* 585-597.

Rogler, L. H., Cortes, D. E., & Malgady, R. G. (1994). The mental health relevance of idioms of distress: Anger and perceptions of injustice among Puerto Ricans. *Journal of Nervous and Mental Disease, 182,* 327-330.

Rogler, L. H., Malgady, R. G., Costantino, G., & Blumenthal, R. (1987). What do culturally sensitive mental health services mean? The case of Hispanics. *American Psychologist, 42,* 565-570.

Rogler, L. H., Malgady, R. G., & Rodriguez, O. (1989). *Hispanics and mental health: A framework for research.* Malabar, FL: Krieger.

Root, M. P. P. (1985). Guidelines for facilitating therapy with Asian American clients. *Psychotherapy, 22,* 349-356.

Rosenheck, R., & Fontana, A. (1994). Utilization of mental health services by minority veterans of the Vietnam era. *Journal of Nervous and Mental Disease, 182,* 685-691.

Rowe, W., Bennett, S. K., & Atkinson, D. R. (1994). White racial identity models: A critique and alternative proposal. *Counseling Psychologist, 22,* 129-146.

Roy, C., Choudhuri, A., & Irvine, D. (1970). The prevalence of mental disorders among Saskatchewan Indians. *Journal of Cross-Cultural Psychology, 1,* 383-392.

Ruiz, A. S. (1975). Chicano group catalysts. *Personnel and Guidance Journal, 53,* 462-466.

Ruiz, A. S. (1990). Ethnic identity: Crisis and resolution. *Journal of Multicultural Counseling and Development, 18,* 29-40.

Ruiz, R. A., & Casas, J. M. (1981). Culturally relevant behavioristic counseling for Chicano college students. In P. B. Pedersen, J. G. Draguns, W. J. Lonner, & J. E. Trimble (Eds.), *Counseling across cultures* (pp. 181-202). Honolulu: University of Hawaii Press.

Rumbaut, R. G. (1985). Mental health and the refugee experience: A comparative study of Southeast Asian refugees. In T. C. Owan (Ed.), *Southeast Asian mental health* (pp. 433-486). Rockville, MD: National Institutes of Mental Health.

Rumbaut, R. G. (1989). Portraits, patterns, and predictors of the refugee adaptation process. In D. W. Haines (Ed.), *Refugees as immigrants: Cambodians, Laotians, and Vietnamese in America* (pp. 138-182). Totowa, NJ: Rowman & Littlefield.

Rutledge, J. P. (1992). *The Vietnamese experience in America.* Bloomington: Indiana University Press.

Ryan, A. S. (1985). Cultural factors in casework with Chinese Americans. *Social Casework, 66,* 333-340.

Sabnani, H. B., & Ponterotto, J. G. (1992). Racial/ethnic minority-specific instrumentation in counseling research: A review, critique, and recommendations. *Measurement and Evaluation in Counseling and Development, 24,* 161-187.

Sabnani, H. B., Ponterotto, J. G., & Borodovsky, L. G. (1991). White racial identity development and cross-cultural counselor training. *Counseling Psychologist, 19,* 76-102.

Sabogal, F., Marín, G., Otero-Sabogal, R., VannOss Marín, B., & Perez-Sable, E. J. (1987). Hispanic familism and acculturation: What changes and what doesn't? *Hispanic Journal of Behavioral Sciences, 9,* 397-402.

Sampath, H. M. (1974). Prevalence of psychiatric disorders in a southern Baffin Island Eskimo settlement. *Canadian Psychiatric Association Journal, 19,* 363-367.

Sampson, E. E. (1988). The debate on individualism: Indigenous psychologies of the individual and their role in personal and societal interventions. *American Psychologist, 43,* 15-22.

Sampson, E. E. (1993). Identity politics: Challenges to psychology's understanding. *American Psychologist, 48,* 1219-1230.

Sanders Thompson, V. L. (1996). Perceived experiences of racism as stressful life events. *Community Mental Health Journal, 32,* 223-233.

Sandoval, M. C. (1977). Santeria: Afrocuban concepts of disease and its treatment in Miami. *Social Science and Medicine, 138,* 137-151.

Sandoval, M. C. (1979). Santeria as a mental health care system: An historical overview. *Social Science and Medicine, 138,* 137-151.

Santiago, J. M. (1992). The fate of mental health services in health care reform: I. A system in crisis. *Hospital and Community Psychiatry, 43,* 1091-1094.

Santiago, J. M. (1993). Hispanic, Latino, or Raza? Coming to terms with diversity. *Hospital and Community Psychiatry, 44,* 613.

Sapp, M., Farrell, W., & Durand, H. (1995). Cognitive behavioral therapy: Applications for African American middle school at-risk students. *Journal of Instructional Psychology, 22,* 169-177.

Saraceno, B., Briceno, R. A., Asioli, F., & Liberati, A. (1990). Cooperation in mental health: An Italian project in Nicaragua. *Social Science and Medicine, 31,* 1067-1071.

Sasaki, Y. (1986). Nonmedical healing in contemporary Japan: A psychiatric study. In T. S. Lebra & W. P. Lebra (Eds.), *Japanese culture and behavior: Selected readings* (Rev. ed., pp. 344-353). Honolulu: University of Hawaii Press.

Sasao, T., & Sue, S. (1993). Toward a culturally anchored ecological framework of research in ethnic-cultural communities. *Journal of Community Psychology, 21,* 705-727.

Sattler, J. M. (1970). Racial "experimenter effects" in experimentation, testing, interviewing, and psychotherapy. *Psychological Bulletin, 73,* 137-160.

Schacht, A. J., Tafoya, N., & Mirabela, K. (1989). Home-based therapy with American Indian families. *American Indian and Alaska Native Mental Health Research, 3*(2), 27-42.

Schein, L. (1983). The Miao in contemporary China: A preliminary overview. In G. L. Hendricks, B. T. Downing, & A. S. Deinard (Eds.), *The Hmong in transition* (pp. 73-85). Staten Island, NY: Center for Migration Studies of New York; Southeast Asian Refugee Studies, University of Minnesota.

Schlesinger, A. M., Jr. (1991). *The disuniting of America: Reflections on a multicultural society.* Knoxville, TN: Whittle.

Schwarz, B. (1995, May). The diversity myth: America's leading export. *Atlantic Monthly, 275,* 57-67.

Seaman, G. (1981). In the presence of authority: Hierarchal roles in Chinese spirit medium cults. In A. Kleinman & T. Y. Lin (Eds.), *Normal and abnormals behavior in Chinese culture* (pp. 61-74). Dordrecht, Holland: Reidel.

Selker, L. G. (1988). *Associate degree nursing and the nursing home.* New York: National League for Nursing.

Sena-Rivera, J. (1979). Extended kinship in the United States: Competing models and the case of la familia chicana. *Journal of Marriage and the Family, 41,* 121-129.

Shadish, W. R., Jr. (1984). Policy research: Lessons from the implementation of deinstitutionalization. *American Psychologist, 39,* 725-738.

Shen, W. W., Sanchez, A. M., & Huang, T. D. (1984). Verbal participation in group therapy: A comparative study on New Mexico ethnic groups. *Hispanic Journal of Behavioral Sciences, 6,* 277-284.

Shon, S. P., & Ja, D. Y. (1982). Asian families. In M. McGoldrick, J. K. Pearce, & J. Giordano (Eds.), *Ethnicity and family therapy* (pp. 206-228). New York: Guilford.

Shore, J. H., Kinzie, J. D., Hampson, J. L., & Pattison, E. M. (1973). Psychiatric epidemiology of an Indian village. *Psychiatry, 36,* 70-81.

Simons, R. C., & Hughes, C. C. (1985). *The culture-bound syndromes: Folk illnesses of psychiatric and anthropological interest.* Boston, MA: Reidel.

Singer, J. L., & Opler, M. K. (1956). Contrasting patterns of fantasy and motility in Irish and Italian schizophrenics. *Journal of Abnormal and Social Psychology, 53,* 42-47.

Siskin, E. E. (1983). *Washo shamans and peyotists: Religious conflict in an American Indian tribe.* Salt Lake City: University of Utah Press.

Slagle, A. L., & Weibel-Orlando, J. (1986). The Indian Shaker Church and Alcoholics Anonymous: Revitalistic curing cults. *Human Organization, 45,* 310-319.

Slavin, L. A., Rainer, K. L., McCreary, M. L., & Gowda, K. K. (1991). Toward a multicultural model of the stress process. *Journal of Counseling and Development, 70,* 156-163.

Smart, J. F., & Smart, D. W. (1995). Acculturative stress: The experience of the Hispanic immigrant. *Counseling Psychologist, 23,* 25-42.

Smith, B. (1995). *Embracing change: How to survive and thrive in managed care '95.* Irvine, CA: Practice Builder Press.

Smitherman, G. (1973). White English in Blackface, or who do I be? *Black Scholar, 4*(8-9), 32-39.

Solomon, B. B. (1976). *Black empowerment.* New York: Columbia University Press.

Solomon, P. (1987). Racial issues in mental health services. *Psychosocial Rehabilitation Journal, 11*(2), 3-12.

Soto-Fulp, S., & DelCampo, R. L. (1994). Structural family therapy with Mexican American family systems. *Contemporary Family Therapy, 16,* 349-362.

Speck, R. V., & Attneave, C. L. (1973). *Family networks.* New York: Pantheon.

Spires-Robin, R., & McGarrahan, P. (1995). The healing practices of Mexican spiritism. In L. L. Adler & B. R. Mukherji (Eds.), *Spirit versus scapel: Traditional healing and modern psychotherapy* (pp. 121-135). Westport, CT: Bergin & Barvey.

Srole, L., Langer, T. S., & Mitchell, S. T. (1962). *Mental health in the metropolis: The Midtown Manhattan Study* (Vol. 1, rev. ed.). New York: New York University Press.

Starr, B. J., & Wilson, S. F. (1980). Some epistemological and methodological issues in the design of cross-cultural research. In M. P. Hamnett & R. W. Brislin (Eds.), *Research in culture learning: Language and conceptual studies* (pp. 143-153). Honolulu: University Press of Hawaii.

Steele, S. (1990). *The content of our character: A new vision of race in America.* New York: St. Martin's.

Stern, G. G. (1970). *People in context: Measuring person-environment congruence in education and industry.* New York: John Wiley.

Stricker, L. J. (1980). "SES" indexes: What do they measure? *Basic and Applied Socisl Psychology, 1,* 91-101.

Suazo, A. (1990). *Window of opportunity: Disabled Hispanics in the labor force* (Switzer Monograph). Washington, DC: National Institute on Disability and Rehabilitation Research.

Sue, D. W., Arredondo, P., & McDavis, R. J. (1992). Multicultural counseling competencies and standards: A call to the profession. *Journal of Multicultural Counseling and Development, 20,* 64-88.

Sue, D. W., & Sue, S. (1972). Counseling Chinese Americans. *Personnel and Guidance Journal, 50,* 637-644.

Sue, S. (1973). Community intervention: Implications for action. In S. Sue & N. N. Wagner (Eds.), *Asian American psychological perspectives* (pp. 274-280). Palo Alto, CA: Science and Behavioral Books.

Sue, S. (1977). Community mental health services to minority groups: Some optimism, some pessimism. *American Psychologist, 32,* 616-624.

Sue, S. (1996). Measurement, testing, and ethnic bias: Can solutions be found? In G. R. Sodowsky & J. C. Impara (Eds.), *Multicultural assessment in counseling and clinical psychology* (pp. 7-36). Lincoln, NE: Buros Institute of Mental Measurements, University of Nebraska–Lincoln.

Sue, S., Allen, D. B., & Conway, L. (1978). The responsiveness and equality of mental health care to Chicanos and Native Americans. *American Journal of Community Psychology, 6,* 137-146.

Sue, S., Chun, C. H., & Gee, K. (1995). Ethnic minority intervention and treatment research. In J. F. Aponte, R. Y. Rivers, & J. Wohl (Eds.), *Psychological interventions and cultural diversity* (pp. 266-282). Boston: Allyn & Bacon.

Sue, S., Fujino, D., Hu, L., Takeuchi, D., & Zane, N. (1991). Community mental health services for ethnic minority groups. *Journal of Consulting and Clinical Psychology, 59,* 533-540.

Sue, S., Sue, D. W., Sue, L., & Takeuchi, D. T. (1995). Psychopathology among Asian Americans: A model minority? *Cultural Diversity and Mental Health, 1,* 39-51.

Sue, S., & Zane, N. (1987). The role of culture and cultural techniques in psychotherapy: A critique and reformulation. *American Psychologist, 42,* 37-45.

Suinn, R. M. (1985). Research and practice in cross-cultural counseling. *Counseling Psychologist, 13,* 673-684.

Suinn, R. M., Rickard-Figueroa, K., Lew, S., & Vigil, P. (1987). The Suinn-Lew Asian Self-Identity Acculturation Scale: An initial report. *Educational and Psychological Measurement, 47,* 401-407.

Swenson, C. H., Jr. (1973). *Introduction to interpersonal relations.* Glenview, IL: Scott, Foresman.

Swerdlow, M. (1992). "Chronicity," "nervios," and community care: A case study of Puerto Rican psychiatric patients in New York City. *Culture, Medicine, and Psychiatry, 16,* 217-235.

Swinomish Tribal Mental Health Project. (1991). *A gathering of wisdoms. Tribal mental health: A cultural perspective.* Mt. Vernon, WA: Veda Vangarde.

Szapocznik, J., & Kurtines, W. M. (1993). Family psychology and cultural diversity: Opportunities for theory, research, and applications. *American Psychologist, 48,* 400-407.

Szapocznik, J., Kurtines, W. M., Foote, F. H., Perez-Vidal, A., & Hervis, O. (1983). Conjoint versus one-person family therapy: Some evidence for the effectiveness of conducting family therapy through one person. *Journal of Consulting and Clinical Psychology, 51,* 889-899.

Szapocznik, J., Kurtines, W. M., Foote, F., Perez-Vidal, A., & Hervis, O. (1986). Conjoint versus one-person family therapy: Further evidence for the effectiveness of conducting family therapy through one person with drug-abusing adolescents. *Journal of Consulting and Clinical Psychology, 54,* 395-397.

Szapocznik, J., Rio, A., Murray, E., Cohen, R., Scopetta, M., Rivas-Vasquez, A., Hervis, O., Posada, V., & Kurtines, M. (1989). Structural family therapy versus psychodynamic child therapy for problematic Hispanic boys. *Journal of Consulting and Clinical Psychology, 57,* 571-578.

Szapocznik, J., Scopetta, M. A., Aranalde, M. A., & Kurtines, W. (1978). Cuban value structure: Treatment implications. *Journal of Consulting and Clinical Psychology, 46,* 961-970.

Tafoya, T. (1990). Circles and cedar: Native Americans and family therapy. In G. W. Saba, B. M. Karrer, & K. V. Hardy (Eds.), *Minorities and family therapy* (pp. 71-98). New York: Haworth.

Takasashi, T. (1993). Hospital care for the mentally disabled in Japan. In J. M. Mandiberg (Ed.), *Innovations in Japanese mental health services* (pp. 35-44). San Francisco, CA: Jossey-Bass.

Takemoto, Y. (1984, March). *Amae as metalanguage: A critique of Doi's theory of amae*. Paper presented at the 73rd annual meeting of the American Psychoanalytic Association, San Diego, CA.

Takeuchi, D. T., Sue, S., & Yeh, M. (1995). Return rates and outcomes from ethnicity-specific mental health programs in Los Angeles. *American Journal of Public Health, 85,* 638-643.

Takeuchi, D. T., & Uehara, E. S. (1996). Ethnic minority mental health services: Current research and future conceptual directions. In B. L. Levin & J. Petrila (Eds.), *Mental health services: A public health perspective* (pp. 63-80). New York: Oxford University Press.

Taki, R (1985). *Reflected current problems in Japanese society: The thematic content analysis of Jinsei Annai and Dear Abby*. Unpublished master's thesis, University of Arkansas, Fayetteville.

Tanaka-Matsumi, J., & Higginbotham, H. N. (1989). Behavioral approaches to counseling across cultures. In P. B. Pedersen, J. G. Draguns, W. J. Lonner, & J. E. Trimble (Eds.), *Counseling across cultures* (pp. 269-298). Honolulu: University of Hawaii Press.

Tapp, J. L., Kelman, H., Triandis, H., Wrightsman, L., & Coehlo, G. (1974). Advisory proposals for ethical considerations in the conduct of cross-cultural research: Fall 1973 revision. *International Journal of Psychology, 9,* 231-249.

Teicher, A. (1995). Proposal for a psychological classification system. *Independent Practitioner, 15*(2), 82-84.

Terrell, F., & Terrell, S. L. (1981). An inventory to measure cultural mistrust among blacks. *Western Journal of Black Studies, 5*(3), 180-184.

Thao, X. (1986). Hmong perception of illness and traditional ways of healing. In G. L. Hendricks, B. T. Downing, & A. S. Deinard (Eds.), *The Hmong in transition* (pp. 365-378). Staten Island, NY: Center for Migration Studies of New York; Southeast Asian Refugee Studies, University of Minnesota.

Thomas, M. E., Herring, C., & Horton, H. D. (1994). Discrimination over the life course: A synthetic cohort analysis of earning differences between black and white males, 1940-1990. *Social Problems, 41,* 608-626.

Thompson-Sanders, V. L. (1995). The multidimensional structure of racial identification. *Journal of Research in Personality, 29,* 208-222.

Topper, M. D., & Curtis, J. (1987). Extended family therapy: A clinical approach to the treatment of synergistic dual anomic depression among Navajo agency-town adolescents. *Journal of Community Psychology, 15,* 334-348.

Toupin, E. S. W. A. (1980). Counseling Asians: Psychotherapy in the context of racism and Asian American history. *American Journal of Orthopsychiatry, 50,* 76-86.

Toupin, E. S. W. (1981). Counseling Asians: Psychotherapy in the context of racism and Asian American history. *American Journal of Orthopsychiatry, 50,* 76-86.

Tracey, T. J., Leong, F. T. L., & Glidden, C. (1986). Help-seeking and problem perception among Asian Americans. *Journal of Counseling Psychology, 33,* 331-336.

Tran, T. V. (1993). Psychological traumas and depression in a sample of Vietnamese people in the United States. *Health and Social Work, 18*(3), 184-194.

Trimble, J. E. (1992). A cognitive-behavioral approach to drug abuse prevention and intervention with American Indian youth. In L. A. Vargas & J. D. Koss-Chioino (Eds.), *Working with culture: Psychotherapeutic interventions with ethnic minority children and adolescents* (pp. 246-275). San Francisco, CA: Jossey-Bass.

Trimble, J. E., & Fleming, C. (1989). Providing counseling services for Native American Indians: Client, counselor, and community characteristics. In P. Pedersen, J. Draguns, W. Lonner, & J. Trimble (Eds.), *Counseling across cultures* (3rd ed., pp. 145-168). Honolulu: University Press of Hawaii.

Trimble, J. E., Fleming, C. M., Beauvais, F., & Jumper-Thurman, P. (1996). Essential cultural and social strategies for counseling Native American Indians. In P. B. Pedersen, J. G. Draguns, W. J. Lonner, & J. E. Trimble (Eds.), *Counseling across cultures* (pp. 177-209). Thousand Oaks, CA: Sage.

Trimble, J. E., Lonner, W. J., & Boucher, J. D. (1983). Stalking the wiley emic: Alternatives to cross-cultural measurement. In S. H. Irvine & J. W. Berry (Eds.), *Human assessment and cultural factors* (pp. 259-271). New York: Plenum.

Trimble, J. E., Manson, S. M., Dinges, N. G., & Medicine, B. (1984). American Indian concepts of mental health. In P. B. Pedersen, N. Sartorius, & A. J. Marsella (Eds.), *Mental health services: The cross-cultural context* (pp. 199-220). Beverly Hills, CA: Sage.

Trimble, J. E., & Medicine, B. (1993). Diversification of American Indians. In U. Kim & J. W. Berry (Eds.), *Indigenous psychologies: Research and experience in cultural context* (pp. 133-151). Newbury Park, CA: Sage.

Trotter, R. T. (1979). Evidence of an ethnomedical form of aversion therapy on the United States-Mexico border. *Journal of Ethnopharmacology, 1,* 279-284.

Truax, C. B., & Carkhuff, R. R. (1964). For better or for worse: The process of psychotherapeutic personality change. In *Recent advances in the study of behavior change* (pp. 118-163). Montreal, Canada: McGill University Press.

Tsui, P., & Schultz, G. L. (1985). Failure of rapport: Why psychotherapeutic engagement fails in the treatment of Asian clients. *American Journal of Orthopsychiatry, 55,* 561-569.

Tung, M. (1991). Insight-oriented psychotherapy and the Chinese patient. *American Journal of Orthopsychiatry, 61,* 186-194.

Tung, T. M. (1972). The family and the management of mental health problems in Vietnam. In W. T. Lebra (Ed.), *Mental health research in Asia and the Pacific: Transcultural research in mental health* (Vol. 2, pp. 107-113). Honolulu: University Press of Hawaii.

Tung, T. M. (1985). Psychiatric care for Southeast Asians: How different is different? In T. C. Owan (Ed.), *Southeast Asian mental health: Treatment, prevention, services, training, and research* (pp. 5-40). Washington, DC: National Institute of Mental Health.

Turner, J. C., & TenHoor, W. J. (1978). The NIMH Community Support Program: Pilot approach to a needed social reform. *Schizophrenia Bulletin, 4,* 319-349.

Turner, S. M., & Jones, R. T. (Eds.). (1982). *Behavior modification in black populations.* New York: Plenum.

Tweed, D. L., Goldsmith, H. F., Jackson, D. J., Stiles, D., Rae, D. S., & Kraemer, M. (1990). Racial congruity as a contextual correlate of mental disorder. *American Journal of Orthopsychiatry, 60,* 392-403.

U. S. Bureau of the Census. (1984). *The Hispanic population in the United States* (Current Population Reports, Series p. 20, No. 431). Washington, DC: Government Printing Office.

U.S. Bureau of the Census. (1990a). *1990 census of the population, general population characteristics, United States.* Washington, DC: Government Printing Office.

U.S. Bureau of the Census. (1990b). *1990: Census of population: Asians and Pacific Islanders in the United States* (CP-3-5). Washington, DC: Government Printing Office.

U.S. Bureau of the Census. (1993). *Statistical abstract of the United States, 1993* (113th ed.). Washington, DC: Government Printing Office.

U.S. Congress, Office of Technology Assessment. (1993, November). *International health statistics: Background paper* (OTA-BP-H-16). Washington, DC: Government Printing Office.

U.S. Department of Health and Human Services. (1987). *Report of the Secretary's Task Force on black and minority health, August 1985*. Washinton, DC: Government Printing Office.

U.S. Department of Health and Human Services, Centers for Disease Control and Prevention. (1993, June). Diversity in the health care database: A preamble for policymakers. 1992 Annual Report of the National Committee on Vital and Health Statistics, 3-19.

Ulbrich, P. M., Warheit, G. J., & Zimmerman, R. S. (1989). Race, socioeconomic status, and psychological distress: An examination of differential vulnerability. *Journal of Heallth and Social Behavior, 30,* 131-146.

Usdansky, M. L. (1993, November 5). Immigrants' status: Many factors in the mix. *USA Today,* p. 10A.

Valentine, C. A. (1971). Deficit, difference, and bicultural models of Afro-American behavior. *Harvard Educational Review, 41*(2), 137-157.

Van den Berg, J. H. (1961). *The changing nature of man.* New York: Norton.

van der Veer, G. (1992). Counseling and therapy with refugees: Psychological problems of victims of war, torture, and repression. New York: John Wiley.

Van Esterik, J. L. (1985). Lao. In D. W. Haines (Ed.), *Refugees in the United States: A reference handbook* (pp. 149-165). Westport, CT: Greenwood.

Vega, W. A., Khoury, E. L., Zimmerman, R. S., Gil, A. G., & Warheit, G. J. (1995). Cultural conflicts and problem behaviors of Latino adolescents in home and school environments. *Journal of Commmunity Psychology, 23,* 167-179.

Vega, W. A., & Murphy, J. W. (1990). *Culture and the restructuring of community mental health.* New York: Greenwood.

Vega, W. A., & Rumbaut, R. G. (1991). Ethnic minorities and mental health. *Annual Review of Sociology, 17,* 351-383.

Velasquez, R. J., Butcher, J. N., Garrido, M., & Cayiba, J. J. (1996). *Dana's culturally competent MMPI assessment of Hispanics: A case of "rounding up" the usual suspects.* Unpublished manuscript.

Vontress, C. E. (1991). Traditional healing in Africa: Implications for cross-cultural counseling. *Journal of Counseling and Development, 70,* 242-249.

Wade, J. C. (1993). Institutional racism: An analysis of the mental health system. *American Journal of Orthopsychiatry, 63,* 536-544.

Waldram, J. B. (1990). The persistence of traditional medicine in urban areas: The case of Canada's Indians. *American Indian and Alaska Native Mental Health Research, 4*(1), 9-29.

Wallen, J. (1992). Providing culturally appropriate mental health services for minorities. *Journal of Mental Health Administration, 19,* 288-295.

Wang, Z. M. (1993). Psychology in China: A review dedicated to Li Chen. *Annual Review of Psychology, 44,* 87-116.

Warheit, G., Holzer, C. E., & Arey, S. A. (1975). Race and mental illness: An epidemiological update. *Journal of Health and Social Behavior, 16,* 243-256.

Warren, R. C., Jackson, A. M., Nugaris, J., & Farley, G. K. (1973). Differential attitudes of black and white patients toward treatment in a child guidance clinic. *American Journal of Orthopsychiatry, 43,* 384-393.

Watkins-Duncan, B. A. (1992). Principles for formulating treatment with black patients. *Psychotherapy, 29,* 452-457.

Weclew, R. (1975). The nature, prevalence, and level of awareness of "Curanderismo" and some of its implications for mental health. *Community Mental Health Journal, 11,* 145-154.

Wei, W. (1993). *The Asian American movement.* Philadelphia, PA: Temple University Press.

Weidman, H. H. (1979). Falling-out: A diagnostic and treatment problem viewed from a transcultural perspective. *Social Science and Medicine, 13B,* 95-112.

West, C. (1993). *Race matters.* Boston: Beacon.

Westermeyer, J. (1985). Psychiatric diagnosis across cultural boundaries. *American Journal of Psychiatry, 142,* 798-805.

Westermeyer, J. (1986). Indochinese refugees in community and clinic: A report from Asia and the United States. In C. L. Williams & J. Westermeyer (Eds.), *Refugee mental health in resettlement countries* (pp. 113-130). New York: Hemisphere.

Westermeyer, J. (1988). Folk medicine in Laos: A comparison between two ethnic groups. *Social Science and Medicine, 27,* 769-778.

Westermeyer, J., Neider, J., & Callies, A. (1989). Psychosocial adjustment of Hmong refugees during their first decade in the United States. *Journal of Nervous and Mental Disease, 177,* 132-139.

Westermeyer, J., & Wintrob, R. (1988). "Folk" explanations of mental illness in rural Laos. *Psychiatry, 136,* 901-905.

Whatley, P. R., & Dana, R. H. (1989). *Racial identity and MMPI group differences.* Fayetteville: University of Arkansas.

Whitmore, J. K. (1985). Chinese from Southeast Asia. In D. W. Haines (Ed.), *Refugees in the United States: A reference handbook* (pp. 59-76). Westport, CT: Greenwood.

Wiggins, J. S. (1995). *Interpersonal Adjectives Scales: Professional manual.* Odessa, FL: Psychological Assessment Resources.

Williams, D. F., & Anderson, L. P. (1996). The acculturated stress scale. In R. L. Jones (Ed.), *Handbook of tests and measurements for black populations* (pp. 351-358). Hampton, VA: Cobb & Henry.

Williams, D. H. (1986). The epidemiology of mental illness in Afro-Americans. *Hospital and Community Psychiatry, 37,* 42-49.

Williams, D. R. (1996). Racism and health. *Ethnicity & Disease, 6*(1, 2), 1-201.

Williams, J., Karls, J., & Wandrei, K. (1991). The person in environment system for describing problems of social functioning. *Hospital and Community Psychiatry, 40,* 1125-1127.

Williams, R. (1975). *Ebonics: The true language of black folks.* St. Louis, MO: Robert L. Williams and Associates.

Williams, R. L. (1981). *The collective black mind: An Africentric theory of black personality.* St. Louis, MO: Williams & Associates.

Willie, E. (1989). The story of Alkali Lake: Anomaly of community recovery or national trend in Indian country? *Alcoholism Treatment Quarterly, 6*(3/4), 167-174.

Wilson, L. G., & Young, D. (1988). Diagnosis of severely ill inpatients in China: A collaborative project using the Structured Clinical Interview for *DSM-III* (SCID). *Journal of Nervous and Mental Disease, 176,* 585-592.

Wilson, W. J. (1980). *The declining significance of race: Blacks and changing American institutions.* Chicago: University of Chicago Press.

Wilson, W. J. (1987). *The truly disadvantaged: The inner city, the underclass, and public policy.* Chicago: University of Chicago Press.

Winkleby, M. A., & Rockhill, B. (1992). Comparability of self-reported Hispanic ethnicity and Spanish surname coding. *Hispanic Journal of Behavioral Sciences, 14,* 487-495.

Wittig, M. A. (1985). Metatheoretical dilemmas in the psychology of gender. *American Psychologist, 40,* 800-811.

Wong, B. (1982). Chinese-Americans. In L. D. Buenker & L. A. Katner (Eds.), *Multiculturalism in the United States: A comparative guide to acculturation and ethnicity.* New York: Greenwood.

Woodard, A. M., Dwinell, A. D., & Aarons, B. S. (1992). Barriers to mental health care for Hispanic Americans: A literature review and discussion. *Journal of Mental Health Administration, 19,* 224-236.

Wrenn, C. G. (1962). The culturally encapsulated counselor. *Harvard Educational Review, 32,* 444-449.

Wyatt, G. A. (1977). A comparison of the scaling of Afro-American life-change events. *Journal of Human Stress, 26,* 13-18.

Wyatt, G. E., Powell, G. J., & Bass, B. A. (1982). The Survey of Afro-American Behavior: Its development and use in research. In B. A. Bass, G. E. Wyatt, & G. J. Powell (Eds.), *The Afro-American family: Assessment, treatment, and research issues* (pp. 13-33). New York: Grune & Stratton.

Yamamoto, J. (1977). An Asian view of the future of cultural psychiatry. In E. F. Foulks, R. M. Wintrob, J. Westermeyer, & A. R. Favazza (Eds.), *Current perspectives in cultural psychiatry* (pp. 209-215). New York: Spectrum.

Yamamoto, J. (1978). Therapy for Asian Americans. *Journal of the National Medical Association, 70,* 267-270.

Yamamoto, J., Lam, J., Fung, D., Tan, F., & Iga, M. (1977). Chinese speaking Vietnamese refugees in Los Angeles: A preliminary investigation. In E. F. Foulks, R. M. Wintrob, J. Westermeyer, & A. R. Favezza (Eds.), *Current perspectives in cultural psychiatry* (pp. 113-118). New York: Spectrum.

Yang, D., & North, D. (1988). *Profiles of the Highland Lao communities in the United States: Final report.* Washington, DC: Educational Research Association.

Yansen, E. A., & Shulman, E. L. (1996). Language assessment: Multicultural considerations. In L. A. Suzuki, P. A. Meller, & J. G. Ponterotto (Eds.), *Handbook of multicultural assessment: Clinical, psychological, and educational applications* (pp. 353-393). San Francisco, CA: Jossey-Bass.

Yeatman, G. W., & Dang, V. V. (1980). Cao Gio (coin rubbing)—Vietnamese attitudes toward health care. *Journal of the American Medical Association, 244,* 2748-2749.

Yee, A. H., Fairchild, H. H., Weizmann, F., & Wyatt, G. E. (1993). Addressing psychology's problems with race. *American Psychologist, 48,* 1132-1140.

Young, T. Y., Ekeler, W. J., Sawyer, R. M., & Prichard, K. W. (1994). Black student cubcultures in American universities: Acculturation stress and cultural conflict. *College Student Journal, 28,* 504-508.

Yucun, S. (1989). China looks ahead: Mental health program for 1986-1990. *International Journal of mental Health, 18*(3), 47-54.

Ziter, M. L. P. (1987). Culturally sensitive treatment of black alcoholic families. *Social Work, 32,* 130-135.

Zuckerman, M. (1990). Some dubious premises in research and theory on racial differences: Scientific, social, and ethical issues. *American Psychologist, 45,* 1297-1303.

Zuoning, J. (1987). Community psychiatry in China: Organization and characteristics. *International Journal of Mental Health, 16*(3), 30-42.

Index

About the Author

Richard H. Dana has academic appointments at Portland State University (Research Professor, Honorary) and Southern Oregon University (Adjunct Professor) and is Director for Research and Training, Mentor Research Institute, Portland, Oregon. He was Principal Investigator, Minority Cultural Initiative Project (1989-1991), Research and Training Center, Regional Research Institute, Portland State University. He has been Professor, Director of Clinical Training, Psychology Department Chair, or Dean in various universities and retired in 1988 as University Professor Emeritus, University of Arkansas. He has published or edited 10 books, 15 book chapters/monographs, and more than 100 articles in the areas of multicultural clinical psychology, assessment, interventions, personality, and health psychology. His most recent book is *Multicultural Assessment Perspectives for Professional Psychology* (1993); he is editor of *Handbook of Cross-Cultural and Multicultural Personality Assessment,* which will be published in 1998. He has a Diplomate in Clinical Psychology (ABPP/ 1960) and received the Bruno Klopfer Distinguished Contribution Award from the Society for Personality Assessment (1984). He is currently developing an assessment-intervention model for services to multicultural populations in the United States. This model emphasizes an understanding of the cultural self as the locus for psychological services.